5-99
C10
W24

SUBHAS CHANDRA BOSE IN NAZI GERMANY

ROMAIN HAYES

Subhas Chandra Bose in Nazi Germany

*Politics, Intelligence and Propaganda
1941–43*

HURST & COMPANY, LONDON

First published in the United Kingdom in 2011 by
C. Hurst & Co. (Publishers) Ltd.,
41 Great Russell Street, London, WC1B 3PL
© Romain Hayes, 2011
All rights reserved.

The right of Romain Hayes to be identified as the author
of this publication is asserted by him in accordance with
the Copyright, Designs and Patents Act, 1988.

A Cataloguing-in-Publication data record for this book
is available from the British Library.

ISBN: 978-1849-041-140 *hardback*

This book is printed using paper from registered sustainable
and managed sources.

www.hurstpub.co.uk

For my parents without whom this would not have been possible.

CONTENTS

Acknowledgments	ix
Chronology	xiii
Glossary	xxiii
Prologue	xxv
Photographs	xxix
Introduction	1
1. Forging an Alliance: Indian Nationalism and National Socialism	29
Initiating Indo-Nazi Co-operation, April 1941	29
Co-ordinating Indo-Nazi Policy, April–May 1941	41
2. Extending the Boundaries: Aspiring for Nazi Liberation	49
Kabul, Rome and Venice, May–June 1941	49
Barbarossa, Indian Reversals and Intelligence Planning, June–October 1941	56
Free India, November–December 1941	65
3. Tripling the Effect: Berlin, Rome, Tokyo	73
Co-ordinating Tripartite Policy, Stalag IV D/Z and Collaboration Dilemmas, December 1941–February 1942	73
Chiang Kai-shek, Tojo and the Impact of Singapore, February–March 1942	83
4. Offensive from Berlin: The Cripps Mission	91
Bose's Propaganda Campaign and Japanese Intervention, March–April 1942	91

CONTENTS

    Bose, Gandhi, Churchill and Nehru: Convergence and Collision April 1942   99
5. Sustaining the Offensive: Politics, Intelligence and Propaganda   105
    Hitler, Mussolini and Bose, April–June 1942   105
    Bangkok, Regenwurm and Rome, June–July 1942   118
6. Transition to Tokyo: *I-30* to *U-180*   125
    Interactions with the Nazi Leadership: Bose, Himmler and Goebbels July 1942   125
    I-30 August 1942   127
    Congress Compulsions and Post-War Plans   128
    'Quit India', August–September 1942   131
    'On the Path of Danger', October 1942–February 1943   137
7. Epilogue: Indo-Nazi Collaboration   145
    Post-War Legacy   145
    Misconceptions and Political Divergences   147
    Military Intervention and Soviet Sabotage   151
    Nazi Realpolitik   153
    Political Realities and Renewal   158
    Bose and the 'Jewish Question'   165

Appendices   169
1. Plan for Co-operation between the Axis Powers and India, 9 April 1941   171
2. Mohammed Iqbal Shedai Letter to the German Embassy (Rome), 21 September 1941   177
3. Bose-Ribbentrop Conference Minutes, 29 November 1941   183
4. Tripartite Declaration on India, 1942   189
5. British Intelligence Assessment on German Recruitment of Indian POWs, 22 June 1943   193

Notes   199
Bibliographical Essay   231
Index   241

ACKNOWLEDGMENTS

Years ago when first embarking on this book, I remember reading the opening lines of Hugh Toye's biography on Subhas Chandra Bose, *The Springing Tiger*, in which he refers to the many years he spent preparing it and in the process acquiring the reputation of being a troglodyte. Little did I know that this would one day apply to me as well. Nevertheless over the years several individuals and institutions proved to be of considerable assistance. I am grateful to the All India INA Committee in New Delhi which was not only encouraging but also made it possible for me to meet veterans of the Indian Legion. In this regard I am particularly grateful to Captain S. S. Yadava. Lieutenant K. V. Chandran and the Tamil Nadu INA Forum were equally helpful in Chennai. Again in Delhi, the staff at the Nehru Memorial Museum & Library was most accommodating. In Calcutta, the staff at the Netaji Institute for Asian Studies was equally helpful. My thanks to the late Director of the Netaji Research Bureau, Sisir K. Bose and his successor Sugata Bose for granting me access to the extensive archives of the Netaji Research Bureau. The former also kindly described his involvement in arranging Bose's escape to Berlin. I am also grateful to the staff of the German Federal Archives and of the Webster Library at Concordia University in Montreal.

For contributing to my general understanding of Bose by sharing their wartime recollections—in some cases close involvement

ACKNOWLEDGMENTS

with him—I am especially grateful to the late Air Commodore Ramesh S. Benegal, Lieutenant-Colonel N. S. Bhagat, Captain D. Dasan, the late Colonel Gurbakhsh S. Dhillon, Natesan Govindaswamy, Govindarasu Muthukrishnan, Captain Puan Sri Datin Janaky Nahappan, Lieutenant R. Lakshmi Devi Naidu, Lieutenant Hari Ram, Lieutenant-Colonel Lakshmi Sahgal, Malkiat Singh, Natesan Swamiyappan and John Patrick Thomson. My gratitude also extends to Rama Rao, M. Shinnasamy and M. K. Valampuri Thevar for their eagerness to share their experiences.

For providing valuable sources on the Indian Legion—in many cases documents as well as surviving witnesses—I am grateful to Claude Jeay, the Director of the Archives Départementales in Bourges, Philippe Gitton of the Section Historique of the Archives Municipales in Bourges, M. Galand and Michel Lafitte of the Histoire et Archives section of the Marie of Libourne and Jean Arnoux of the Groupe d'Histoire Locale in Luzy. Also of significant help were the Mayor of Ardentes, Didier Barachet, the Deputy Mayor of de Beaune, Alain Suguenot, the Mayor of Luzy, Jean-Louis Rollot, the Mayor of Ruffec, Bernard Charbonneau and the Mayor of Saint Laurent Médoc, Henri Laurent. I am also grateful to Sarah Ducoudray at the Marie of Le Poinçonnet, Martine Faury at the Marie of Angoulême and Christian Martin, a Municipal Councillor in Libourne. My thanks as well to the Mayors of Bourges, Châteauroux, Jussey, Le Poinçonnet, Sainte-Hélène and Soulac-sur-Mer. I am also particularly grateful for providing information and sharing their recollections of the Indian Legion to Francis Cordet, Henri Gendreau, Marcel Jarraud, Pierre Pirot, L. C. Renault, Nicole Richebon and Josette Tessier. Rudolf Hartog, a former German officer in the Legion, was very helpful in providing a different perspective in some regards.

Anyone writing in the field of Boseian studies is inevitably indebted to T. R. Sareen, the former Director of the Indian Council of Historical Research, for his pioneering work and the valuable collection of documents he has assembled over the

ACKNOWLEDGMENTS

years. Professor Milan Hauner facilitated my research into his monumental work through an act of generosity. Jan Kuhlmann responded to a query in a most helpful manner. I am also very grateful to Maurice Gerard with whom I had a most enriching time conducting interviews and partially retracing the footsteps of the Indian Legion in France. Brian Schouten was also of help in this regard for the coastal region. Gilles Sigro proved to be very generous when we met in Versailles. My thanks as well to Martin Bamber, Romen Bose, Rudolf Hebig, Stéphane Pauli and Tomasz Sudol. A special thank you to Rahul Srivastava. The same applies to Michael Dwyer who believed in this book from the beginning. Last—but certainly not least—during my stay in Calcutta, Victor and Maya Banerjee proved to be wonderful hosts and true to the Indian proverb that a guest is treated like a God in India.

CHRONOLOGY

1941

17 February	Hitler orders the Operations Staff of the High Command to plan an invasion, via Afghanistan, of India.
2 April	Bose arrives in Berlin from Moscow.
7 April	The Chief of Staff of the High Command, General Halder, makes estimates on the number of divisions required to invade India.
9 April	Bose completes his 'Plan for Co-operation between the Axis Powers and India'.
12 April	Bose submits his plan to the Foreign Office and warns of the possibility of his leaving if an agreement is not reached.
29 April	Ribbentrop receives Bose at the Imperial Hotel in Vienna.
2 May	Hitler confides to Goebbels that he is considering establishing an Indian provisional government in Berlin. Fighting breaks out in Iraq between British and Iraqi troops.
3 May	Bose prepares an extensive note for the Foreign Office requesting in part a German declaration on Indian independence.

CHRONOLOGY

10 May	Hitler approves Bose's request for a declaration on India.
16 May	The first Indian POWs begin to be transferred from North Africa, via Sicily, to Germany.
20 May	Bose prepares an elaborate 'Detailed Plan of Work' for the Foreign Office and instructs his agent in Kabul, Talwar, to prepare for anti-British operations in India.
23 May	Hitler issues 'Directive No. 30 Middle East' on German involvement in the region.
24 May	Woermann informs Bose that the declaration is postponed.
25 May	Ribbentrop approves one million Reichsmarks for subversive operations in the Tribal Territory.
29 May	Bose and Emilie Schenkl arrive in Rome.
1 June	Bose meets Mohammed Iqbal Shedai, Ajit Singh and Labh Singh.
6 June	Ciano receives Bose to discuss the declaration on India.
8 June	British troops invade pro-Axis Syria.
11 June	Bose visits the German embassy in Rome.
22 June	Germany invades the Soviet Union causing condemnation from political parties in India.
24 June	Woermann writes to Bose urging him to return to Berlin.
5 July	Bose replies to Woermann protesting the invasion of the Soviet Union.
17 July	Woermann receives Bose who vigorously emphasises the urgency of a declaration on India.

19 July	Two *Abwehr* agents *en route* to meet the Fakir of Ipi are ambushed by an Afghan patrol.
11 August	The High Command, the *Abwehr* and the Special India Bureau convene an intelligence meeting on India and the Tribal Territory attended by Bose.
12 August	Shedai arrives in Berlin.
14 August	Roosevelt and Churchill issue a joint Anglo-American Declaration of Principles.
15 August	Bose writes a letter to Ribbentrop emphasising the urgency of a declaration on India.
18 August	Bose presents his letter to Woermann who in a memorandum recognises the urgency of a declaration.
22 August	A senior *Abwehr* officer reviews German commandoes trained in preparation for Operation Tiger.
25 August	British and Soviet troops invade Iran.
6 September	Hitler decides to postpone the declaration on India to prevent an invasion of Afghanistan.
10 September	Ribbentrop instructs Woermann to inform Bose that Germany still remains committed to the declaration.
17–18 September	During a private conversation with his entourage Hitler compares his plans to colonise Russia with British rule in India.
27 September	Bose makes extensive enquiries of Talwar on developments in India.
3 October	Shedai meets German officials in Rome.
16 October	Ribbentrop makes enquires of the High Command on Indian POWs.

CHRONOLOGY

2 November	Bose inaugurates the Free India Centre in Berlin.
4 November	The *Abwehr* plans to send agents to the North-West Frontier.
10 November	The Indian Central Legislative Assembly and the All India Radio station announce that Bose is in Berlin.
11 November	The British and American press launch a campaign denouncing Bose as a Quisling.
13 November	Ribbentrop informs Hitler of the propaganda campaign against Bose.
7 December	The Japanese attack Pearl Harbor.
8 December	Woermann instructs the German embassy in Tokyo to inform the Japanese government of the need to co-ordinate a declaration on India.
8–9 December	Bose, Shedai, German and Italian officials attend an emergency conference on India in Berlin.
11 December	Germany declares war on the United States.
17 December	Bose meets with Woermann and the Japanese ambassador, Oshima, to reiterate the importance of an urgent Tripartite declaration.
22 December	Shedai also emphasises the urgency of the declaration in a letter to a German official.
25 December	The first Indian Legion volunteers set-off for a training camp in Frankenberg.
1942	
2 January	The Special India Bureau prepares for a major propaganda campaign.
9 January	Bose writes to Nambiar asking for Indian recruits from France.

CHRONOLOGY

10 January	The Special India Bureau begins preparing a Tripartite declaration on India.
12–13 January	Hitler expresses scepticism over the Japanese invading India.
26 January	Indian Independence Day is celebrated with fanfare at the Kaiserhof Hotel in Berlin.
28 January	Bose and Colonel Yamamoto attend an *Abwehr* meeting on India.
29 January	Shedai attacks Gandhi and Nehru on Radio Himalaya.
6 February	Bose attends a second *Abwehr* meeting on India. Hitler claims that Japan is incapable of 'digesting India' during a conversation with his entourage.
11 February	Azad and Nehru meet Chiang Kai-shek.
15 February	The Japanese capture Singapore.
16 February	Tojo urges Indians to revolt against the British.
17 February	Bose writes to Woermann asking him to make the necessary press arrangements for a statement he is preparing.
22 February	The Special India Bureau completes the Tripartite declaration on India. Chiang Kai-shek's mission to India ends in failure.
26 February	Bose attends a third *Abwehr* meeting on India.
28 February	Bose broadcasts on the Free India Radio. The Foreign Office prepares a press communiqué in response.
1 March	Goebbels praises Bose's propaganda.
11 March	The British government announces the dispatch of Sir Stafford Cripps to India.
13 March	Bose launches a propaganda offensive against the Cripps Mission.

CHRONOLOGY

22 March	Cripps arrives in India.
23 March	The Japanese seize the Andaman Islands in the Bay of Bengal.
27 March	Cripps meets Gandhi who advises him to return to London. Linlithgow dismisses the effects of Bose's broadcasts. Hitler claims that Nehru has been 'eclipsed' by Bose.
31 March	Bose broadcasts an open letter to Cripps.
1 April	Cripps warns Churchill of an impending crisis in India.
5 April	The Japanese bomb Ceylon.
6 April	Tojo again urges Indians to revolt while the Japanese bomb the eastern coast of India. Bose responds to Tojo's appeal with a broadcast.
11 April	The Japanese government approves the Tripartite declaration on India.
12 April	As Cripps leaves India, Nehru denounces Bose in a press conference.
13 April	Bose attacks the Roosevelt administration in a broadcast.
16 April	Ribbentrop sends the Japanese version of the Tripartite declaration to Hitler.
17 April	Hitler rejects the Tripartite declaration but approves Bose's transfer to Southeast Asia.
19 April	Nehru denounces the Forward Bloc in a speech in Calcutta.
20 April	Goebbels dismisses Gandhi as a 'fool'.
23 April	The Japanese Foreign Minister summons the German ambassador in Tokyo urging a quick decision on the Tripartite declaration.
24 April	Nehru condemns Hitler and Japan and states that he is prepared to 'fight Mr. Subhas Chandra Bose and his party' if he comes to India.

CHRONOLOGY

29 April	Hitler, Mussolini, Ribbentrop and Ciano confer in Salzburg and decide to postpone the declaration on India.
30 April	The Special India Bureau and the *Abwehr* hold an intelligence meeting on India.
4 May	Ciano informs Bose in Rome that the declaration is postponed.
5 May	Bose persuades Mussolini to reconsider issuing the declaration.
7 May	The Special India Bureau prepares a note on the need for Hitler to receive Bose.
9 May	Bose writes to Ribbentrop reemphasising the urgency of the Tripartite declaration.
14 May	Ribbentrop writes to Hitler urging the declaration be issued immediately.
22 May	Bose writes to Ribbentrop asking to be transferred to Southeast Asia.
23 May	The Special India Bureau expresses reservation over Bose leaving.
25 May	Ribbentrop writes to Hitler again urging the declaration is issued.
29 May	The German press announces that Bose has been received by Hitler.
11 June	Bose makes preparations for Free India operations in France.
12 June	Bose holds a press conference in Berlin.
17 June	Bose makes a broadcast praising Gandhi.
26 June	Ribbentrop opposes Bose travelling by air to Asia.
15 July	Himmler receives Bose at his headquarters.
21 July	Goebbels receives Bose at the Propaganda Ministry.
23 July	Bose writes to Ribbentrop expressing his desire to proceed to Asia urgently.

CHRONOLOGY

5 August	The Japanese submarine *I-30* reaches Lorient.
7 August	The Congress convenes in Bombay to vote on the 'Quit India' resolution.
11 August	Bose writes to Ribbentrop protesting plans by the High Command to deploy the Indian Legion in Greece.
13 August	The *Abwehr* makes plans to launch large-scale subversion in the North-West Frontier.
14 August	The High Command cancels plans to deploy the Indian Legion in Greece.
30 August	The *Afrika Korps* reports that there are 14,000 Indian POWs in North Africa.
31 August	Linlithgow informs Churchill that he is 'engaged here in meeting by far the most serious rebellion since that of 1857' as a result of the 'Quit India' movement.
11 September	Bose inaugurates an Indian-German cultural organisation in Hamburg.
16 September	Bose urges Talwar in Kabul to be more active in operations against India.
14 October	Ribbentrop hosts a farewell party for Bose at the Foreign Office.
24 October	Shedai writes to the Italian Foreign Ministry blaming Bose for his downfall.
6 November	Bose leaves for Rome hoping to board an Italian aircraft.
9 November	The Italian-sponsored Free India Battalion is disbanded.
5 December	Bose writes to Ribbentrop asking that arrangements be resumed to send him to Asia.
1943	
26 January	Bose makes his last major public appearance for Indian Independence Day celebra-

	tions at the Kaiserhof Hotel in Berlin where his speech is relayed live on radio.
8 February	Bose writes a letter to his brother informing him that he has married and has a daughter before boarding *U-180*, the German submarine bound for the Indian Ocean.

GLOSSARY

Abwehr	German Armed Forces High Command foreign and counter-intelligence service
All India Congress Committee	Central committee of the Indian National Congress
Congress Working Committee	Executive committee of the Indian National Congress
Cripps Mission	British attempt in March–April 1942 to secure an agreement with Indian political parties on the basis of dominion status
Fakir of Ipi	Fanatical anti-British political and religious leader in the Tribal Territory
Forward Bloc	Political faction within the Indian National Congress founded by Bose in 1939
Free India Battalion	Italian military formation recruited from Indian POWs in 1942 and disbanded that year
Free India Radio	Broadcast station of the Free India Centre in Berlin
I-30	Japanese submarine which Bose hoped to board upon its arrival in German-occupied France
Indian National Army	Organised by the Japanese from Indian POWs captured primarily in Malaya
Indian National Congress	Gandhi-dominated party from the 1920s which led opposition to British rule

GLOSSARY

Indian Princely States	Several hundred Indian principalities affiliated to the British Crown
Kirti Kisan	Indian radical left-wing party
Mahatma	'Great Soul' a term of reverence used for Gandhi
Muslim League	Indian party seeking a separate Muslim state
National Congress Radio	German station purporting to broadcast in the name of the Indian National Congress
Netaji	'Leader' a popular term of reverence for Bose
North-West Frontier Province	Indian region bordering Afghanistan and the Tribal Territory
Operation Barbarossa	German invasion of the Soviet Union in 1941
Operation Tiger	German intelligence plan to destabilise the North-West Frontier Province of India
Radio Himalaya	Italian-sponsored Indian station in Rome
Special India Bureau	Section of the Foreign Office responsible for formulating Indian policy in co-ordination with the Free India Centre
Special India Detachment	Commando formation of the Indian Legion trained to spearhead a German offensive into India
Tribal Territory	Non-administered area between the North-West Frontier Province of India and Afghanistan from which the Germans hoped to destabilise India
U-180	German submarine assigned to transport Bose to the Indian Ocean
Völkischer Beobachter	National Socialist party newspaper
Waziristan Radio	German station intended to incite an anti-British revolt in the Tribal Territory

PROLOGUE

On the morning of 3 April 1941, 'Orlando Mazzotta', a man who had arrived from Moscow the previous afternoon posing as an Italian diplomat, walked up the steps of the German Foreign Office on the Wilhelmstrasse in Berlin. The Under-Secretary of State, Dr Ernst Woermann, immediately received him and listened carefully as he spoke of the need to establish a government-in-exile and launch a new military offensive. The government he had in mind was Indian and the target of his offensive was India.[1] Although Woermann was rather surprised by the nature of these proposals, he should not have been: 'Orlando Mazzotta' was in fact Subhas Chandra Bose, an Indian radical leftist nationalist and former president of the Indian National Congress. He had escaped a few months earlier from Calcutta and made his way to Kabul where the German and Italian legations assisted him in reaching Berlin, via Moscow, using Italian diplomatic cover.[2]

Bose was India's most important nationalist leader after Mohandas Gandhi and Jawaharlal Nehru. He had worked closely with them from the 1920s onwards before assuming leadership of the Congress in 1938. Differences not only in regard to temperament, but tactics as well, ensured that Gandhi ousted him from that position in 1939. While both men nevertheless retained mutual respect for each other, their politics diverged more fundamentally with the outbreak of the Second

World War. Bose saw the war as an opportunity to take advantage of Britain's parlous situation while Gandhi and Nehru were reluctant to do so, fearing this would weaken the democracies in the face of totalitarian aggression and expansion. They perceived Nazism and Fascism, as much as British imperialism, as posing a threat to India. Bose, in contrast, was increasingly inspired by Nazi victories, perceiving Germany, Italy and Japan as India's natural allies.

This was not unprecedented: throughout the 1930s, Bose had consistently reached out to the Fascist and Nazi regimes, even meeting secretly with Nazi party officials in Bombay while Congress president in 1938,[3] but it was his overtures to Fascist Italy which proved most successful. The Italian Duce, Benito Mussolini, received him on several occasions in Rome where he was seen as a potential ally in Fascist designs against the British Empire. Bose was considerably less successful in Berlin. Although received by Nazi dignitaries, his proposals for Indo-German co-operation failed to elicit a response from a regime which sought a rapprochement, if not an alliance, with Britain.[4] Hitler's admiration of the British Empire influenced much of his strategic foreign policy calculations. He was particularly fascinated by British rule in India which served as a source of inspiration for his own ambitions in Russia.[5]

Britain's determination to wage war in 1939, in the aftermath of the Nazi invasion of Poland, forced Germany to alter course. This was reinforced by repeated British rejections of Nazi peace offers.[6] Indian nationalism was perceived suddenly as a useful means of applying pressure on the British Empire. When the German legation in Kabul informed the Foreign Office in Berlin of Bose's arrival there in early 1941, the latter responded positively.[7] Elaborate arrangements were made quickly to transfer Bose to Berlin. Soviet reticence caused weeks of delay which ended only when Berlin, Rome and Tokyo combined forces to apply pressure on Moscow. On March 3, Bose was finally permitted to enter Soviet territory after a precarious existence hiding in the bazaars of Kabul.[8]

With his arrival in Berlin, the Nazis had to decide what to do with their recalcitrant Indian guest. This was complicated by his defiant and radical antecedents, including public quarrels with Gandhi and Nehru, criticism of Nazi policies, not to mention the fact that he had come to Germany with an elaborate, preordained political and military programme, and it seemed little concerned with what his hosts might have had in mind. Bose had certainly not come to obey Nazi directives.[9]

All this bode ominously for the future as it became increasingly evident that neither Bose nor the Germans were inclined to compromise. Their future co-operation would be most complex. Neither was it a simple ideological consequence of what has been described as Bose's 'flirtation with fascism' in the 1930s.[10] If his presence in wartime Berlin is to be fully understood, one must first trace his pre-war political activities, particularly in regard to the Nazi regime.

LIST OF PHOTOGRAPHS

Between pages xxxii and 1

Joachim von Ribbentrop—Bundesarchiv, Bild 102–18086, Fotograf: Pahl

Heinrich Himmler, Hermann Goering, Galeazzo Ciano, Hitler and Mussolini—Bundesarchiv, Bild183-H12939, Fotograf: o.Ang.

Ribbentrop and Joseph Goebbels—Bundesarchiv, Bild101I-808-1236-08, Fotograf: o.Ang.

Bose surrounded by high-ranking and senior SS officials—Bundesarchiv, Bild101III-Alber-064-16A, Fotograf: Alber

Bose conversing amicably with Himmler—Bundesarchiv, Bild101III-Alber-064-03A, Fotograf: Alber

Former Indian prisoners of war—Bundesarchiv, Bild101I-823-2704-10A, Fotograf: Aschenbroich

Indian Legionaries swear an oath to Adolf Hitler—Bundesarchiv, Bild 101I-823-2704-14, Fotograf: Aschenbroich

Nazi propaganda condemning British rule in India—Bundesarchiv, Plak003-028-101, Fotograf: o.Ang.

A Free India ceremony held in Berlin—Bundesarchiv, Bild 183-J08488, Fotograf:Hoffmann

An Indian Legionary in France—Bundesarchiv, Bild 101I-263-1580-06, Fotograf: Wette

LIST OF PHOTOGRAPHS

Field Marshal, Erwin Rommel, reviewing troops of the Indian Legion—Bundesarchiv, Bild 101I-263-1598-04, Fotograf: Müller

Rommel looks on at former Indian prisoners of war in German uniform—Bundesarchiv, Bild 183-J16796, Fotograf: Jesse

An Indian Legionary with a standard 'Free India' patch—Bundesarchiv, Bild 101I-577-1912-12, Fotograf: Stocker

Indian Legionaries relaxing after playing hockey against a German team—Bundesarchiv, Bild101I-264-1604-05A, Fotograf: Wette

Indian Legionaries on duty in German-occupied France—Bundesarchiv, Bild 183-J16695, Fotograf:Werner

Wilhelm Keppler addresses a Free India gathering at the Kaiserhof Hotel, Berlin—Bundesarchiv, Bild 183-J08486, Fotograf: Hoffmann

SUBHAS CHANDRA BOSE IN NAZI GERMANY—PHOTOGRAPHS

Bundesarchiv, Bild 102-18086, Fotograf: Pahl.

Joachim von Ribbentrop, the Nazi Foreign Minister, who had the reputation of being an extremely vain and arrogant man. He was even despised by his Nazi colleagues although Bose succeeded in establishing cordial relations with him based on their mutual hostility to Britain.

Bundesarchiv, Bild 183-H12939, Fotograf: o.Ang.

Heinrich Himmler, Hermann Goering, Galeazzo Ciano, Hitler and Mussolini (*left to right*) each of whom interacted differently with Bose and often held opposing views on India. Goering never formally received Bose. In the 1930s Bose had rebuked him for criticising Gandhi.

Bundesarchiv, Bild 1011-808-1236-08, Fotograf: o.Ang. Ribbentrop and (*on the right*) the Minister of 'Public Enlightenment and Propaganda', Joseph Goebbels, who proved an ardent admirer of Bose much in contrast to the disdain he felt for Gandhi.

Bundesarchiv, Bild 101III-Alber-064-16A, Fotograf: Alber

Bose surrounded by high-ranking and senior SS officials during a visit to Himmler's headquarters in 1942.

Bundesarchiv, Bild 101III-Alber-064-03A, Fotograf: Alber

Bose conversing amicably with Himmler. His 'outstanding intelligence' made a 'deep impression' on Himmler in the words of an SS official.

Bundesarchiv, Bild 101I-823-2704-10A, Fotograf: Aschenbroich

Former Indian prisoners of war at the training camp of the Indian Legion in Königsbrück. At first the Legion attracted few volunteers but it expanded drastically following Gandhi's launching of the 'Quit India' campaign in August 1942.

Bundesarchiv, Bild 101I-823-2704-14, Fotograf: Aschenbroich

Indian Legionaries touch a German officer's sword as they swear an oath to 'obey the leader of the German state and people, Adolf Hitler, Commander of the German Armed Forces, in the fight for the freedom of India, in which fight the leader is Subhas Chandra Bose'.

Bundesarchiv, Plak 003-028-101, Fotograf: o.Ang.

Nazi propaganda condemning British rule in India in the aftermath of the Churchill and Roosevelt declaration on the 'sovereign rights' of nations of August 1941 which compelled Bose to urge Ribbentrop to respond with a counter declaration on India.

Bundesarchiv, Bild 183-J08488, Fotograf: Hoffmann
A Free India ceremony held in Berlin in 1943.

Bundesarchiv, Bild 101I-263-1580-06, Fotograf: Wette

An Indian Legionary in France manning defences along the Atlantic Wall in anticipation of an Anglo-American landing. Bose had specified that the Indian Legion was not to be used against Soviet troops.

Bundesarchiv, Bild 101I-263-1598-04, Fotograf: Müller

Field Marshal, Erwin Rommel, reviewing troops of the Indian Legion during an inspection tour of the Atlantic Wall in France in February 1944.

Bundesarchiv, Bild 183-J16796, Fotograf: Jesse

Rommel looks on with irony at former Indian prisoners of war in German uniform as they had been captured by the *Afrika Korps* while fighting in North Africa.

Bundesarchiv, Bild 101I-577-1912-12, Fotograf: Stocker

An Indian Legionary with a standard 'Free India' patch depicting a springing tiger superimposed on the Indian National Congress colours.

Bundesarchiv, Bild 101I-264-1604-05A, Fotograf: Wette

Indian Legionaries relaxing after playing a game of hockey against a German team. An official of the Free India Centre in Berlin is seen standing discreetly in civilian cloths.

Bundesarchiv, Bild 183-J16695, Fotograf: Werner

Indian Legionaries on duty in German-occupied France. The Indian Legion was responsible for defending a significant area along the south western coast of France.

Bundesarchiv, Bild 183-J08486, Fotograf: Hoffmann

The Secretary of State, Wilhelm Keppler, addresses a Free India gathering at the Kaiserhof Hotel in Berlin in 1943 in the presence of Italian and Japanese diplomats to commemorate Bose's establishment of a Free India government in Southeast Asia recognised by Japan, Germany, Italy, Croatia, Thailand, Burma, Manchukuo, China (Nanking) and the Philippines.

INTRODUCTION

Bose was born into a prominent Bengali family on 23 January 1897 in Cuttack, in the present day state of Orissa. His father was a government pleader who was appointed to the Bengal Legislative Council in 1912. Bose was expected to pursue a similar path in the service of the British Raj, yet from an early age he displayed a rebellious streak. His childhood was shaped by the passionate nationalism that gripped Bengal, particularly in the aftermath of Lord Curzon's disastrous partition of the province in 1905, and which then swept across the rest of India in the years leading up to the First World War. His generation ceased to view British rule as either progressive or even as a benevolent form of despotism.

Bose first manifested a violent nationalist impulse in 1916, while studying at Presidency College in Calcutta. An English professor who had allegedly made disparaging remarks about Indian civilisation was assaulted by several students as he came down a flight of stairs. The incident stunned Calcutta. Bose, who is said to have masterminded, if not directly participated in, the assault was rusticated and temporarily became the despair of his family.[1] Nevertheless he resumed his studies in 1917 and at the insistence of his father even sailed for England in 1919, to study for admission into the prestigious Indian Civil Service.

No further incidents involving professors were to occur. Bose studied diligently in Cambridge and passed his exams successfully. Upon being admitted into the Indian Civil Service he was presented with the dilemma of choosing a promising career, as he put it, with 'a nice fat income' and a 'good pension in afterlife' in the service of the Raj or remaining true to his nationalist convictions.[2] With little difficulty Bose embarked on the latter course, becoming a cause célèbre upon resigning from the Indian Civil Service. He failed to heed the desperate appeals by embarrassed officials at the India Office in London, urging him to reconsider.

When Bose arrived in Bombay on 16 July 1921, he was immediately received by Gandhi that very afternoon. The latter was then busy transforming Indian politics through the use of passive resistance and civil disobedience and had launched a massive non-co-operation campaign promising self-rule before the year ended. The meeting came symbolically to define the relationship between Bose and Gandhi. To put it simply, Bose, in his words, was left 'depressed and disappointed'.[3] When in his typically non-subservient approach he questioned Gandhi on his plans, Bose promptly concluded that they suffered from a 'deplorable lack of clarity'.[4] Indeed, Gandhi's promise to bring about self-rule within the year ultimately took more than a quarter of a century to achieve. While Bose admired Gandhi's saintly demeanour and his ability to mobilise the Indian masses, he disdained his opposition to modernity, his veneration of non-violence and his glorification of rural India. Bose was a nationalist, but as a progressive man of his times a socialist too, in growing measure. His ambitious vision for post-independent India included not only dispensing with caste, class and communalism through elaborate social engineering but also transforming India's agricultural economy into a modern industrial one. The political and economic contrast between the two men could not have been greater. To make matters worse, Bose was also drawn to totalitarian and dictatorial political models which were anathema to the Mahatma. As a product of the political ferment in which he lived, Bose was inevitably affected by the establishment of totalitarian regimes, not only in Russia but also in Italy and Germany. They appeared to offer a vibrant and challenging alternative to parliamentary democracy. For subject nations preoccupied with post-emancipation economic and political matters, the radical and seemingly egalitarian progressive polices of the Soviet Union, combined with its anti-imperialist posturing, often proved irresistible. Yet Bose—who was too intensely nationalist to adopt a second motherland—refused to become a Bolshevik. Moreover being dictated to from Moscow would have contradicted his fiercely anti-imperialist principles. Bose also perceived the rational and materialist nature of communism as incompatible with India's spiritual traditions.

Bose was therefore left to reconcile his right-wing nationalism with left-wing socialism. This fusion of nationalism and socialism is sometimes seen as a fundamental precursor to fascism, a particular political trajectory best personified by Benito Mussolini. But fascism was more than such a fusion. Nehru, for example, was both a nationalist and socialist yet vehemently anti-Fascist. His commitment to liberal democracy differentiated him from Bose who was increasingly drawn towards dictatorship and totalitarianism. Yet if Bose never became a Bolshevik, neither did he become a fascist; he even reacted with indifference at first to the rise of fascism in Italy and Germany.

There was little to attract Bose initially to Italian Fascism, even less so to Nazism, as confirmed by a cursory reading of *Mein Kampf*, written in prison following Hitler's failed Bavarian beer-hall *putsch* of 1923, while Bose was emerging as a prominent politician in Bengal.[5] Hitler referred to Indian nationalists as 'Asiatic mountebanks' claiming that he had no time for them.[6] 'England will never lose India', he wrote, 'unless she admits racial disruption in the machinery of her administration' or 'unless she is overcome by the sword of some powerful enemy'. Further, as a German he would 'far rather see India under British domination than under that of any other nation'.[7] For Hitler, Germany's humiliation in the aftermath of the Versailles Treaty, which reduced her territory and military strength, was not to be compounded through association with anti-colonial movements. While both sides shared common grievances, the fundamental difference was that Hitler intended not only to restore, but also to exceed Germany's former imperial achievements. This included obtaining the restitution of German colonies in Africa and the Pacific, as well as, more radically, colonising parts of Europe and Russia. This was anathema to British and French imperialism which could conceive of colonising Africans, Arabs and Asians but certainly not Europeans or Russians. Nevertheless, Hitler envisaged replicating a vast New World in the east where Germans would assume the role of conquistadors and Slavs that of natives. Such a vision only ensured contempt for Indian nationalist aspirations and was central to Hitler's refusal to ally himself with Indian nationalists. British rule in India epitomised for him Aryan achievement: a small island race had made themselves the masters of hundreds of millions of people with an ancient civilisation. It was for this reason that the British Raj served not so much as a model—for Nazi Germany's actions in Russia were to be immeasurably more brutal and savage than Britain's in India—but rather as a source of inspiration for Hitler's own imperial ambitions. There were to be no princely states, maharajas or sepoys in his vision of empire.

This peculiar Hitlerian vision of utopia was not shared by all Nazis, particularly those who attached genuine importance to the socialist claims of the party, constituting as they did its left-wing. They sought to integrate the Nazi struggle into the wider anti-imperialist movement against Britain and France. One of its leading proponents, Otto Strasser, was reproached by Hitler precisely for articulating this. The Indian independence movement, Hitler assured him was 'a rebellion of the inferior Hindu race against the valorous Anglo-Nordic' which only itself had the 'right to dominate the world'.[8] 'That right', Hitler continued, would 'be the guiding principle of our foreign policy' and it was for this reason that 'any alliance with Russia, a Slav-Tatar body surmounted by a Jewish head, is out of the question'.[9] Hitler was prepared, even eager, to guarantee the existence of the British Empire if Germany received a free hand in eastern Europe and Russia. 'The land for us, the seas for England' was how he put it.[10]

Hitler articulated this concept on numerous occasions including once during a meeting with the Aga Khan, the leader of a prominent Indian Muslim sect. Hitler was willing to meet such Anglicised conservative Indians as they were perceived to be loyal subjects of the British Raj. In any case, Hitler only did so in the latter's capacity as president of the League of Nations, aware that the contents of their discussion would eventually filter back to London. He therefore went out of his way to act as a reassuring host, stating that 'if England gives us a free hand on the continent, we will not meddle in its affairs overseas'.[11] Hitler and Bose were therefore ideologically unappealing to each other, and Bose attempted in vain throughout his life to have Hitler's references to Indians excised from *Mein Kampf*. It was one of two points he even brought up when the two men finally met, in 1942.

While Hitler spewed his hatred from behind bars, Bose gradually emerged from his role as a provincial political leader to become a national one in India. Despite the unsatisfactory nature of his meeting with Gandhi, he worked within the Gandhi-dominated Indian National Congress under the guidance of its leader in Bengal, Chittaranjan Das. In him 'I had found a leader and I meant to follow him' Bose would later write, while recounting his disastrous encounter with the Mahatma.[12] Bose's rise in Bengali politics was spectacular and he was soon imprisoned for six months as a result of a government crackdown on the Non-Co-operation Movement.

Following his release in August 1922, Bose and Jawaharlal Nehru rapidly emerged as the 'Young Turks' of the party, representing the new generation which was less inclined to compromise with the British. Bose functioned as secretary of the Bengal Provincial Congress Committee while Nehru—a few years his senior—did so as general secretary of the All India Congress Committee. In 1924, Das, now Mayor of Calcutta, appointed Bose chief executive officer of what was in effect the second city of the empire. When Das died shortly afterwards, Bose gradually inherited his legacy. In October 1924, as Hitler awaited release, Bose was arrested again, this time on suspicion of conspiring with revolutionaries in Bengal. There were also allegations of contact with dreaded Bolshevik agents. Although there was no evidence to prove such links, Bose was held without charge before being deported to Burma.

While Bose resented imprisonment without trial, he realised that he was already at an early age following symbolically in the footsteps of prominent anti-British Indians who had been exiled to Burma, notably the last Mughal emperor, Bahadur Shah II, and Bal Gangadhar Tilak, the former leader of the Extremist faction of the Congress. Bose's imprisonment and exile therefore only enhanced his nationalist credentials, just as it did for many other nationalists who faced a similar fate. It practically became a mandatory requirement for promotion within Congress ranks.

In 1926, Bose was elected by a significant majority to the Bengal Legislative Council, albeit while still imprisoned, which served as a form of public vindication. The following year, after two and a half years in gaol, he was finally released. Bose spent much of 1927 convalescing in Shillong as his health had deteriorated badly in prison. While unable to attend the annual Congress meeting in Madras, he nevertheless strongly supported a resolution presented by Nehru calling for independence instead of dominion status.

In 1928 Bose organised the Congress meeting in Calcutta. To the discomfort of many, and in one of the first indications of his future ambitions, he appeared in military uniform, riding a

INTRODUCTION

brown horse in his capacity as Commander of the Congress Volunteers militia. As one observer put it 'the strutting, clicking of boots, and saluting' was not at all to Gandhi's liking.[13] Matters were made worse when Bose publicly challenged Gandhi's willingness to continue negotiating with the British while reiterating Nehru's call for unconditional independence.

Gandhi's more conciliatory approach failed. The British showed no inclination to respond in 1929 with an offer of prompt dominion status. As a result, Gandhi launched a civil disobedience campaign the following year culminating in the famous Salt March. Gandhi and Nehru, along with tens of thousands of Congressmen, were arrested. Bose was already back in prison having been charged with sedition and unlawful procession and sentenced in January 1930 before the other Congress leaders were arrested. With ample time now on his hands, his attention turned increasingly to ideological matters. Bose became preoccupied with political developments in Italy after reading two books by former prime ministers: Francesco Nitti's *Bolshevism, Fascism and Democracy* and Ivanoe Bonomi's *From Socialism to Fascism*.[14] Bose concluded that Fascism was a new, aggressive form of nationalism and that dictatorship—with the Fascist and Soviet models in mind—was a necessary means of consolidating state power.

In August 1930, while still in prison, Bose was elected Mayor of Calcutta. He was released in September and in his mayoral address to the Calcutta Corporation, on 27 September 1930, he made his first major public reference to Fascism. He did so rather awkwardly, by praising what he described as the Socialist and Fascist aspects of Das' political legacy, which he defined as the 'justice, the equality, the love, which is the basis of Socialism' combined with the 'efficiency and the discipline of Fascism as it stands in Europe today'.[15] To reduce Fascism to mere efficiency and discipline was of course profoundly to misunderstand its true nature. Nevertheless, the speech was significant for its positive, if naive, reference to Fascism although what Bose had in mind was Italian Fascism rather than its more extreme variants. Mussolini was then a highly respected statesman admired by politicians as diverse as Winston Churchill and Gandhi. The former, for example, claimed that Fascism had 'rendered service to the whole world' and that he too would be a Fascist if he was an Italian.[16] Bose was therefore unexceptional at the time in attributing positive qualities to the Fascist regime. Neither was he wrong in claiming—albeit with a streak of admiration—that Mussolini was 'a man who really counts in the politics of modern Europe'.[17] Such comments did not confer on Bose the status of a Fascist but they did reveal a growing fascination and preoccupation with Fascism.

On 26 January 1931, Bose organised a procession in Calcutta to commemorate 'Independence Day' which was now the official Congress aim. The demonstration was charged by mounted British police leaving many, including Bose, wounded. He was again arrested and imprisoned. Gandhi, who by now had been released, immediately alerted the press in London, appalled by the incident. Nevertheless, Gandhi and the Viceroy, Lord Irwin, soon concluded an agreement, known as the Gandhi-Irwin Pact, whereby civil disobedience was called off and a Round Table Conference was to be held to discuss constitutional reform. There was a collective sense of disappointment within the Congress. A distressed Nehru spoke for many when he asked 'was it for this that our people had behaved so gallantly for a year? Were all our brave words and deeds to end in this?'[18] Bose, who was released under the terms of the Pact, was equally aghast and rushed off to confront the Mahatma in Bombay.[19]

To make matters worse, only days before the annual Congress meeting in Karachi, the Indian people erupted in anger when Bhagat Singh and two other nationalists were executed by the British for having thrown a bomb into the Indian Central Legislative Assembly. Despite the violent nature of their actions they were considered national heroes and there was much criticism of Gandhi for his failure to prevent their execution. When Gandhi arrived in Karachi, he was received by angry demonstrators waving black flags, a 'welcome' that had been organised by Bose.

Bose was further disillusioned when Gandhi left India in August 1931 to attend the Round Table Conference in London. The only satisfaction he derived was Gandhi's acceptance of an invitation from Mussolini to visit Italy on his return voyage. The Duce ended up hosting Gandhi in his typically pompous style. To Gandhi's amusement this included reviewing a black-shirted Fascist youth honour guard. Mussolini even invited him—along with the goat that accompanied him everywhere—to his family residence. Despite their ideological opposition the two men greatly respected each other. Mussolini hailed Gandhi as a 'genius and a saint',[20] admiring as he did his ability to challenge the British Empire. His praise contrasted markedly with Churchill's response to the Mahatma: he had recently described Gandhi as a 'half-naked' fakir whose actions posed a danger to 'white people' and refused to meet him in London.[21] Gandhi in turn was impressed by what he saw as Mussolini's 'care of the poor, his opposition to super-urbanisation, his efforts to bring about co-ordination between capital and labour' and his 'passionate love for his people'.[22]

Bose concluded that the Mahatma had rendered India 'great public service' by visiting Fascist Italy.[23] Gandhi's encounter with Mussolini nurtured Bose's increasingly favourable impression of the Fascist regime, such that when Gandhi returned to Bombay, on 28 December 1931, Bose was there to meet him in person. He was also gratified to learn that the Round Table Conference in London had failed and Gandhi was now resolved to resume civil disobedience.

The British pre-empted this, however, by arresting Gandhi, Bose and other nationalist leaders in early 1932, rendering the Congress ineffective. Throughout his incarceration Bose's health again deteriorated. Signs of tuberculosis were detected, along with abdominal problems. As a result—following protracted negotiations—Bose was placed on board a ship bound for Europe on 23 February 1933. The British did not want him dying on their hands, fearing the trouble that might ensue.

Bose's first stop was Venice but it was devoid of political significance as it was merely in transit *en route* to Vienna where he was to consult doctors. Nevertheless, Bose was impressed by the elaborate arrangements the Italian authorities had made to receive him. This included a large press contingent eager to hear his views on Indian political events now that he was free.

Bose's arrival in Europe coincided with Hitler's seizure of power a few months earlier, and he quickly sought to establish a friendly rapport with the Nazis aware that the British would perceive a resurgent Germany not as a potential ally but rather as a major threat.[24] In April 1933, Bose wrote to the Nazi party newspaper, the *Völkischer Beobachter*, condemning the British press for denouncing Nazi repression in Germany while remaining silent about the oppression of the nationalist movement in India.[25] This attempt to establish an anti-British rapport failed miserably as the Nazis declined to reciprocate.[26] This should not have come as a surprise as the Indian-sponsored League Against Imperialism and the League of Oppressed Nations had already been disbanded.[27] Hitler's contempt for 'Asiatic mountebanks' was now official policy. The essential aim of German foreign policy was first to secure a rapprochement, then an alliance, with Britain. Any suggestion of sympathy for Indian independence would only prejudice such an aim. In Nazi Germany, Britain found an enthusiastic, albeit unwished for, defender of British imperialism in India.

Nevertheless, Bose persisted in portraying India and Germany as mutual victims of British perfidy. This was even the subject of a debate held—rather ironically—at the English Club in Vienna that June. Bose went so far as to claim that repression in India was worse than in Nazi Germany.[28] His aim of course was not to defend the Nazi regime as much as it was to demonise British rule.

During the summer of 1933 Bose made the first of several journeys across Europe. As a former mayor of Calcutta, he was usually received by mayors of the respective cities he visited and as the principal political representative of India in Europe, at times by heads of state and foreign ministers as well. When Bose arrived in Berlin, in July 1933, the mayor received him but his desire to meet Hitler remained unfulfilled. Bose wanted to 'convince him' in the words of a Nazi party member 'of his entirely wrong judgment of the Indian people' in their 'fight for freedom'.[29] Bose also wanted Hitler's statements on Indians to be excised from future editions of *Mein Kampf*.

Despite his status as a foreign dignitary, Bose declined an invitation from the government to be hosted at the state's expense during his several week long visit to Germany, preferring instead to pay for a private hotel out of his own pocket. While willing to reach out to the Nazi leadership, he was steadfast when it came to maintaining his independence. When Bose met Nazi officials at the Foreign Office they proved reluctant to arrange a meeting with Hitler, claiming that Germany had to remain neutral over India. Bose was under no illusion as to the direction in which this 'neutrality' tilted. He therefore sought to establish relations with the rival foreign affairs section of the Nazi party but neither was this initiative successful. Its head, Alfred Rosenberg, who was also the party's ideologue, had written *The Myth of the Twentieth Century*—the second most important Nazi text after *Mein Kampf*—in which he had portrayed Indians as descendants of a degenerate Aryan civilisation. As Bose put it in a letter written from Berlin to a nephew studying in Munich, attempts at 'tackling the authorities here over the statements of Herr Hitler & Dr Rosenberg' had brought 'no result'.[30] Nevertheless, Bose did befriend Lothar Frank, a Nazi party member who sympathised with Indian independence. He put Bose in contact with the left-wing of the party—increasingly disturbed by Hitler's compromise with big business, the army and the conservatives—and promising discussions were held on smuggling Nazi arms and ammunition into India.[31]

After a few weeks in Berlin, Bose was back in Vienna, which served as his base for his travels in Europe. He returned to Italy at the end of the year to attend a meeting of the Asiatic Students' Congress which was to be addressed by Mussolini. 'The speech was a fine one', Bose wrote to a friend, but added cautiously 'whatever we might think of the speaker'.[32] This reserved attitude was radically transformed following two meetings with the 'big boss' as Bose soon called Mussolini.[33] The two men established an excellent rapport as Mussolini, in contrast to Hitler, sympathised with Indians in their struggle against British imperialism. Bose was also escorted by Fascist officials who familiarised him with the various institutions and works of the regime. He was particularly impressed by the Fascist Hall of Martyrs which he wanted to replicate in Calcutta for nationalist martyrs.[34]

In early 1934, Bose was approached in Rome by the local correspondent of the *Völkischer Beobachter* who asked him to contribute an article on India. Bose agreed although he was apprehensive that the piece might not even appear.[35] The situation nevertheless had changed considerably from a year earlier when it was Bose who had approached the *Völkischer Beobachter*, only to be rebuffed. The Nazis had come belatedly to realise—in the aftermath of his visit to Berlin and prominent role at the Oriental Conference in Rome—that Bose could not be ignored.

This improvement in relations was to prove only temporary as the German Reich Marshal, Hermann Goering, in an interview with the *Daily Mail*, denounced Gandhi as a 'Bolshevik agent' in a deliberate, if misguided, attempt to impress British public opinion.[36] While Bose himself was openly critical of Gandhi, even describing him as a 'useless piece of furniture' shortly after his arrival in Europe for calling off the Civil Disobedience campaign, he never accepted foreigners doing so.[37] Bose acknowledged Gandhi as the political symbol of India and perceived any insult to him as one to the wider Indian nation too. In an official memorandum to the German government he protested vehemently, insisting that 'the statement about M. Gandhi being a Bolshevik agent is entirely false', adding that it was 'widely known that M. Gandhi is hated by all Communists, whether in India, or outside India'.[38]

The incident did not deter Bose from returning to Germany in March 1934. The Reich Minister of Economics, Kurt Schmitt, arranged to meet him,[39] suggesting that Bose was being taken more seriously, yet this was indicative more of an economic rather than a political interest in India. Nevertheless, Bose seized the opportunity to present a long list of grievances to Schmitt, ranging from complaints by Indian university students on deteriorating conditions in Germany to a recent incident in which he had been called a 'negro' by children in the street. Bose attributed this to 'present "race" propaganda in the schools and universities of Germany'.[40] Schmitt assured Bose that he would bring up the matter with Hitler. To reinforce his point, Bose also submitted his complaints in a formal memorandum which included his rebuttal of Goering's remarks to the Foreign Office. He insisted that a drastic change in policy was required 'if friendly relations' were 'to be maintained between Germany and India'.[41]

During a visit to Munich, Bose met Karl Haushofer, the founder of the notion of 'Geopolitics', who was the mentor of Hitler's deputy, Rudolf Hess and had even advised Hitler himself.[42] Bose and Haushofer soon established friendly relations although the latter did not wield sufficient influence to arrange the meeting with Hitler which Bose still desired. He also hoped that Haushofer might at least serve as a conduit to Hess and Ernst Röhm, the Chief of Staff of the brown-shirted storm-troopers (SA) who represented the dissatisfied and militant left-wing of the Nazi party. Bose's plan to meet Röhm came to nought, as he was soon liquidated, along with much of the SA leadership, in the 'Night of the Long Knives' in 1934 which effectively purged the party of its left-wing. This only left Bose further disillusioned with the Nazi regime.

In April 1934 Bose returned to Rome where he was again received by Mussolini.[43] The two men by now enjoyed a warm relationship, as was reflected in a book Bose spent several months writing that summer in Vienna. This was on Indian politics from the perspective, as he put it, of a 'Left-Wing Nationalist', and was entitled *The Indian Struggle 1920–34*.[44] In it Bose for the first time discussed the ideological implications of Fascism for India. He denounced Nehru's claim that the choice facing humanity was between Communism and Fascism, insisting that not only was an ideological synthesis possible, but that it was actually desirable in India.[45] What appealed to Bose in totalitarian ideology was the supremacy of the state, planned industrialisation, one-party rule and the suppression of opposition.[46] He also harboured hopes that an ideological synthesis of Fascism and Communism would occur first in India. 'Nothing less than a dictator is needed to put our social customs right', Bose wrote privately to a friend.[47]

Bose also argued adamantly in *The Indian Struggle* that India's 'salvation' could 'not be achieved' through Gandhi's leadership, while nevertheless acknowledging his immense contribution to Indian nationalism.[48] Bose referred to him as a 'virtual dictator', albeit one who was not as effective as 'Dictator Stalin, or Il Duce Mussolini or Führer Hitler' and who had already committed many 'blunders'.[49] The only concession Bose was willing to make was rather awkwardly comparing Gandhi's Salt March of 1930 with Mussolini's March on Rome of 1922.[50] Bose was also critical of Nehru, dismissing him as a 'loyal follower of the Mahatma'.[51] Bose's free and unrestrained criticism of his colleagues, including those on the executive

Congress Working Committee, was indicative of his future ambitions.

While writing *The Indian Struggle*, Bose also hired a secretary by the name of Emilie Schenkl. They eventually fell in love and married secretly in accordance with Hindu rites.[52] Bose's book was well received by the British press although it was, ironically, proscribed in India. Bose sent a copy to the *Völkischer Beobachter* hoping it would be reviewed and translated into German.[53] He also presented a copy to Mussolini at another meeting, in January 1935.[54]

Bose was developing an increasingly positive impression of Italy's Fascist regime, stimulated by his undeniable rapport with Mussolini. In a letter to the Indian newspaper, *Amrita Bazar Patrika*, he wrote of his attempt to 'study something of the work of the Fascist Party and how it was working in co-operation with the government for the uplift of the nation'.[55] 'The Fascist Party was out to create a new nation', he asserted, in which 'every individual in the state, regardless of age or sex' was taken care of.[56] His assessment was free of criticism of Mussolini or Fascism.

In September 1935, Bose and Nehru met in Badenweiler, in Germany, where the latter's wife was undergoing medical treatment. The contrasting attitudes of Bose and Nehru to the Nazis were revealing. Nehru deliberately snubbed Nazi officials, insisting on treating his visit as a purely private one devoid of political significance yet at the same time making a point of frequenting Jewish shops.[57] Not that Bose was much more pleased with the Nazis at the time. He wrote a long letter to Dr Franz Thierfelder, the Director of the German Academy in Munich, who served as an intermediary with the Foreign Office, dismissing recent assurances from the race-relations political office of the Nazi party and the Ministry of Propaganda offering to 'co-operate against any anti-Indian attacks in the press'.[58] 'Just offering empty words would not be enough', Bose warned, adding that 'we nationalists will do as much for Germany as Germans do for us Indians'.[59] He made it clear that he was prepared for an 'absolute worsening' in Indo-German relations.[60] 'Nazi Germany today believes only in force and looks down with contempt on enslaved nations like the Indians' Bose confided to a friend a few days later.[61]

The forceful and threatening nature of Bose's complaints finally got the attention of the Nazi leadership. On 6 December 1935, Hitler received A. L. Sinha, the representative of the Indo-German News Exchange in Berlin, to emphasise that the Nazi regime was not antagonistic towards Indians.[62] The significance of the meeting for Bose was in Hitler deliberately receiving a political non-entity rather than himself. The harsh reality was that Bose was seen as too much of a liability. Hitler was in the habit of lecturing; not being lectured at. Nevertheless, his reception of Sinha was counter-productive as it left Bose more frustrated than ever before. Not surprisingly, when he returned to Berlin in January 1936 and met officials at the Foreign Office, the result was 'practically nil', as he put it.[63] Bose was further aggravated a month later when Hitler in a speech spoke of white superiority. Bose responded by writing to the Indian press, advocating a trade boycott of Germany which was already gaining support in India.[64] He went further during a press conference in Geneva, publicly expressing his disillusionment with the Nazi regime:

> During the last few weeks my mind has been greatly disturbed at the insulting remarks made by the German Führer. [...] This is not the first time that India has been insulted by the [...] leaders of Nazi Germany. It is quite clear that Germany today is determined to curry favour with England by insulting India. I can have no objection if the Germans desire to lick the boots of the Britishers, but if they think that [...] an insult hurled at India will be quietly pocketed by us, they are sadly mistaken. [...] the Indian people can no longer be insulted with impunity.[65]

INTRODUCTION

In a letter to Thierfelder, on 25 March Bose was no less restrained, fully aware that its contents would be transmitted to the Foreign Office:

When I first visited Germany in 1933, I had hopes that the new German nation which had risen to a consciousness of its national strength and self-respect, would instinctively feel a deep sympathy for other nations struggling in the same direction. Today I regret that I have [...] the conviction that the new nationalism of Germany is not only narrow and selfish but arrogant. [...] I am still prepared to work for an understanding between Germany and India. This understanding must be consistent with our national self-respect. When we are fighting the greatest empire in the world for our freedom and for our rights [...] we cannot brook any insult from any other nation or any attack on our race or culture.[66]

Bose could afford to be so critical as he had decided to return to India despite the risk of incarceration. Indeed, upon disembarking in Bombay, on 8 April 1936, he was immediately arrested. Nehru, now Congress president, organised an 'All India Subhas Day' in protest. The matter was even discussed in the House of Commons but the Government of India was adamant on keeping him in custody. Only when Bose's health deteriorated seriously did it release him, in March 1937, confident that he was too sick actively to engage in politics. While recuperating in Dalhousie, Bose was still partly preoccupied with Nazi Germany and attempted to procure a book entitled *Hitler's Drive to the East*.[67] In October that year Bose hosted an All India Congress Committee meeting in Calcutta. Gandhi now resolved that Bose should succeed Nehru as Congress president yet paradoxically warned a confidante that he was 'not at all dependable'.[68] The presidency was in recognition of Bose's many years of imprisonment and exile, his role in Europe as well as the importance he had assumed in India. As Gandhi simply put it 'there is no nobody but he who can be the president'.[69] Bose's appointment was also an attempt by Gandhi to rally the radical left-wing elements of Congress. Aware of the serious burden that Bose was about to assume, Gandhi advised him to recuperate fully in Europe before assuming the presidency in 1938.[70]

Bose arrived in Naples by air on 21 November 1937 *en route* to Bad Gastein, a spa resort in Austria, only to find himself harassed by Italian officials. Infuriated, he made a scene and later wrote to one of Mussolini's aides claiming that he took a 'very serious view' of the matter. 'I have naturally no desire of passing through Italy if I am to be insulted once again', he added.[71] He even threatened to raise the matter with the Indian press.[72] Il Duce's adviser immediately sent a telegram and two letters profusely apologising for the incident. Bose, realising that it was the result of overzealous officials rather than deliberate policy, accepted the apology and expressed his willingness to meet Mussolini on his way back to India but only *'under conditions of absolute secrecy'*.[73] As Congress president-elect, Bose did not want to compromise himself by publicly meeting a man who had become a political pariah following the Italian invasion of Abyssinia and the forging of closer relations with Nazi Germany. He had little to gain by such an encounter now.

Bose was even more cautious when it came to the Nazis, carefully avoiding any contact while passing through Munich on his way to London. The sentiment was reciprocal. The Nazis were by now fed-up with Bose's constant criticism. Hitler had also just compromised himself again with the British political establishment in an extremely rash intervention on the India question. This occurred during a controversial visit to Germany by Lord Halifax, who as Viceroy, when known by his previous title of Lord Irwin, had concluded the 1931 Pact with Gandhi. Anxious to impress Halifax with his Anglophilia, Hitler expressed astonishment over political unrest in India. 'All you have to do', he said, by way of a solution, 'is to shoot Gandhi. If necessary, shoot more leaders of Congress. You will be surprised how quickly the trouble will die down'.[74] Halifax stared at Hitler first in bewilderment, then in contempt. While recognising Gandhi as an adversary, many Britons nevertheless greatly admired him. When Hitler's comments inevitably made the rounds of political circles in London, they reinforced fears that Hitler was completely irresponsible. The Foreign Secretary, Anthony Eden, for one, interpreted Hitler's remarks as proof that returning to Germany its former colonies might prove impossible.[75]

Fortunately, Bose was not informed of the controversy during his visit to London in January 1938, which generated much attention. He was received at Victoria Station by representatives of at least a dozen Indian organisations and made his way through a cheering crowd to a limousine flying the Congress flag. For several days, in his capacity as Congress president-elect, Bose met prominent Labour and Conservative politicians, including Halifax, Clement Attlee, Sir Stafford Cripps, George Lansbury and Arthur Greenwood. He addressed several gatherings across England, including one with Harold Laski. Bose's responsibilities as Congress president, combined with the increasingly aggressive and expansionist nature of Fascist and Nazi foreign policy, made it necessary for him to distance himself from the ambiguous position he had taken towards Fascism in *The Indian Struggle*. During a speech at St Pancras Town Hall on 11 January 1938, for example, Bose carefully emphasised that the Indian nationalist struggle was part of the larger struggle for freedom, democracy and socialism in the world while specifically referring to events in Abyssinia, China and Spain. Bose went further in an interview which appeared in the communist *Daily Worker* on 24 January 1938, admitting that the manner in which he had spoken of Fascism was 'not a happy one'.[76] 'My political ideas have developed further since I wrote my book three years ago' Bose assured his interviewers.[77] 'Fascism had not started on its imperialist expedition', he added, 'and it appeared to me merely an aggressive form of nationalism'.[78] Bose now joined Churchill and Gandhi in disavowing Mussolini.

SUBHAS CHANDRA BOSE IN NAZI GERMANY

Bose finally assumed the Congress presidency in India in February 1938. His long inaugural speech at the annual meeting in Haripura before the Congress leadership and thousands of delegates vigorously denounced British rule. He quoted Lenin, not Mussolini, and praised the British communist party as he sought to reaffirm his left-wing credentials while being careful not to antagonise the conservative Gandhian right-wing.[79] Bose's presidency greatly enhanced his reputation. He appeared, for example, on the cover of *Time* magazine on 7 March 1938.

Nevertheless, as rumours multiplied of an impending war in Europe, Bose felt the need to reach out again to the Nazi regime and it was at the end of the year that he secretly met with Nazis officials in Bombay. The meeting achieved little, as it was essentially a rehash of much that Bose had discussed earlier, from excising critical references to Indians in *Mein Kampf* to rebutting Goering's remarks on Gandhi. The Nazis in turn complained of the hostile attitude of the Congress and the Indian press towards Nazi Germany. Nevertheless, with an Anglo-German war increasingly becoming a possibility, both sides recognised the importance of improving relations.

As Bose's presidency neared its end, to the surprise of many, in particular Gandhi, he sought re-election for a second term. Gandhi, who wanted a moderate Gandhian to succeed Bose, appointed his own candidate to challenge him. When Bose resolutely defeated Gandhi's nominee, the latter publicly interpreted this as a personal defeat:

> Subhas Bose has achieved a decisive victory. [...] I must confess that from the very beginning I was decidedly against his re-election. [...] Nevertheless, I am glad of his victory [...] the defeat is more mine than his [...] it is plain to me that the delegates do not approve of the principles and policy for which I stand. I rejoice in this defeat.[80]

Matters worsened when the majority of the Gandhian-dominated Congress Working Committee collectively resigned. Nevertheless, this presented Bose with an opportunity to constitute

INTRODUCTION

a non-Gandhian Committee. The founder of the Indian communist party, Manabendra Nath Roy, advised Bose, for example, that Gandhi's recognition of defeat presented an opportunity for a 'new leadership, entirely free from the principles and preoccupations of Gandhism which until now determined Congress politics'.[81] Bose was reluctant to proceed, for fear of splitting the Congress between the minority left-wing which largely supported him and the conservative right-wing wing which backed Gandhi. 'It will be a tragic thing for me', Bose announced with unusual humility, 'if I succeed in winning the confidence of other people but fail to win the confidence of India's greatest man'.[82] That man, however, was not inclined to assist Bose in forming a Congress Working Committee, after a resolution was passed by the right-wing requiring his prior approval. Gandhi soon described Bose as the 'spoilt child of the family'.[83] As for Nehru, despite his left-wing sympathies, he abandoned Bose, fearing that his policies were not only alienating Gandhi but also dividing the Congress. 'I am sorry you find it difficult to understand me. Perhaps it is not worth trying' he finally wrote to Bose in disillusionment following protracted correspondence.[84]

During a meeting of the All India Congress Committee in April 1939, Bose conceded defeat, unable as he was to form a committee with Gandhi's approval, and resigned. He responded shortly by forming his own party, the Forward Bloc, with himself as president, although still very much within the Congress. Nehru dismissed this as 'evil'.[85] Bose certainly used his party to attack what he perceived to be the conservative, if not reactionary, policies of the new Gandhi-controlled Congress Working Committee and for this he was eventually barred from holding any Congress office for three years. Bose was now in effect at war with the Congress leadership.

As criticism mounted of the Forward Bloc, including accusations that it was recruiting fascists, Bose responded with an article in the party newspaper in August 1939, asserting that if what was meant by fascists were 'those who call themselves Hitlers, Super-Hitlers, or budding-Hitlers' such 'specimens of humanity' were to be found in the Congress right-wing.[86] As war appeared increasingly inevitable at the end of the month, in another article Bose warned of 'enforced participation' in an 'imperialist war' and lamented British preoccupation with 'self-determination for the Poles' when, as he put it to the 'east of the Suez Canal there is a land inhabited by an ancient and cultured people who have been deprived of their birth right of liberty and have been groaning under British yoke'.[87] While ostensibly claiming a policy of neutrality, Bose secretly welcomed the war as an opportunity to hasten Indian freedom. He was deeply impressed by German victories, and while conceding that Germany might be 'fascist or imperialist, ruthless or cruel', one could not 'help admiring these qualities of hers—how she plans in advance, prepares accordingly, works according to a timetable and strikes with lightening speed' he wrote on 13 March 1940.[88] Bose was soon praising German 'dynamism and mobility' while still acknowledging that the Nazi regime was 'imperialist'.[89]

When Germany invaded Holland and Belgium in preparation for the final and decisive push into France in 1940, Bose emphasised the need to 'utilise the international crisis to India's advantage', claiming freedom was 'almost within reach'.[90] Not that Gandhi's attitude was any more encouraging: he responded to the defeat of France by advising the British to 'invite Herr Hitler and Signor Mussolini to take what they want of the countries you call your possessions. Let them take possession of your beautiful island with your many beautiful buildings. You give all these, but neither your souls, nor your minds'.[91] He had already written to the Viceroy, Lord Linlithgow, stating that Hitler was not 'as bad as he is portrayed' and that 'if the British Cabinet desire it, I am prepared to go to Germany' to 'plead for peace'.[92] The British inevitably scoffed contemptuously at such an offer. If Gandhi was perceived as naive but harmless, Bose in contrast was seen as dangerous and in July 1940, he was finally arrested under the Defence of India Act.

A few months into his imprisonment Bose threatened to 'fast unto death' in protest over his incarceration.[93] As a result, on 5 December 1940 he was released temporarily. Bose soon reached out to Gandhi, offering unconditionally to support a limited civil disobedience campaign he had launched.[94] The Mahatma only reiterated the 'fundamental differences' between them.[95] 'Till one of us is converted to the other's view, we must sail in different boats', he advised Bose.[96] The latter could not have been more disillusioned. He had already written in disgust to his brother Sarat wondering whether it was the British bureaucracy or the Gandhian hierarchy which posed a 'greater menace to India's political future'.[97] 'Gandhism', he concluded, 'is sickening to a degree'.[98]

By the end of 1940, this utter disillusionment with Gandhi, combined with his more radical approach to achieving liberation, converged with the other factors finally to convince Bose that he had to leave India. First, the realisation that he would eventually face trial and most likely be imprisoned for the duration of the war proved to be a powerful motive. The entire Congress leadership was itself to be imprisoned for much of the war following a short-lived revolt in 1942, rendering the Indian nationalist movement largely ineffective. This allowed Bose, as he had anticipated correctly, to develop a more aggressive and militant alternative outside India. Secondly, Bose's marginalisation within the Congress made it necessary for him to reinvent himself politically. Finally, he had a growing conviction—not all that unjustified in the second half of 1940—that Germany would win the war. His desire to leave for Berlin was therefore not the result of latent ideological fascination with fascism but purely a strategic and political decision.

In February 1941, disguised as a Muslim, Bose slipped out of his family residence in Calcutta and proceeded to the North-

West Frontier Province where local Forward Bloc activists smuggled him into Afghanistan. Bose approached both the Nazi and Soviet legations in Kabul, but while welcomed at the former he was rebuffed by the latter. This should not have come as a surprise as he had already been denied entry into the Soviet Union in the 1930s. His transit through Moscow *en route* to Berlin was devoid of any political contact with Soviet officials as they refused to acknowledge his real identity.

....

Bose's arrival in Germany raises important questions regarding the nature of his involvement with the Nazis. Was he forced to abandon or compromise his nationalist principles of the 1930s in search of accommodation with the Nazi regime? Was there any basis to the systematic portrayals of Bose as an Indian Quisling in the Allied press? And did he turn a blind eye to Nazi atrocities, or rather condemn them?

Bose's arrival in Germany also raises important questions regarding Nazi foreign policy. To what extent was the regime flexible in reorienting its policies to exploit the opportunities presented by anti-British sentiment in India? Was it forced to compromise its racial and political ideology to accommodate Indian nationalist aspirations? Was this merely rhetoric brought on by the compulsions of war? In essence, was Nazi policy purely exploitative and cynical, or able when required to interact on a basis of parity with an ally? What was Hitler's specific role? Did he abandon or alter his own reactionary ideological positions of the 1920s and 1930s when it came to India? Finally, what are the implications of Bose's alliance with Nazi Germany for Indian independence? Should it be integrated into the freedom struggle, despite its embarrassing implications, or should it be seen as an aberration?

Bose's alliance with the Nazis, and more generally with the Axis powers, also challenges Gandhi-centric portrayals of the

INTRODUCTION

Indian independence movement. With time it has become clear that the nationalist movement organised outside India during the Second World War cannot be ignored, forming as it does an integral part of the struggle for Indian freedom. While this is certainly more true of events in Southeast Asia, which were of a more substantial nature, this does not justify excluding the preceding period in Nazi Germany. In fact, it was a necessary prelude to events in Southeast Asia.

This in turn challenges the popular perception that Indian independence was achieved through largely pacifist Gandhian means as opposed to the more violent and military alternative provided by Bose. This is what also makes Bose such a highly controversial figure. His arrival in Berlin in April 1941 was not akin to one of his 1930s visits to Germany but rather a deliberate attempt to engage the Nazi regime during its most aggressive, expansionist and brutal phase. By using one imperialist power to challenge another, Bose's approach was pragmatic as much as it was opportunistic, creating a fundamental ethical dilemma in the process. How did one of the most prominent, popular and progressive Indian politicians of the 1930s end up allying himself with the Nazis? That Bose is a national icon in India today on par with Gandhi and Nehru only fuels this controversy. Can a man who collaborated with the Nazis be celebrated as a progressive and heroic figure?

Bose's presence in Nazi Germany also challenges simplistic notions of the Second World War as being a conflict between purely progressive forces and reactionary ones. In this particular case, Nazi Germany found itself supporting a popular and progressive cause while its opponents—fighting ostensibly for freedom—remained largely silent. The actions of pro-Axis Indian nationalists are an example of the complex political ambiguities of the Second World War.

The controversial implications of Bose's involvement with the Nazi regime and the Axis Powers also raises the question of historiography and the manner in which it has addressed the issue. It has been divided essentially into two schools of thought, one of which has been extremely hostile, seeing Bose as a disgraceful pro-Nazi collaborator. This is particularly evident in the works of Christopher Sykes and Gerhard L. Weinberg. It must be emphasised, however, that this school of thought represents minority opinion which is not rooted in Indian history although it has had an impact in conventional accounts of the Third Reich and of the Second World War.

The opposing and more specialised school of thought essentially sees Bose as a progressive figure despite his involvement with Nazi Germany and the Axis powers. The first major study to take this approach was by Hugh Toye, who as a former British intelligence officer had interrogated some of Bose's soldiers at the end of the war. He concluded that Bose's actions were largely understandable and this came to be reflected in his pioneering work. This was the approach also taken by Indian historians, largely dominated by a nationalist school of thought. Bose's popularity in India at the end of the war only reinforced this approach. Even Marxist historians were gradually forced to adopt this position by the 1970s as Bose once again became an increasingly popular figure in the post-Nehru years. This was a radical shift from Marxist portrayals of Bose during the war.

Nevertheless, much emphasis was placed on Bose's activities in Southeast Asia to the detriment of the crucial period in Nazi Germany precisely because of its awkward implications. What little early writing was produced on the subject tended to reduce Bose's period in Germany to essentially being a continuation of his anti-Nazi criticisms and rhetoric of the 1930s, causing constant tension with the regime and thwarting the emergence of meaningful collaboration. It was even suggested that Bose's intention had never been to go to Berlin, but rather to Moscow. Only the unhelpful attitude of Soviet diplomats in Kabul forced him to turn to Berlin. In other words, his presence in Berlin was purely

INTRODUCTION

accidental. This analysis is not, however, borne out by historical fact. Second, neither was Bose under any illusion as to the nature of Nazi rule. His criticisms of the 1930s were sufficient proof. While it would be absurd to deny that there were not fundamental differences—even moments of despair—it is too simplistic to reduce Bose's activities in Nazi Germany to a mere continuation of his anti-Nazi pre-war rhetoric. Unconvincing attempts were also made to associate Bose with certain German anti-Nazi symbols although again there is no evidence to substantiate this. This early approach was particularly evident in the works of Alexander Werth, Girija K. Mookerjee and N. G. Jog.

A significantly more nuanced approach, in which Bose was still largely seen as a progressive figure but his activities in Germany and with the Axis Powers assessed in a more critical manner, emerged in the 1980s, first in the work of Milan Hauner, and then in that of Mihir Bose and Leonard A. Gordon. This was further developed in the 1990s and 2000s by Peter Ward Fay, Jan Kuhlmann, Anton Pelinka and T. R. Sareen. There is still a tendency, however, to refrain from focusing exclusively on Bose's wartime activities in Nazi Germany. It therefore remains the least known although most controversial aspect of his life. It is for this reason, along with the implications it has for the Second World War, Nazi foreign policy and Indian independence, that it requires greater investigation.

1

FORGING AN ALLIANCE

INDIAN NATIONALISM AND NATIONAL SOCIALISM

Initiating Indo-Nazi Co-operation, April 1941

The Berlin that Bose arrived in was the unofficial capital of Europe, with German troops positioned from the Arctic to the Pyrenees and from the Atlantic to the Black Sea. Four days after his arrival, they smashed their way into Yugoslavia and Greece, the last pro-British bastions on the continent. In North Africa, meanwhile, General Erwin Rommel's newly deployed *Afrika Korps* launched its first offensive, sending thousands of British troops reeling across the Libyan desert. With Germany seemingly invincible, Bose was determined to take advantage of the situation as quickly as possible. His meeting with the Under-Secretary of State, Woermann, on 3 April, was the first step in this direction. Bose suggested that his proposed Indian government be modelled on the London based Polish, Czech, Dutch and Norwegian governments-in-exile.[1] Woermann was particularly surprised to hear Bose also speak casually of sending 100,000 German troops to invade India. It became evident to Woermann at that moment that Bose's aspirations and German intentions were fundamentally disconnected. Bose had come to

Berlin with an extremely radical agenda, naively convinced that Germany was out to destroy the British Empire. The notion that the Nazi leadership was hopeful of reaching peace with Britain appeared to have eluded him completely.

In a memorandum to the Foreign Minister, Joachim von Ribbentrop, summarising the conversation and specifically referring to Bose's proposal for a Nazi invasion of India, Woermann noted that he had 'maintained a purely non-committal attitude on this point'. He skirted making any commitment by asking Bose to first submit his proposals in writing. All that was agreed to in the interim was Bose making a series of English and Hindustani broadcasts to India as soon as the German press and radio had publicised his arrival in Berlin—with 'appropriate ceremony'.[2] The details of his journey would be kept secret so as not to embarrass the Afghan or Soviet governments.

During the next few days, Bose worked hard in his hotel room, hammering out an agenda,[3] growing increasingly anxious that success or failure might well depend on the words he chose. Ambitiously entitled 'Plan for Co-operation between the Axis Powers and India', his memorandum consisted of an elaborate blueprint as how to destabilise the British Empire and achieve Indian independence.[4] His proposals remained centred around the establishment of a 'Free India' government. Bose's determination to set-up such a government was revealed in an extensive nine-page 'Explanatory Note' attached to his plan:

> It is one of the cardinal principles of British diplomacy to adopt a sanctimonious role when she is fighting in reality for her own selfish interests. We saw in the World War that Great Britain posed as the champion of smaller nations and we see it now again. At the present time...the King of Norway, the Queen of Holland, De Gaulle of France, etc. are allowed to set up their own governments in London under the name of 'free' governments. They are given the full diplomatic status of independent governments by virtue of special legislation and most, if not all, of those 'governments' are financed by the British. By this clever

subterfuge Great Britain endeavours to show to the world that she is in reality the champion of smaller nations. Why should not the Axis Powers adopt the same policy and pay England back in her own coin?[5]

Bose had other motives too for establishing an Indian government in Berlin. Apart from making Indian independence a reality in the sphere of international politics, it would be one significant step on the road to independence without waiting for British approval. A government would also provide an alternative to what he perceived as the politically stagnant Gandhi-dominated Congress and a new pivot around which to mobilise Indian public opinion. German recognition also implied recognition of a future independent Indian state. This was of critical importance at a time when Germany seemed destined to win the war. At worst, India might earn a seat at the negotiating table.

To ensure that it would not be a mere static structure in Berlin, Bose proposed that the government—acting through the Forward Bloc in India—organise boycotts, strikes (to paralyse the British war effort), sabotage, civil disobedience (intended to appeal to a larger segment of the population than the more violent tactics preferred by the Bloc) and infiltration of the armed forces—all as a 'springboard for the revolution'.[6] In Afghanistan and the Tribal Territory, the Bloc would co-ordinate its operations with German intelligence. In particular, Bose hoped that the notoriously anti-British Fakir of Ipi, Mirza Ali Khan,[7] and his tribesmen, who had waged a ferocious campaign against British troops in 1936–37, would be incited to do so again. This would weaken British defences in the Indian North-West Frontier province in preparation for German penetration. As Bose elaborated in his *Explanatory Note*:

The British position is not as strong as it appears from the outside [...] only a strong blow is needed to make the house of cards topple [...] British troops [...] number 70,000. [...] Indian troops number about 180,000. [...] The British section of the Army [...] is the only loyal force [...] on whom the British government can fully depend [...] after the fall of France in June, 1940, the Indian Army was in a mood in which there was utter lack of confidence in British military strength. [...] A similar opportunity will come again when Britain receives another severe blow [...] in that revolutionary crisis, the [...] government will have only [...] British soldiers to fall back on. If at that juncture, some military help is available from abroad (i.e. a small force of 50,000 men with modern equipment) British power in India can be completely wiped out.[8]

Bose did not explain how he expected 50,000 German troops to reach India. The only routes available—via the Soviet Union or the Middle East—were equally untenable as in the first case the Soviets would hardly grant a right of passage to such a large number of troops on a mission of this type while in the second, British military presence prevented any penetration. Nevertheless, in making a proposal of this kind Bose reaffirmed that he had come to Berlin not to engage merely in propaganda, but rather, that he was determined to expel the British from India and that he expected as much from Germany.

Significantly, Bose reduced the number of troops from the initial 100,000 he had mentioned to Woermann, to 50,000. Was he developing second thoughts? Bose had already considered the risks of such an operation—in particular if the Germans overstayed their welcome in India. He brushed aside his anxieties, realising that once the Indian masses revolted, it would be too late to stop their revolutionary momentum. Indians would not accept German rule as a substitute for British rule. In any case, the Germans would have 180,000 Indian troops to contend with—nearly three times the size of the expeditionary force he envisaged.[9] Ultimately what mattered most was that India did not feature among Germany's territorial ambitions. Paradoxically, this made persuading the Nazis to send troops to India all the more difficult. Nevertheless, the real risk, as far as Bose was concerned, was losing this opportunity to inflict a potentially devastating blow on the British Empire.

Bose also expressed hope that Japan would attack Singapore, the biggest British naval base in Southeast Asia, as this would 'automatically weaken British military strength and prestige in India'.[10] In doing so, Bose revealed his ultimate aim as being not a German military campaign as much as a concerted Axis one against British India. To limit ambiguity over external intervention, Bose emphasised the need for a treaty clearly stipulating that the Axis powers guaranteed Indian independence—in return for 'special privileges' after the war.[11] Bose did not define these 'special privileges', but they were economic (concessions) or military (bases) in nature as he had nothing else to offer.

The Indian government would also have its own Free India radio station and legations in as many countries as possible.[12] Bose could at least count on the support of Germany's numerous allied and satellite states in Europe.[13] The existence of a treaty and the establishment of legations would 'convince the Indian people' he wrote that their independence had been guaranteed by the Axis powers and that the status of independence was 'being recognised' already in practise.[14] Bose was concerned with substance as much as with form. When it came to financing, he proposed a loan which independent India would reimburse in full after the war. Counterfeit currency could also be used to finance subversive operations in India.

Bose's attempt to establish a government in Berlin (without the consent of the Congress—if anything its vigorous opposition), while appearing dubious, if not suspiciously ambitious in retrospect, was at the time only an exercise in anti-British *realpolitik*. Where Bose was deficient was in his failure to reveal with whom he intended to constitute such a government. The few available Indians—mostly stranded journalists and university students in German-occupied Europe—lacked the necessary political legitimacy with which to establish a credible government.[15]

Bose's overall plan nevertheless suffered from a lack of realism as it expected too much of the Germans. He simply assumed that they shared his preoccupation with destroying the British Empire. What he failed to realise was that they were engaged in preparing an entirely different operation in the East, code-named Barbarossa, intended in Hitler's words to 'crush Soviet Russia in a rapid campaign'.[16] India and the British Empire were, and would remain, peripheral to this strategy.[17] Not aware of German planning, Bose naively assumed that the war would remain an Anglo-German one, not yet foreseeing the entry of the United States nor of the Soviet Union and the devastating impact this would have on Germany.

This was consistent with the flawed manner in which he essentially perceived things from a purely Indian nationalist perspective, little troubled by German interests. His theoretical formula 'the enemy of my enemy is my friend' was not so simple, however, when applied practically. On the positive side, the audacity of Bose's plan ensured that it at least received attention and that something of substance might well emerge from it. It certainly forced bureaucrats at the Foreign Office to do what they had failed to do so far—namely develop a comprehensive policy on India.[18]

The plan also signalled a complete rejection of Gandhian non-violence and opposition to securing foreign assistance. Bose's principal concern was Independence, rather than the manner in which it was achieved. He was prepared to do whatever had to be done to bring this about—even if it meant defying his Congress colleagues. It was after all his disillusionment with them that had brought him to Berlin in the first place. Bose was convinced that national liberation movements required foreign assistance in one form or another (usually military). He had no moral qualms over such issues. If successful, he would accept acclaim for achieving independence, if not, universal condemnation.

Nevertheless, even before completing his plan, Bose showed signs of anxiety as to how the Germans would react. He held on to the document nervously for two days before finally handing it to Woermann on 12 April.[19] What prompted this anxiety? Three days earlier, while still completing his plan, Bose had been forced to take shelter in the basement of his hotel as Berlin experienced one of its worst explosive and incendiary air raids. This was courtesy of the Royal Air Force, in retaliation for a massive *Luftwaffe* bombing of Belgrade. Bose may have been badly shaken by the incident—not physically—but politically. With bombs crashing down from the skies he was forced to ponder the reality of British military might. It was obvious that England was far from defeated. Bose had ample opportunity to question whether it had been such a good idea after all to have come to Berlin. Germany certainly did not appear as invincible from within as it had from without.

It was immediately after this incident that Bose held on nervously to his original plan. That he evinced last-minute reservations became evident on 12 April, when he asked Woermann to cancel all press and radio announcements regarding his arrival so that he could return to the Indian frontier if an agreement could not be reached.[20] He did not explain how he expected to return to Afghanistan after the Soviets had made it so difficult to allow him through in the first place. Yet there is good reason to believe that Bose was sincere. A few weeks later, during a meeting with Indian nationalists in Rome, he again spoke of going back to India if nothing substantial could be accomplished in Germany.[21]

Bose was not bothered by the political embarrassment he would bring upon himself. Nor did he fully appreciate that it would only be a matter of time before British intelligence would detect his presence. Bose's sudden reversal reflected his extremist nature and emotional approach to politics. It was always all or nothing; now or never.

His reservations were not expressed in vain though. Woermann advised Ribbentrop, in a memorandum attached to Bose's plan, to 'consider' his 'misgivings'.[22] Indeed these 'misgivings' where not without basis. Simply put, Bose's plan did not elicit the kind of reaction from the Foreign Office he might have hoped for. Quite the contrary. First, there was concern that recognition of an Indian government presided by Bose would be perceived as German preference for the 'leftist Forward Bloc' faction within the Congress[23] which would antagonise Gandhi and Nehru. The Germans were not prepared to do this merely to gain Bose as an ally. Gandhi was rightly recognised as the key force in Indian politics, regardless of the contempt his pacifist ideology aroused in Berlin.[24] As Woermann put it 'there would hardly be any direct political advantage for us in elevating Bose as chief of an Indian government', even claiming that this would be met with an 'unfavourable response in large parts of India'. The impression would be of Bose having been 'bought' by the Axis powers.[25]

In reality, Woermann greatly underestimated Bose's political appeal in India. When he did eventually set up an Indian government in Southeast Asia, in 1943, which was recognised by Germany, it struck an intensely popular chord among Indians. It is true, however, that the context was different. At that time, the entire Congress leadership was behind bars. In retrospect, the Germans did him a favour in rejecting a government at the time as it would have met with fierce condemnation from Congress circles and also because he lacked the resources, including manpower, particularly the Indian National Army, that he would have at his disposal in Southeast Asia, to back such a government. A Boseian government set up in Berlin in 1941 risked being perceived as little more than a German propaganda stunt. The German response was nevertheless indicative of an initial lack of confidence in Bose.

There were also other factors—not explicitly stated—which generated opposition to Bose's proposal for an Indian government. All along he seemed not to have appreciated to what extent German policy was subservient to Soviet interests when it came to India. This was a result of the 1939 German-Soviet Non-Aggression Pact and Friendship Treaty which had indirectly relegated India to the Soviet sphere of influence. This policy was reinforced in the course of a state visit by the Soviet Commissar for Foreign Affairs, Vyacheslav Molotov, to Berlin,[26] whom Bose had tried desperately (and in vain) to meet in Moscow.

Although the Soviets were not particularly interested in India, seeing British rule as a sufficient stabilising factor, a sudden change in German policy—particularly the establishment of an Indian government in Berlin—might have aroused Soviet suspicions. This is the last thing the Germans wanted at a time when they were in the midst of preparing Operation Barbarossa—the massive invasion of Russia. While Barbarossa would put an end to German preoccupation with Soviet concerns, there was little Germany could do till then effectively to assist Indian independence. The situation was not helped by Bose's naive conviction that the Soviet Union would only be too willing to assist Germany in bringing about Indian independence.[27] This perception of Soviet foreign policy being guided—unlike Germany—by genuinely anti-imperialist principles was something that he would have difficulty shaking off.[28]

There was also concern within the German Foreign Office that the establishment of an Indian government in Berlin might preclude any future Anglo-German compromise. Apart from the Nazi leadership, a not inconsiderable number of bureaucrats in the Foreign Office still remained hopeful this might be accomplished. The problem was that Bose attached too much importance to the Anglo-German war, accepting the Nazi argument that they were fighting Britain only because the island nation resisted, not realising that, if it persisted, it was because the British under Churchill had determined never to concede defeat. Finally, there was also opposition to Bose's proposal for a military operation in India.[29] An adventure of this type was seen as purely hypothetical as long as Germany was not in a military position to carry it out. 'This subject should not be discussed with Bose' was how Woermann tersely put it.

Some interest, however, was shown in Bose's intelligence and subversion proposals concerning Afghanistan, the Tribal Territory and India.[30] This could weaken the British, contribute to Indian independence while at the same time avoid any irreversible political engagements. It was precisely the vague, clandestine, nature of this work that appealed to the conservative mindset of the Foreign Office. Bose's proposal to establish an Indian radio station met with a similarly positive response.

The rejection of Bose's two most important proposals—namely the establishment of a government and a military intervention—came as a rude awakening to him. He began to fear that his mere presence in Berlin would compromise him politically unless he at least obtained a public declaration of support, if not a guarantee, on Indian independence. Bose's last minute reservations or 'misgivings' were therefore not without justification.

Nevertheless, help arrived from unexpected quarters. When Hitler was informed of Bose's proposal to set up an Indian government, he uncharacteristically responded positively, confiding to his Minister of Public Enlightenment and Propaganda, Joseph Goebbels, on 2 May, that he was seriously contemplating such a move.[31] Why did Hitler do so when it so clearly contradicted Foreign Office policy? There were several reasons. Unlike the conservative—at times reactionary—bureaucrats of the Foreign Office (a class Hitler despised and referred to as 'sluts'[32]) he was not constrained by such compulsions. On the contrary, his politically extremist nature made Bose's radical agenda all the more appealing.

Hitler also had pragmatic reasons to consider an Indian government. First, it offered him an opportunity of launching one last political offensive against Britain before turning his attention to Barbarossa in the East. He also realised that the establishment of an Indian government would radicalise German foreign policy, in part by projecting Nazi Germany as a state committed to achieving a New Order, not only in Europe, but throughout the world. Hitler fully appreciated the devastating impact Indian independence would have on the British Empire. Indeed, he was motivated more by anti-British sentiment than by any genuine desire to liberate India. Indian independence was for him essentially a means of getting at Britain. He never appreciated the complexities of the sub-continent, as he demonstrated consistently by resorting to basic—often Victorian—clichés when speaking of India.[33]

Nevertheless, with Barbarossa imminent, Hitler's thoughts turned increasingly to India. The question he pondered over and over again was what his troops would do after defeating the Soviet Union. The next logical move was the annihilation of British power in India. Hitler, without consulting his generals, had already considered such a move for months. In reality, he overestimated his abilities,[34] not realising that he had already miscalculated badly in assuming German troops would be able to smash the Soviet Union in a matter of weeks. In the end it would be the Soviets, not the Germans, who would do the smashing. Nevertheless, at the time, Hitler believed that striking at the heart of the British Empire would force the British to their knees. What they had not done for England, they might just do for India in a desperate, last minute attempt to salvage what wreckage they could from their Empire.

Hitler gave little thought to what his troops would achieve once in India. Did he really expect Indians to acclaim him as their liberator? While he would have now only been too pleased to assume such a role,[35] this was certainly not his primary aim in entering the country. The Führer was showing disturbing signs of losing touch with reality.[36] A few weeks before Bose's arrival in Berlin, he had ordered the Operations Staff of the High Command to plan an invasion of India.[37] Bose's proposals, in particular the establishment of an Indian government and a military operation, therefore could not have come at a better time. In fact, while he had been writing up his proposals, the

Chief of Staff of the High Command, General Franz Halder, had already been making estimates on the types and numbers of divisions that would be required to attack Afghanistan as a preliminary to the offensive in India. He concluded that a combination of seventeen armoured, motorised, infantry and mountain divisions would be required in all.[38] This was at least three times the number of troops had Bose envisaged. Indeed, the German aim was not intervention but outright invasion.

To ease German troop penetration into India, the High Command's intelligence service, the *Abwehr*, prepared an operation code-named Tiger, aimed at inciting the Frontier tribes to attack the British much in the manner that Bose had recommended in his plan. The German legation in Kabul had coincidentally just dispatched a report on the Fakir of Ipi.[39] Even the Naval High Command had reason to welcome Bose's plan. His emphasis on the importance of a Japanese attack on Singapore fitted perfectly with its strategic aims. Hitler, in 'Directive No. 24 Co-operation with Japan' had unequivocally stated that the aim of the Tripartite Italo-German-Japanese Pact of 1940 was to 'induce Japan to take action in the Far East as soon as possible'.[40] 'The seizure of Singapore, England's key strategic position in the Far East', he went on 'would represent a decisive success in the combined strategy of the three powers'.[41] This was partly the result of persistent efforts by the Naval Commander-in-Chief, Grand Admiral Erich Raeder, to convince Hitler of the need for such a move, precisely because it would destabilise India and the surrounding region.[42]

There was another reason why Bose's proposals could not have come at a better time. In the course of its first offensive, Rommel's *Afrika Korps* had just captured part of an Indian motorised brigade at Mechili in Libya. This, the first major interaction of the war between German and Indian troops, went surprisingly well. The Germans treated the Indian prisoners of war (POWs) in accordance with the Geneva Convention, unlike the manner in which they would soon treat Soviet POWs. As such the Indians had no cause to complain. On the contrary, many of them quickly befriended their German and Italian guards. They considered themselves to be mercenaries fighting to feed their families and not for the glory of the British Raj, and blamed the British, not the Germans, for their plight. Anti-British sentiment ran high in the aftermath of defeat. A group of nationalist officers even wrote a letter to Mussolini offering to organise Indian POWs alongside the Axis to fight the British.[43] Realising the significance of this, the Italian Supreme Command promptly notified the German High Command, which in turn, informed Bose.

Co-ordinating Indo-Nazi Policy, April–May 1941

Captain Walter Harbich was assigned to establish liaison and co-ordinate policy with Bose.[44] Not wanting to be excluded, the Foreign Office ensured that one of its own representatives was always present at these meetings. What it feared above all was Bose and the High Command formulating policy on their own. There was also cause for concern, as Harbich later would recall, that the High Command approached Bose 'from the very first moment with the respect to which he was entitled because of his position in India'.[45] This ensured an amicable relationship, no doubt helped by Bose's enthusiasm over the capture of Indian POWs and the prospects of military collaboration. This was in contrast to his dealings with the Foreign Office. Bose now envisaged the creation of a 'Free Indian Legion' which would serve as the military wing of an eventual Indian government.[46] The High Command, however, was not prepared to do this yet. It first wanted to screen and train the POWs in preparation for combat operations on the frontline with German troops. It sought nothing less than a genuine military formation; not a propaganda stunt. It also was contrary to basic principles of military psychology to put POWs into new uniforms and simply throw them back at the very lines they had just come from. Organising a credible and effective military formation required both time and effort. Bose gradually accepted these views, satisfied that a promising basis of military co-operation had at least been found.

Bose's increasingly close relations with the High Command remained a source of consternation within the Foreign Office. Junior officials simply could not get accustomed to the idea that Bose had come to Berlin not to engage merely in radio propaganda but, rather, that he had an ambitious political and military agenda. Nevertheless, on 29 April, the Foreign Minister, Ribbentrop, arranged to meet Bose. The two men had every reason to get along as they both shared a profound dislike of Great Britain. For Bose it was purely political, but for Ribbentrop it was more personal. He had not forgotten the manner in which the British establishment had rebuffed and ridiculed him while serving as Hitler's ambassador before the war. This naturally gave him a sympathetic predisposition towards Bose. The latter offered him an opportunity of getting back at England.[47] For Bose, the encounter was equally important, realising as he did that it was a critical opportunity to influence the German government at the highest level. He knew that Ribbentrop was very close to Hitler. If he could gain Ribbentrop's confidence, it would be one significant step towards gaining Hitler's support. Bose would have taken additional comfort had he known that Ribbentrop looked down on the very bureaucrats of the Foreign Office who had responded so sceptically to his proposals.[48]

Ribbentrop began by enquiring about the general political situation in India, making no effort to conceal his ignorance of the matter. Bose attributed the lack of revolt to insufficient arms. The impression he sought to engender—in keeping with his ideological outlook—was that Gandhian pacifist ideology was not particularly relevant to the political context. When Ribbentrop inevitably enquired about the latter's role in Indian politics, Bose quickly dismissed him as a 'man of compromise' who did not want to 'shut the door in the face of the English'. Nevertheless, Ribbentrop—as ignorant as he may have been about India—was not so easily fooled, insisting on the need in the course of the conversation to take Gandhi 'always' into consideration. Much to Bose's surprise, he was also reluctant to simply dismiss Gandhian non-violence or 'passive resistance' out of hand.[49]

Bose emphasised in turn the importance of Indian troops in the discussion and the desire of the Indian POWs in North Africa to fight the British. This would have a 'very strong effect' on the armed forces he claimed. Indian officers already listened attentively to German broadcasts and some troops had even mutinied in North Africa and India, he added. Ribbentrop in turn hoped that it might also be 'possible to prepare the ground and organise the resistance from within the armed forces themselves'.[50]

One issue which Bose repeatedly brought up was a possible Anglo-German peace compromise although he had not referred to this in either his 'Plan for Co-operation between the Axis Powers and India' or extensive 'Explanatory Note'. A few weeks in Berlin was enough to make him realise that such a prospect existed and that he would be its first victim, with the British, no doubt, insisting on his head as the prerequisite to any peace talks. Ribbentrop, sincerely committed to fighting Britain, went out of his way to assure Bose that this was no longer possible. While conceding that one of the primary aims of pre-war German foreign policy had been a rapprochement, if not an alliance, with Britain, Ribbentrop now insisted that it was too late as the 'English had gone too far and it would be all over with them this time'. This was followed by a tirade on the military inevitability of a British defeat. Ribbentrop ended up sounding as though he was trying to convince himself as much as he was tying to convince Bose.[51]

Bose also emphasised the importance of a German declaration on Indian independence in order to 'win over the Indian masses completely'. Although Ribbentrop did not specifically respond to this, he did assure Bose in the course of the conversation of his conviction that India would attain 'her freedom in the course of this war'. He was 'quite sure of this'. Bose was delighted by this statement as it was the first expression of unconditional support he had heard for Indian independence since arriving in Berlin. If only for this reason, he left the discussion satisfied and relieved. Even if Ribbentrop had not gone beyond mere verbal expressions of support, even stressing at one point the need to proceed cautiously, 'step by step and not too hurriedly', it was clear that there was still room in which to manoeuvre.[52] Bose understood that he had to be patient and persistent in his efforts to win over the Nazi leadership if his plans were to be implemented. He had accomplished the first step by establishing correct—if not cordial—relations with a man very few people, from foreign statesmen to his own staff, found easy to get along with. Almost without exception the entire Nazi leadership despised Ribbentrop.[53]

Significant by their omission from the meeting—they were not even alluded to—were an Indian government and the training of Indian POWs. There was good reason for this. Hitler was still considering an Indian government-in-exile, leaving Ribbentrop as much in the dark as Bose as to what the outcome would be. Aware of the reservations of his staff over the issue—and Hitler's favourable tilt—Ribbentrop maintained cautious neutrality. As for the POWs, Bose preferred to keep what was essentially a military decision away from the Foreign Office, now that he enjoyed close relations with the High Command. In any case, Ribbentrop again seemed quite content to leave matters as they were.

One subject which had changed considerably since Bose's arrival was his handling of Gandhi. In his 'Plan for Co-operation between the Axis Powers and India' as well as in his 'Explanatory Note', Bose had not mentioned Gandhi once.[54] In contrast, his meeting with Ribbentrop was replete with constant critical references to Gandhi. Bose was determined to convince the Germans that Gandhi was not indispensable to achieving Indian independence. He wanted to convince them that his voice was as important and legitimate as Gandhi's. The extent to which Gandhi's political significance was appreciated in Berlin was not something he had anticipated. Bose was determined to prove that only he could provide a viable alternative leadership capable of bringing about a successful alliance between Indian nationalism and National Socialism.

Immediately after his meeting with Ribbentrop, Bose realised that he had not sufficiently emphasised the importance of a declaration on India. He was convinced that such a declaration was indispensable in the absence of a government. Not only would it help legitimise his presence in Berlin and reassure Indian public opinion, but it would also deflect potential Congress criticism. Accordingly, on 3 May, Bose prepared an extensive note for the Foreign Office, re-emphasising the necessity and urgency of a declaration.[55] He recommended one for Arab nations as well, realising that this would alter the perception of Germany throughout the region while uniting Arab and Indian opposition to the British. Bose wrote of a 'strong under-current of unrest' which could be 'worked up into an open revolt'. He was clearly prepared to exploit the frustrations of Arab nationalism if it could help India. Bose went as far as suggesting that these nations would take on a pro-German position in case of a German 'conflict' (a euphemism for war) with either Turkey or the Soviet Union.

In the case of India, Bose conceded that while there had been a 'large measure of pro-Soviet feeling' it was accepted now that it was 'the Axis Powers alone (and not the Soviet)' which could help bring about liberation.[56] He downplayed the Soviet factor, despite knowing that powerful pro-Soviet forces would have nothing to do with the Axis regardless of any convergence of aims. What Bose was really implying was that he was prepared to do everything in his power to encourage his countrymen to adopt a pro-Axis position if the latter made a significant contribution to Indian independence. He did express a preference, however, for maintaining the 'status quo' between Germany and the Soviet Union.

Bose did not restrict himself to the declaration. He also advocated destabilising the Afghan regime so that the Axis could 'concentrate on attacking the heart of the British Empire, that is, British rule in India'. Further, military assistance, if required, was to be provided to the pro-German regime in Iraq which was on the verge of war with Britain. The implementation of these proposals, Bose argued, would produce a pro-German 'chain' stretching from 'North Africa on the one side and right up to Japan in the Far East'.[57] He would have taken great comfort in knowing that this is precisely what the British Prime Minister, Winston Churchill, feared most, realising that a successful German intervention in Iraq might allow 'Hitler's hand' to stretch 'very far towards India' and beckon 'to Japan'.[58]

To 'strike at British power' in India, Bose envisaged proceeding via Russia (on the naive assumption that the Soviets would agree), the Middle East (ignoring Britain's military presence there) or, more realistically, from the Suez Canal (although this was dependent on the *Afrika Korps* first capturing Egypt).[59]

Bose's ambitious note indicated a significant resurgence of optimism. In the aftermath of his meeting with Ribbentrop, he was more confident of his position, now taking it upon himself to advise the Germans not only on India but North Africa and the Middle East too. He was increasingly looking at things from a wider perspective, prepared fully to exploit the global conflagration to India's advantage, even if it meant turning against the Soviet Union, violating Afghan sovereignty or exploiting Arab nationalism. The reality was that Bose was prepared to do just about anything to liberate India. What he did not realise was

FORGING AN ALLIANCE

that his optimism and ambitions were not necessarily matched by those of the Germans.

Nevertheless, after finishing his note, Bose found even more cause for optimism. German radio flashed news reports that Iraqi troops had opened hostilities against the British and that a full-fledged war was now in progress. In an addendum to his note, an excited Bose wrote: 'This will have a powerful reaction in all Oriental countries and particularly among the Arabs. The need of an immediate decision regarding the Oriental policy of Germany has thus become all the more urgent'.[60]

This time Bose's memorandum was very well received by the Foreign Office as it coincided with a similar official note written the same day by Ribbentrop urging Hitler to assist Iraq militarily while generally seizing the initiative in the Middle East.[61]

As a result, and following similar advice from the High Command, Hitler soon issued 'Directive No. 30 Middle East':

The *Arab Freedom Movement* is our natural ally against England in the Middle East. In this connection the rising in Iraq is particularly important. It strengthens the forces hostile to England beyond the Iraqi frontier, disturbs English communications, and ties up English troops and shipping at the expense of other theatres of war. I have therefore decided to hasten developments in the Middle East by supporting Iraq. [...] The victory of the Axis will free the countries of the Middle East from the English yoke, and will give them the right to self-determination. All who love freedom will therefore join in the fight against England.[62]

Hitler also approved Bose's request for declarations on India and Arab nations, realising that they would politically reinforce his directive by furthering anti-British sentiment and mobilising public opinion alongside Germany.[63] He was still debating whether to set-up an Indian government but in the end allowed the Foreign Office to shelve it indefinitely, much to its relief and satisfaction. Ribbentrop clouded matters by eschewing a clear position on the matter. His main priority was to avoid contradicting Hitler. The most the Foreign Office came up with as a substitute was a 'Free India Centre' or an 'Indian Independence Committee'.

Although it is not clear to what extent Bose's note influenced German policymaking, what is certain is that it was not without some impact. Proof of this was the embarrassed manner in which officials at the Foreign Office now asked Bose to draft the declaration on India. There was nothing ambiguous about his draft:

Germany [...] recognises the inalienable right of the Indian people to have full and complete independence. [...] She assures the Indian people that the New Order which she is out to establish in the world will mean for them a free and independent India. [...] It will, of course, be for the Indian people to decide what form of government they should have. [...] Germany conveys its sincerest good wishes to the Indian people in their struggle for freedom and declares that she is prepared to render them such assistance as lies in her power, so that the goal of liberty may be reached without delay.[64]

Although the last sentence went beyond a mere expression of support for Indian independence, amounting as it did to a pledge of assistance, the Foreign Office accepted the draft without alteration. It was to be released along with similar declarations on South Africa, Ireland and Arab nations as part of a propaganda offensive against the British Empire.[65] Bose, who played a key role in bringing this about, considered these declarations to be 'morally invincible' and an 'historic event in world politics'.[66] He was now more enthusiastic than ever about the prospects for Indo-Nazi co-operation.

2

EXTENDING THE BOUNDARIES

ASPIRING FOR NAZI LIBERATION

Kabul, Rome and Venice, May–June 1941

On 20 May, Bose sent a long message, via the German legation in Kabul, to Bhagat Ram Talwar, a Forward Bloc activist who was setting-up a regional intelligence apparatus:

> Big events will happen soon in the sphere of international politics which will help the overthrow of British imperialism. [...] I am expecting from the Axis powers within a fortnight an open declaration regarding Indian independence. Immediately after this declaration, I intend starting propaganda activity. [...] Have you attempted to organise a big *jirga* (conference) [...] for organising an attack on the British [...] we can begin sending help for India from June. [...] We can also send propaganda leaflets and booklets. Please arrange for these and sabotage materials [...] to be taken to India [...] bring from India report regarding reaction of the Indian people [...] to the Anglo-Iraq war.[1]

Talwar was also instructed to liaise with German intelligence operatives in Nepal and anti-British organisations in Burma via other agents. Bose hoped to create an extensive regional underground ready to pounce on the British when the time came. Finally, all major military installations in India were to come under surveillance.[2]

Bose also prepared an important 'Detailed Plan of Work' the same day for the Foreign Office in which he recommended setting-up a secret military training centre and airstrip in the Tribal Territory. This would allow much needed equipment including arms, sabotage material, portable radio transmitters and printing machinery, to be sent. The airstrip could also be used to eventually deploy advance German and Free Indian units for the offensive into India.[3]

Having been informed officially of the decision to defer an Indian government for now, Bose rejected an 'Indian Independence Committee', claiming that it would be a 'democratic body and from the practical point of view it will be unworkable'.[4] This was the first indication of Bose's latent dictatorial tendencies that were to be manifested during the war.[5] An Indian committee, it is true, was reminiscent of one set-up by Indian nationalists in Berlin during the First World War and which, in spite of grandiose actions, including establishing a provisional government in Kabul, had gone from one failure to another. Not wanting to share in its legacy, Bose was satisfied for now with a 'Free India Centre'. He was insistent, however, on establishing as many branches as possible—official and clandestine—in numerous countries.[6]

Now that he was prepared to launch a major propaganda campaign, Bose proposed that the Free India Radio station broadcast with four distinct aims:

(a) For India, the object will be to work up a revolution. (b) For other Oriental countries, the object will be to inspire revolts against Britain in Egypt, Palestine, other Arab countries etc. (c) For America, the object will be to attack the argument that Britain and America are really fighting for democracy. (d) For other countries, the object will be to explain what a curse British imperialism has been to other countries.[7]

This was indicative of the manner in which Bose sought to integrate the Indian struggle for freedom into the wider global conflagration. He saw the latter as an opportunity to rid not only India, but other nations as well, of British imperialism. This prompted him, in a moment of unjustified optimism, to contradict his note of 3 May by naively raising the possibility of a 'German-Soviet agreement' on India. In the event that this was not possible, he suggested turning instead to Iran.

Four days later, Berlin received a positive response from Kabul. The first *Abwehr* agents had arrived in connection with Operation Tiger and established contact with Talwar.[8] They confirmed that preparations for a major revolt in the Tribal Territory were underway.[9] It was even hoped that the Iraqi legation in Kabul would provide assistance.[10] One of the agents made an urgent request for sabotage material, thereby legitimising Bose's recommendation on the matter. Half a million Reichsmarks were deemed necessary to keep the Fakir of Ipi and his tribesmen fighting the British,[11] a small price to pay. Ribbentrop, in the event, allotted one million Reichsmarks for overall operations in the region.[12]

Ribbentrop was more reserved, however, about the political offensive against Britain. Fearing that German intervention in Iraq might not prove successful, he preferred to wait for the outcome, especially now that Iraqi-British fighting was nearing its peak.[13] Woermann informed Bose of this on 24 May, while assuring him that preparations to open the Free India Centre were under way.[14] Bose did not protest.[15] On the contrary, this was convenient for him as he was about to leave for Rome in an attempt to persuade the Italians to join Germany in issuing the declaration on India—thereby doubling its impact.

When Ribbentrop was informed of this he was dismayed, concerned that the Italians might entice Bose to remain in Rome. For all their pretence of being close allies, the reality was that there was much distrust between Berlin and Rome. After being reproached by Ribbentrop for casually approving Bose's departure, an embarrassed Woermann advised the German embassy in Rome by telegram on 28 May:

SUBHAS CHANDRA BOSE IN NAZI GERMANY

The well-known Indian nationalist, Subhas C. Bose [...] will arrive in Rome by plane on May 29. [...] The intention is to work together very closely with him in all Indian matters. Extensive confidential plans of large scope are being considered here [...] which in certain circumstances are to be executed on short notice. We are therefore interested in Bose's curtailing his stay in Rome as much as possible and returning here as soon as possible. [...] receive him in a friendly manner and afford him any help he desires. [...] report regularly by telegram regarding Bose's stay in Rome and the people who receive him.[16]

The Germans need not have worried: Bose's visit was a complete disaster. First, he could not have chosen a worse time in which to arrive, as Mussolini and his Foreign Minister, Count Galeazzo Ciano, were on the eve of leaving to meet Hitler and Ribbentrop at the Brenner Pass. Bose spent his time sightseeing with Emilie Schenkl who accompanied him as his 'secretary'.

The Italian Foreign Ministry did arrange for Bose to meet three former members of the Indian revolutionary organisation *Ghadar* which had been active during the First World War. These men, Mohammed Iqbal Shedai, Ajit Singh and Labh Singh, broadcast to India on the Italian-sponsored Radio Himalaya. Although amateurs, their broadcasts were not without significance—at least that is what they succeeded in convincing the Italians. They had offered their services as soon as Italy entered the war and their hosts were only too happy to oblige. Neither side envisaged anything as extensive as Bose and the Germans did. The Italians seemed quite content to let these disgruntled old men rave and rant on the radio (as much against the British as the new generation of nationalists that had emerged in India) as part of their anti-British efforts. Nevertheless, decades away from India had cut them off from the mainstream of the Indian nationalist movement. They had little understanding of or sympathy for the Congress. This posed an immediate problem for Bose. That he was a former Congress president on intimate terms with Gandhi and Nehru was a matter of absolute indifference to them. They had resorted to force, including terrorism, in the past and Gandhi's pacifist ideology only aroused their contempt. Bose's efforts to emphasise his differences with Gandhi—precisely over such matters—failed to have any impact.[17] He was and would remain in their eyes a dubious Congress politician.

Several meetings did nothing to improve matters. Neither was the realisation that Bose's underground organisation was weak and dependent on the Kirti Kisan, a party these men believed themselves affiliated with through a loose network of contacts.[18] Bose's assertion that Axis financial assistance did not pose an ethical dilemma did not go down very well either.[19] Bose nevertheless was determined to win them over. Even when they made it quite clear that he should not expect much from them, he persisted, realising what a significant political failure it would be on his part if he failed to win over the three Indians who could be of use to him in Europe. Not only did they already broadcast to India but they also boasted of extensive contacts with Indian revolutionary organisations and had already initiated contact with Indian POWs.

What Bose did not realise was that their reservations regarding co-operation stemmed from a fear of subordination. They had succeeded in convincing Italian officials that they were important nationalists while in reality they were unknown, insignificant, entities. The link with Indian revolutionary organisations existed primarily in their imaginations. Bose's presence in Rome risked exposing this. It was for this reason that they were eager that he return to Berlin as quickly as possible. To achieve this they resorted to fabricating lies intended to portray him as an unreliable, if not dangerous, buffoon. After each meeting Shedai wrote meticulous reports to the Italian Foreign Ministry revealing in detail the contents of what were supposed to have been confidential meetings between Indian nationalists. Shedai in effect became a self-appointed informer. With each passing meeting his reports became more hysterical, until losing all sense of proportion and credibility, they ultimately became self-defeating. One passage suffices:

Mr Bose depends for his revolutionary work on my party—i.e. the Kirti-Kisan Party [...] his work [...] is nothing but imaginary. [...] all parties in India are against Mr Bose and especially the All India National Congress which expelled him from its ranks. [...] It is a pity that none has faith in him [... and] most [...] Bengalis are against him. [...] As far as I can see he has not been able to persuade the Germans to accept his programme if he has any.[20]

Shedai also cast aspersions on Emilie Schenkl, suggesting she was a German spy and that he had to be 'very cautious' in her presence.[21] Again this was a crude attempt to undermine Bose's credibility. The tone and nature of these reports should have alerted Italian officials as to their intention. On the other hand it was not in the interest of the Foreign Ministry to probe too deeply into these reports as the realisation that it was promoting three charlatans while the only Indian of importance was in Berlin, would be another admission of failure on the part of Italy.

On 6 June, the Foreign Minister, Ciano, finally received Bose upon his return to Rome although significantly, Mussolini did not do so on this occasion. After polite preliminaries, Bose got to the point, emphasising the need for an Italo-German declaration on India.[22] Ciano responded defensively, conscious that his country was in no position militarily to issue a declaration without potentially appearing ridiculous. Italian soldiery had just been saved from a humiliating quagmire in Greece and Libya by the Wehrmacht and Italy's armed forces could not guarantee Indian independence. Ciano could not afford to be too explicit. In any case, Berlin had not informed Rome of the declaration and the initiative seemed to come exclusively from Bose. Neither did it help that Ciano was unimpressed by Bose and was particularly sceptical of his accomplishments in Berlin.[23] Doubtless Shedai, operating from behind the scenes, was partly responsible for this state of affairs. Nevertheless, Ciano did not rule out a declaration entirely. He first wanted to check with Berlin before taking a formal decision, thereby revealing the extent to which Italian policy had become dependent on Germany.

In Berlin, meanwhile, Bose was becoming a cause for concern. Before leaving he had assured Woermann that he would maintain regular contact through the German embassy. On 6 June, however, the embassy reported that while Bose was busy conferring left, right and centre, he had not even made a courtesy call.[24] Bose did not bother doing so for nearly two weeks, completely indifferent to the anxiety this was causing. After finally visiting the embassy on 11 June, the relieved Counsellor, Otto von Bismarck, informed Berlin that Bose had shown no indication of wanting to transfer his activities to Rome, as Ribbentrop initially feared. 'He is solely under the impression that his return to Berlin is not so urgent' he reported.[25] This remained the primary concern of the Foreign Office as it had no inkling that Bose's discussions in Rome had come to nought, the Italians having done little to enlighten their German partners on the matter.

A few days later, Ciano and Ribbentrop met during an Axis conference in Venice. In regard to India they agreed on the need to support Bose but that a declaration was premature.[26] There was good reason for this. Even before Bose left Berlin, Iraqi resistance quickly petered out. German intervention proved ineffective as the British quickly regained control of the country. Equally serious, British troops on June 8 invaded pro-Axis Vichy Syria, allowing Britain to regain the initiative and reassert control in the Middle East. This put an end to Bose's hopes for a pro-German 'chain' and Churchill's concerns with 'Hitler's hand' stretching across the region. Clearly, this was not the time to issue a declaration guaranteeing Indian independence. It would only destroy what little was left of German and Italian political credibility.[27]

This was not a perspective Bose was inclined to heed. Indeed, when Ciano conveyed this decision to him upon his return from Venice, Bose evinced little or no understanding of the situation: he only made his disappointment visibly clear. The worst of his sojourn was still ahead of him.

Barbarossa, Indian Reversals and Intelligence Planning, June–October 1941

On 22 June 1941, Germany launched Barbarossa—the long planned invasion of the Soviet Union. It began as a resounding success, prompting much jubilation in the Reich capital, but Bose was not given to rejoicing. On the contrary, his repressed pro-Soviet sympathies now came out to the fore, fully realising as he did that the personal consequences for him would be devastating as Indian public opinion would inevitably side with the Soviet Union. Indeed, all political parties, including the Forward Bloc,[28] promptly passed resolutions expressing sympathy for the Soviet Union and condemning Germany. This was a particularly embarrassing indication that Bose was no longer in control of his own party. Under such circumstances, he postponed his return to Berlin and waited for events to unfold. Anticipating such a response, Woermann wrote to him two days after the invasion, urging him to return promptly as his presence was required in Berlin. Somewhat flattered—and with little to hold him back in Rome—Bose reluctantly agreed to do so in his reply of 5 July. He expressed himself directly:

> I met Count Ciano after his return from Venice [...] the talk was not encouraging for me and soon after that, the war in the east broke out. The prospect for the realisation of my plans looked gloomy in the altered circumstances and I was thinking that an early return to Berlin would not be of much use. [...] The public reaction in my country to the new situation in the east is unfavourable towards your government. [...] I am following the situation as closely as I can and I shall discuss the whole matter with you as soon as I arrive.[29]

Bose was blunter during their meeting on 17 July: 'In the German-Russian war', he told Woermann, 'the feelings of the Indian people were very decidedly on the Russian side' because Germany was the 'aggressor' and another 'imperialist power'. The approach of German troops would be perceived as an attempt to substitute 'British rule' with 'German rule'. He even warned of a possible Anglo-Indian political compromise. Bose could not have expressed himself more pessimistically.[30]

It was the absence of a declaration which caused Bose the greatest distress. Woermann sought to restore his sagging morale by emphasising his government's commitment to the issue while advising Bose to be patient. Bose erupted at the latter suggestion, suddenly insisting in a very agitated state that Ribbentrop issue the declaration urgently. After restoring his equanimity, he glumly conceded that it would have to be issued while considering the war in its entirety. Bose's sudden outburst, the result of weeks of pent up frustration over the delay, his disastrous visit to Rome and the invasion of Russia, surprised Woermann. The latter quickly changed the subject, speaking of a new 'Special India Bureau' which was being organised within the Foreign Office as well as of preparations to open the Free India Centre, but realising that Bose was neither impressed nor interested, stopped.[31]

After the meeting, unused to hearing such blatant criticism of German foreign policy, Woermann wrote a memorandum summarising the conversation for Ribbentrop, claiming: 'Bose's statements indicated that, away from Berlin, he is strongly influenced by the Soviet thesis even in the question of the origin of the German-Russian conflict, so that it will be one of the first tasks to set him right on this point'.[32] Woermann was fooling himself as much as he was fooling the Foreign Minister.

For the next few weeks, Bose did little more than ponder his own dissatisfaction. He refrained from even involving himself with the transfer of Indian POWs from North Africa to

Germany.³³ Only on 11 August did he reappear in public, this time to attend an important intelligence meeting on India and the Tribal Territory, convened by the High Command, the *Abwehr* and the new Special India Bureau. The conference coincided with an extensive report from Kabul on Afghan fortifications, road conditions and troop movements as well as a detailed strategic analysis of the North-West Frontier.³⁴ There had been significant changes in the Tribal Territory since Bose had returned to Berlin. A few weeks earlier, an *Abwehr* agent had been killed and another wounded by an Afghan patrol while on a mission to contact the Fakir of Ipi.³⁵ The Afghan government warned Berlin against such activities in future.³⁶ In spite of this the participants, including Bose, decided to proceed with Operation Tiger.³⁷

Of importance to Bose was the decision to implement his proposal of 20 May, for an airstrip in the Tribal Territory, thereby allowing *Abwehr* agents as well as German commandos (already being specially trained for Tiger) to be deployed in large numbers.³⁸ The main obstacle was that the long distance Focke-Wulf Fw 200 Condor aircraft used to transport troops required large and firm airstrips in a region known for its rugged terrain.³⁹ For the time being, *Abwehr* agents would simply be parachuted into the Tribal Territory. Bose contributed little to the meeting as he was in general agreement with its resolutions. Despite political deadlock over the declaration, he could at least derive satisfaction on the intelligence front.

On 12 August, Shedai arrived in Berlin. Bose had arranged for him to be invited, through the Foreign Office, in the hope of winning him over, particularly if the initiative was seen as coming from Berlin.⁴⁰ He need not have bothered. From the very beginning, Shedai responded with even more hostility than he had shown in Rome. He was particularly annoyed by Bose's lack of enthusiasm for an Indo-Italo-German committee he was propounding.⁴¹ Shedai realised that such an outcome would put him and the Italians on a par with Bose and the Germans, thus

EXTENDING THE BOUNDARIES

ensuring a more egalitarian basis from which to develop Indian policy. This is exactly what Bose wished to avoid. He had already made it clear to the Germans that he opposed committees because of their democratic nature.[42] In this particular case he opposed the inclusion of the Italians, accusing them of indiscretion.[43] Bose might have been influenced by German perceptions of Italian unreliability, if not incompetence. His opposition might have also been in retaliation for Mussolini's failure to receive him. Whatever the reason, Shedai was furious.

Neither did it help that the two men could not even agree on the nature of the declaration on India. Typically, Shedai complicated matters by insisting that only an Axis declaration would do,[44] namely a declaration by Germany, Italy, Hungary, Romania, Bulgaria, Croatia and Slovakia. For good measure he threw in Japan as well although it still maintained diplomatic relations with Britain. Bose tried in vain to explain that this would be impossible to obtain when it was already so difficult to procure a mere Italo-German declaration. Shedai was adamant. He paid an immediate price for his uncompromising attitude and impractical nature of his political agenda as Woermann and the Director of the Special India Bureau, Wilhelm Keppler, suddenly cancelled their meetings with him.[45]

Shedai blamed Bose for this, conveniently ignoring the poorly concealed fact that it had been Bose's idea all along to invite him to Berlin. Indirectly, Bose gave Shedai additional importance by his determined and naive attempt to win him over. It was as though Bose was testing his own political skills rather than acknowledging that it would make little difference whether or not he succeeded in recruiting Shedai. Within days of Shedai's arrival it finally became obvious to Bose that his efforts were not only futile, but counterproductive.

In the end, Shedai was reduced to meetings with junior officials of the Foreign Office. He repeated his arguments for a committee and declaration—to no avail. Adam von Trott, a senior official at the Special India Bureau, tried to entice Shedai by offering him control of the Free India Centre and the POWs, even going as far as to suggest reducing Bose to a figurehead.[46] Trott, who personally disliked Bose,[47] was speaking for himself as he had not received any such instructions from his superiors. In any case, Shedai was not so easily fooled. He set two conditions as the basis for co-operation. First, an Axis declaration, and secondly the approval of the Italian Foreign Ministry. 'I am loyal to my Italian friends and shall not do anything without their consent', he boasted.[48]

Shedai's visit to Berlin was not a complete failure. He did visit some Indian POWs interned in Stalag IV D/Z in Annaburg near Berlin.[49] What he found there was not to his liking at all. The POWs, seething with discontent, complained bitterly about their daily staple of soup, potato and cabbage. There were also concerns about the weather, particularly, with winter approaching. They clearly had absolutely no inkling of the catastrophic conditions in nearby Soviet POW and concentration camps.[50] Not that Shedai was interested in such comparisons, preferring instead to make political capital out of the situation by blaming Bose. What really upset him was the squandering of goodwill. Many of the POWs now spoke of Germany with growing suspicion and resentment. The postponement in recruiting had only reinforced their self-perception as POWs.[51]

Shedai blamed Bose entirely. In an official report to the Italians, he complained that Bose did 'not care a bit for these poor devils' and that he had 'committed the biggest crime by bringing them over to Germany'.[52] Disgusted as he was by his visit to Berlin, Shedai wrote this scathing missive to the Italian Foreign Ministry upon his return to Rome, attributing dubious motives to Bose as well the Germans:

Bose—intentionally or unintentionally—is playing a very dangerous game. [...] He is putting the Germans on the wrong track [...] it is very unwise [...] to help him [...] achieve his selfish and wicked ends. [...]

The Germans hesitate to give any kind of declaration. [...] In my opinion they still believe that after the crash of Russia, England will accept peace. [...] If the Germans declare for the independence of India, there is no card left to begin peace negotiations with England. British Empire means India. The Germans want to use Bose. [...] to frighten the British. Bose has accepted to co-operate with them without any guarantee for the independence of India. I have categorically refused to do anything before the declaration is signed by Germany, Italy, Japan and other allied powers. [...] I was told [...] that without my coming to Berlin, nothing could be done. (A great flattery to my humble soul.)[53]

Bose had other grave concerns to confront. On 14 August, the American President, Franklin D. Roosevelt, and Winston Churchill issued a joint Anglo-American Declaration recognising the 'right of all peoples to choose the form of government under which they will live' and their desire to see 'self-government' and 'sovereign rights' restored to nations deprived of them.[54] Bose realised that this would be enthusiastically received in India and might even bring about a political compromise.[55] He immediately wrote a letter to Ribbentrop. Doing away with the usual diplomatic niceties, he got straight to the point, emphasising the possibility of an imminent political compromise, the danger of increasing American influence, the turning tide of Indian public opinion against Germany and even the possibility of British troops invading Iran. 'The road to Afghanistan which has been open all these months will be cut' he warned in a state of near panic, adding that 'it will then be difficult for us to work out our plans regarding India'. Bose made the case once more for the declaration on India, warning that failure to issue it would mean that the 'march of the German troops towards the east will be regarded as the approach, not of a friend, but of an enemy'. He ended his letter on a desperate note, urging Ribbentrop to come to a quick decision, 'whatever that decision maybe'.[56]

The agitated tone of Bose's letter revealed his lingering suspicion that his presence in Berlin was compromising him politically. Nevertheless, in what appeared to be another incident of nervousness and hesitation, he held on to his letter for three days before handing it Woermann on 18 August.[57] After listening to a summary of its contents—particularly in regard to the declaration—Woermann casually assured Bose in a matter of fact tone that he could have 'full confidence' as he had to 'recognise after all, that the Führer was a master in choosing the moment for political actions'.[58] Bose walked out of Woermann's office in amazement.

Nevertheless, in a memorandum attached to Bose's letter for Ribbentrop, Woermann expressed himself more realistically, even confirming the validity of some of Bose's points:

If one considers the situation in India solely by itself, it would be urgently desirable to have the declaration regarding a free India issued soon, because it would supply the nationalist forces with a weapon against Gandhi's willingness to compromise which is growing under Anglo-American influence. Naturally the question cannot be viewed from this standpoint alone. Rather it is a question of choosing a favourable point of departure with respect to general policy. Thus, the entry of English troops into Iran would perhaps be an event that would offer a plausible occasion for an Indian declaration, which could then be placed in the even larger context of the British rape of the eastern nations.[59]

Indeed, one week later, British and Soviet troops jointly invaded Iran in what Churchill called a 'brief and fruitful exercise of overwhelming force against a weak and ancient state'.[60] It was also ironic, coming as it did, within days of the Anglo-American declaration expressing a desire to 'see sovereign rights and self-government restored' to nations 'forcibly deprived of them'.[61] This allowed Germany to have a propaganda field day, seizing the moral high ground for once, denouncing what it perceived as the 'unscrupulous rape of a small state'.[62] The exaggerated reaction reflected a more genuine concern with reaffirmation of British power in the Middle East.

Hitler, upon being informed of Bose's renewed request for the declaration, decided temporarily to postpone it lest the British now use it as a pretext to invade Afghanistan.[63] After German reversals in Iraq, Syria and Iran, Hitler was not prepared to risk a fourth in Afghanistan. An embarrassed Ribbentrop, fully realising that Bose would not be pleased, instructed Woermann to assure him that:

The Foreign Minister continues to have the greatest interest in his plans, and thanks him sincerely for his letter. If in the past we had desired, and still desire, that the moment for the publication of a declaration regarding a free India should be postponed, it is connected with the situation as a whole. [...] As matters stand today, a proclamation of a free India [...] might possibly have the effect that England would then occupy Afghanistan in order to consolidate her position in India, and that she would muster [...] additional forces to the Near East. [...] We had to avoid bringing about such English measures prematurely.[64]

After a brief visit to Paris in search of staff for the Free India Centre, Bose decided not to return to Berlin but instead went to Bad Gastein, his favourite pre-war spa resort, for a cure. Trott, of the Special India Bureau, was sent to deliver Ribbentrop's message, as well as a letter from Woermann urging Bose to return as soon as possible.[65] It was in vain. Bose continued his 'cure' for several weeks.

Nevertheless, Bose did not abandon his work entirely. At the end of September, he made enquiries of Talwar in Kabul, regarding Indian military desertions, the impact of Radio Himalaya, and the effect of events in Iraq, Syria and Iran on Indian public opinion. Of the eighteen points Bose sought elaboration on, the second was the most revealing: 'Does a concrete revolution plan exist?'[66] he asked. This revealed the extent to which he had now come to question Talwar's activities and German intelligence planning. He had good reason to. Each time Talwar returned to Kabul—ostensibly following a mission to India—he reported not to the German legation but to the Soviet one.[67] With the invasion of the Soviet Union, Talwar suddenly found himself in-between two opposing camps. This covert communist activist resolved that his ideological allegiance lay with Moscow, not Berlin, Bose or Indian independence. Accordingly, he exposed Bose's plans and the entire German regional intelligence apparatus to Soviet intelligence in Kabul.[68]

Bose never fully realised to what extent the invasion of the Soviet Union damaged his plans. Talwar, operating now as a Soviet agent, provided the Germans with meticulously fabricated reports as part of a deliberate Soviet (and British) plan to mislead German intelligence. Talwar succeeded in fooling the Germans into believing that an extensive Boseian underground existed in India.[69] Not surprisingly, whenever local *Abwehr* agents attempted anything substantial, such as organising an airstrip in the Tribal Territory, Talwar always came up with a plausible excuse to deter them. He even succeeded in convincing them to abandon Operation Tiger in accordance with British and Soviet wishes.

A few days later, the German legation in Kabul responded with a report that was not particularly encouraging.[70] With a stagnant political front, and intelligence activities now receding, Bose decided to further extend his 'cure'. It was the low point of his German exile. Nevertheless, the Germans did not abandon Indian activities. On 16 October, Ribbentrop made enquiries of the High Command as to the number of Indian POWs in German custody.[71] This was partly motivated by reports emanating from Rome that the Italians were intensifying their Indian policy, including organising an equivalent to the Free India Centre.[72] The concern was that they might also organise a parallel military formation.[73] Shedai, as usual, was behind this. At this point Bose's compatriots—Shedai and Talwar—were ironically more responsible for hampering his plans than the Germans were.

EXTENDING THE BOUNDARIES

Free India, November–December 1941

At the end of October, finally acknowledging that he could be of greater use in Berlin than feeling sorry for himself in Bad Gastein, Bose decided to return. In his absence the Special India Bureau had worked frantically to get the Free India Centre up and running. It was inaugurated in Bose's presence on 2 November. The Foreign Office had succeeded in recruiting two dozen Indians—mostly stranded journalists, doctors and intellectuals from across German-occupied Europe—to work for the Centre. It was located not without intended symbolism in the Tiergarten, the diplomatic quarter of Berlin. Bose unfurled a Congress flag in the presence of the Indian staff, high-ranking representatives of the Foreign Office as well as the High Command. It proved to be a solemn and emotional affair for the Indians.

Important decisions were taken within days. To give 'Free India' a unique identity, separate from other independence organisations, it was decided to replace the Gandhian spinning wheel on the Congress flag with a springing tiger. The message was clear. All who supported Free India were prepared to achieve independence through more violent means than those advocated by Gandhi.[74] It was as much an affirmation of the need for armed struggle as it was a repudiation of Gandhian non-violence. Within months, hundreds of former Indian POWs would be wearing uniforms with springing tiger patches.

To simplify integration, the Centre adopted *Jana Gana Mana* as the national anthem and Hindustani as the national language, operating very much as though it was as the legitimate government of India.[75] A commission even designed and printed Free India currency and stamps for use in liberated areas. There was also an attempt to revive a national planning commission set up by Nehru and Bose while the latter was Congress president.[76] Although by no means blindly subservient, Bose's staff for the most part went along with him and his plans.

SUBHAS CHANDRA BOSE IN NAZI GERMANY

The emergence of a Free India Centre with a dedicated staff greatly reinvigorated Bose. From total isolation a few weeks earlier to now being surrounded by his compatriots actively working for independence, Bose had reason to feel more satisfied than he had in months. That the Foreign Office conferred diplomatic status on the Indian staff with all the privileges this entailed, including extra rations not available to ordinary Germans, helped bring about an added sense of legitimacy and motivation. The Centre quickly expanded with various departments for propaganda, publishing, intelligence, broadcasting and POWs.[77]

Within a few weeks, Bose's long-planned Free India Radio was on the air broadcasting daily to India. It came as a rude awakening to the British. Unlike the crude and at times vulgar service emanating from Radio Himalaya, Free India provided a more reliable and entertaining alternative to British controlled stations in India. Broadcasts aired in half a dozen Indian languages comprised of not only political but cultural themes as well. Indian classical music, for example, was rebroadcast directly from the Indian service of the BBC.[78] The two daily news bulletins tried to be as accurate as possible so as to ensure long-term credibility and gain public confidence. Nevertheless, Free India Radio did not hide—as its name indicated—its aim. It was just that its political message was subtly enrolled in its broadcasting service. This form of propaganda, while inspired by the Germans, was controlled by the Indians themselves.[79]

Goebbels, the Propaganda Minister, refrained from interfering with these broadcasts, although he showed much interest in their impact abroad. That he was greatly satisfied, no doubt, helped.[80] The service in any case came under the aegis of the Foreign Office, not the Propaganda Ministry.[81] Bose had made it clear from the beginning that the Free India Radio had to operate as a genuinely independent radio station. German interference would be unacceptable. For the time being everything worked well. More Indians were recruited, some to work exclusively on monitoring foreign stations, particularly the BBC.[82] The Centre also published *Free India*, a journal in German and English with a circulation of 5,000.[83]

Many of the intellectuals working at the Centre were anti-Nazi, often with Marxist pasts, but now reconciled to collaborating with Germany. In many cases, having been stranded in different parts of the continent since the outbreak of war they had nothing better to do. The conditions and privileges extended to them were difficult to resist. A tacit agreement between Bose and the Germans existed whereby the left-wing inclinations of his staff were ignored as long as they confined their political activities to India. Everything worked smoothly as long as Indo-German aims remained focused against Britain.

Apart from the Free India Centre, Bose also had another reason to feel satisfied—even comfortable—in Berlin. After months of residing in a hotel, the Foreign Office procured a luxurious residence for him along with a butler, cook, gardener and an *SS*-chauffeured car. Emilie Schenkl moved in openly with him. The Germans, aware of the nature of their relationship, refrained from any involvement. The following year she gave birth to a daughter. The residence quickly became a gathering point for the Indian, Arab and Afghan communities in Berlin. Among them they included the ousted Prime Minister of Iraq, Rashid Ali al-Gaylani, the exiled Grand Mufti of Jerusalem, Mohammad Amin al-Husayni, and the former Afghan Foreign Minister, Ghulam Siddiq Khan. The comfort, combined with the presence of Emilie as well as contact with important anti-British leaders, exiles and the Indian staff, ensured that Bose now began feeling more at 'home' in Berlin.

Bose's growing sense of comfort and confidence was suddenly shattered, however, on 10 November when the Indian Central Legislative Assembly and British-controlled All India Radio station revealed his presence in Berlin, thereby depriving Bose of the opportunity of creating his own sensation at a time of his choosing.[84] The matter was also discussed in the British parliament.[85] Within days, the British and American press launched a campaign denouncing Bose as a pro-Nazi traitor. 'India's Quisling No. 1 flees to Hitler' screamed a typical headline in the *Daily Mail*.[86] Formerly treated as a respected Congress politician by the British press, Bose was now depicted as nothing more than an Indian equivalent of Lord Haw Haw, the fascist Irishman, William Joyce, whose exaggerated anti-British broadcasts on German radio had become a source of public ridicule in Britain. Bose had refrained from having any contact with Lord Haw Haw precisely for such reasons. The latter was an anti-Semitic street fighter and rabble-rouser whereas Bose was determined to maintain his status as a respected national leader and politician.[87]

The intensity of the press campaign was such that within days Ribbentrop informed Hitler in a brief that an 'English counter-propaganda action has recently begun which is intended to discredit Bose with the Indian population as having gone over to the Axis Powers' and to promote his 'antagonist, Pandit Nehru'. He concluded with evident satisfaction: 'The English camp is already beginning to show anxiety as a consequence of Bose's presence in Germany'.[88] He also referred at length to the declaration, realising that Bose would now be more persistent about securing it:

> The point of departure for our policy with regard to India [...] must be the publication of a declaration. [...] We know that Bose has been insistently urging since the Spring that such a declaration be issued. [...] The moment for such a declaration, however, will come only when it is clearly discernible that England does not manifest any willingness to make peace even after the final collapse of Russia. [...] Large-scale propaganda directed at India will become possible only when the declaration regarding a free India has been published. [...] Our decision to defer for the time being a declaration [...] will not have to be altered by us despite the reports circulated by the English.[89]

By making the declaration dependent on peace, Ribbentrop was proposing a complete change in policy. This was an impulsive gesture, designed to impress Hitler, as he soon backtracked and persistently urged Hitler to issue the declaration regardless of British policy.

Ribbentrop made the first of a long series of contradictory statements during a meeting with Bose on 29 November, exactly seven months to the day since their first encounter. Bose expressed gratitude for the help he had received but displayed press clippings from British newspapers, including the *Daily Mail*, which branded him a Quisling.[90] A counter-propaganda campaign, he insisted, had to be launched. By this he implied the declaration although he never actually used the word itself.

Ribbentrop responded with a long monologue explaining that the war would 'result in the destruction of the English possessions everywhere in the world'. He blamed Churchill, with poorly concealed frustration, for prolonging it. As for Russia, it would 'still require some effort to be sure'. When it became apparent that Bose was not particularly interested in Ribbentrop's pronouncements on the war, which included statements such as Ernest Bevin, the Labour Minister, being 'a half-Bolshevik' and assurances that Russia would be 'successfully colonised', he stopped and finally addressed the declaration. 'Germany policy', Ribbentrop explained 'did not think much of declarations with no force behind them, because it was possible that the opposite effect from the one desired could occur'. For example, he referred to the failure of German intervention in Iraq. 'The result was that the Grand Mufti and Gailani were in Germany, the government was forced into exile, and its friends were dead or in prison'. 'It was a guiding principle of German policy not to promise anything which could not be carried out later'. Ribbentrop reminded Bose that propaganda alone would not liberate India. 'This could only be achieved through the destruction of the English positions of power'.[91]

Listening with growing frustration at this long list of excuses, Bose suddenly broke with diplomatic niceties and interrupted to ask in a blatantly sceptical manner if this was also Hitler's view. A rather startled Ribbentrop replied defensively that the 'Führer believed in the final defeat of England; it was simply his view, however, that no action should take place until Germany had the power to support it properly'. Bose insisted that Hitler's views on India needed clarification as *Mein Kampf* was being exploited for propaganda purposes in India by the British. When Ribbentrop spoke of arranging a meeting with Hitler, Bose was very receptive.[92]

Ribbentrop did for the first time provide a time frame as to when a declaration might be issued, suggesting that this would be feasible as soon as German troops captured the Suez Canal or reached the Caucasus. Bose could then establish an Indian liberation committee in Tiflis, 'with a large expenditure and with radio transmitters'. Bose had little to say about this, preferring to wait for events to unfold. In any case, the prospect of reaching the Georgian capital—while it may have been an important military achievement for the Germans and was certainly an improvement over Berlin—did little to motivate him.[93]

The meeting was significantly shorter and more to the point than the first one. With deadlock over the declaration and the Indian Centre now successfully operating on its own, there was little to discuss. Ribbentrop sought to fill the void with a long list of justifications regarding German policy but in the end only betrayed a guilty conscience. Intelligence matters were not even addressed. Neither were the POWs. Ribbentrop was quite content to brush off all such responsibility onto Hitler and the High Command.

Barely concealing his irritation, Bose added little himself. He maintained a cool, distant and sceptical attitude throughout the conversation. It was another low point of Indo-German co-operation. Within days, however, the dynamics of this co-operation would be radically transformed by events in the Pacific. Ribbentrop had already given such a hint when he spoke of a 'serious situation' and 'state of tension' developing rapidly between Japan and the United States.[94]

3

TRIPLING THE EFFECT

BERLIN, ROME, TOKYO

Co-ordinating Tripartite Policy, Stalag IV D/Z and Collaboration Dilemmas, December 1941–February 1942

On 7 December 1941, Japanese aircraft attacked Pearl Harbor, crippling the American fleet and making themselves masters of the Pacific. Hitler responded by declaring war on the United States on 11 December. British rule on the sub-continent was suddenly threatened by Japanese troops rapidly advancing across Southeast Asia. Their speed was so stunning that the Germans—facing their first major setback in the snow on the outskirts of Moscow—were thoroughly reinvigorated.

Even before the attack on Pearl Harbor, Japanese diplomats had been working behind the scenes, urging Berlin and Rome to co-ordinate policy on India.[1] What the two Axis partners had failed to accomplish so far, Japanese diplomacy brought about with astonishing rapidity.[2] Already within hours of the attack on Hawaii, Berlin and Rome convened a two-day emergency conference on India in response to the Japanese initiative. Shedai flew in from Rome where he joined local Italian diplomats. Bose sat on the German side of the table along with representatives of the Special India Bureau, the *Abwehr* and High Command.

Not surprisingly, Bose called for an immediate Tripartite (Italo-German-Japanese) declaration on India.[3] For once, Shedai was in agreement. The Italians were open although the Germans seemed barely able to conceal their lack of enthusiasm. The standard line about the need for military operations to have a greater impact was resorted to, although it was hardly convincing in light of Japanese successes. Nevertheless, Woermann instructed the German embassy in Tokyo to inform the Japanese government that a 'Japanese declaration regarding Indian independence should be co-ordinated with us and Italy with respect to content as well as time'.[4]

In anticipation of anti-Axis statements from Nehru, it was decided to launch a pre-emptive propaganda campaign.[5] There would also be a significant increase of Indian coverage in the European press. Inevitably, Bose was urged to broadcast but he categorically refused to do so in the absence of a declaration. Shedai was delighted to see his rival silence himself. Mohammed Ali Jinnah, the leader of the separatist Muslim League, was also perceived as a serious threat. The League was seen as 'an additional factor in the artificial protraction of the disunity of India by the British'.[6] Nevertheless, so as not to antagonise Muslim public opinion, it was decided not to attack it directly. It was significant that it even came up at all as it was a danger that the Congress was still reluctant to fully acknowledge.

The immediate recruitment of Indian POWs was also approved.[7] The Italians agreed to transfer all captured Indian POWs to Germany. Although a few sabotage and propaganda companies might be retained in North Africa, the main body of the Legion would not, so as to ensure that there would no 'cannon fodder' accusations being emitted from the British. Bose was in agreement as his ultimate aim was deploying the Legion in the North-West Frontier province of British India. With German assurances of a breakthrough on the Eastern Front, he preferred to wait for a greater impact to be made in India rather than in North Africa.

TRIPLING THE EFFECT: BERLIN, ROME, TOKYO

What was not open to debate was the necessity of the Legion operating within the German army—at least until it reached India. A recognised uniform would guarantee all captured legionaries POW status in accordance with the Geneva Convention and prevent them from being shot either as 'deserters', 'partisans' or 'guerrillas'. Bose and Shedai reluctantly agreed, recognising that the interests of the POWs came before political considerations. For the first few months the Legion would be trained as a regular German motorised infantry unit. When Bose emphasised the importance of diversified training, the German military representative assured him that this would include the use of howitzers, anti-tank and anti-aircraft guns.[8] Bose and Shedai were forced to make the best of a potentially awkward situation, leaving the tricky problems of language and diet for later. The main priority now was getting as many Indian POWs into German uniform.

Nevertheless, within days of the meeting Bose was jittery. Reports of continued Japanese successes, particularly the incursion of Japanese troops into Burma, neighbouring India, had discomfited him. It was now only a matter of time before they reached India itself. Accordingly, on 17 December, he re-emphasised to Woermann the urgency of a Tripartite declaration.[9] Woermann assured him that Tokyo had agreed in principle to a joint declaration although he was vague about the timing. Not satisfied, Bose reiterated his concern the same day to the Japanese Ambassador, Hiroshi Oshima.[10] The latter was sympathetic, assuring him that he would bring up the matter directly with Ribbentrop.[11] Bose also used the occasion to express a desire to proceed to Tokyo, realising that he would be more effective there.[12] Oshima regretfully explained that this was now practically impossible owing to the spread of war. That Bose wanted to leave soon became apparent to the Foreign Office as well. The following day it received a report from the German legation in Bangkok on Indian nationalist organisations, already demanding Bose's transfer to Asia.[13] It was not long before Berlin approached Tokyo over the sensitive issue.

Shedai also attempted, meanwhile, to secure a prompt Tripartite declaration. He sent notes to the German embassy and to the Italian Foreign Ministry emphasising the need for urgent action. In his typically blunt style he warned:

If the Axis powers and Japan act on a wait-and-see policy, it can be said without hesitation that the whole of India will accept the British version and will stand by the side of the Anglo-Saxons and their Bolshevik allies.[14]

A few days before Christmas, Bose visited Stalag IV D/Z in Annaburg to begin the recruiting process. He first addressed the assembled officers in a large hall. The atmosphere was 'not very enthusiastic; it was rather reserved and cold' according to a Free India official.[15] Bose's speech on the need to fight for freedom met with an even colder reception.[16] The officers reacted with the distrust and scepticism typical of their class towards politicians—in this case a dissident Congressman in Germany at that. Some coughed and shuffled their boots in an attempt to drown his words.[17] German and Indian officials looked on in dismay.[18]

When Bose addressed the common ranks outside, the reaction was very different. He was more in his element here, speaking, even laughing, informally with the POWs as they formed a huge circle around him, jostling to glimpse their famous compatriot. By the time he left more than a few patriotic slogans had been shouted.[19] The Indian officers watched coldly from a distance.

After Bose's departure, the infuriated camp commandant separated a few ringleaders from among the more hostile Indian officers and ordered them to stand still in the snow. Sentries then loaded their rifles and took pot shots at them.[20] Although no one was killed, the incident proved counter-productive and made the recruiting process all the more difficult.[21] Nevertheless on Christmas Day the first dozen volunteers set off in the freezing cold from Berlin for their training camp in Frankenberg, near Chemnitz.²² Bose, Free India and German officials bade them farewell at the train station. 'For a time Anhalter station was a scene of an Indian platform' wrote an Indian official who was present. 'There was a lot of handshaking and embracing in Indian fashion'.²³ As the train pulled out away there were fierce shouts of 'Long live India'. German civilian and military passers-by watched in bewilderment.²⁴

Thus it was that 1942 started on a high note for Bose, replete with optimism. It was certain to be a momentous year²⁵—that much he knew. Japan would continue its spectacular advance across Asia and the Pacific challenging, possibly even destroying, American and British might. The next twelve months seemed destined to bring India closer to freedom than ever before. Above all, Bose hoped that he would be in Tokyo before it ended. From there he would make his way as close as possible to the Indian border and incite a national revolt.

For the time being, Bose first had to face a bitterly cold and dull January in Berlin. He spent much of the month following Japanese successes with increasing awe and excitement—as did everyone else in Berlin—albeit some with greater apprehension than others as the 'yellow race' contradicted fundamental National Socialist principles of 'Aryan superiority'. It was a problem that Goebbels—as Minister of Public Enlightenment and Propaganda—worked particularly hard to resolve.²⁶ Hitler was also preoccupied with the Japanese advance, particularly in regard to its impact on India. He brought up the subject time and time again in private conversations with his entourage.²⁷

In spite of the Asian focus, Bose persevered with his German work. On 7 and 9 January, he wrote to A. C. N. Nambiar, a former acquaintance and prominent anti-Nazi left-wing Indian journalist whom he had seen in Paris.²⁸ Bose had succeeded in persuading him after considerable difficulty to come to Berlin. Nambiar had good reason to be reluctant as he had been roughed up by Nazi storm-troopers, imprisoned and then thrown out of Germany in the 1930s. It took a concerted effort on Bose's part to change his mind. Having finally acceded, Nambiar was instructed to search for suitable 'Indian collaborators' in Paris before leaving.[29] Their names were to be given to the German embassy in Paris which would then pass them on to Bose for confirmation. As if an afterthought, Bose ended his second letter by writing: 'A Free India Legion for fighting for India's freedom has been started here. A large number of Indians have joined. If any Indian in France will join the Legion, I shall be delighted'.[30] By referring to a dozen volunteers as a 'large number' Bose was sacrificing the truth for political expediency. His hope of recruiting Indians from France revealed the reservations he still had in regard to the POWs.

In the event, Nambiar found only one Indian—for the Free India Centre though—but it was a good catch. Girija K. Mookerjee, another anti-Nazi journalist and former acquaintance of Bose, had co-authored *The Rise and Growth of the Congress in India* with Gandhi's close associate, Charles F. Andrews. Afterwards, he had emerged as the Paris based correspondent of the *Hindustan Times*. He was now stranded there and suffering—badly—from the cold. His main ambition in going to Berlin, as he admitted quite openly was the prospect of heated accommodation,[31] Nambiar having told him nothing of Bose's presence there. It was only when they arrived in Berlin by train on 25 January that Nambiar informed an astonished Mookerjee that they were off to have lunch with Bose.[32] It was also an important meeting for Bose as these were the most prominent Indians he had succeeded in recruiting so far. Bose even postponed his birthday celebrations so that they could be present.

The three men lunched in Bose's residence. Bose initially abjured politics, merely engaging in light talk and cracking a few jokes.[33] He clearly felt at ease with these men, regarding them in many ways as his equals. Mookerjee, who had not seen Bose since 1931, was pleased to note that while he had grown in stature and even acquired a 'certain magnificence', he had not lost his sense of humour.[34] Afterwards, the staff of the Free India Centre arrived to offer their wishes. Mookerjee watched as Bose interacted with them:

> It was with real admiration that I watched him talking and laughing with these people who were by no means very politically-minded, nor did they have a fraction of Subhas's grandeur. He towered above them all by the sheer force of his personality and their attraction for him, curiously enough, was not so much for the leader of men he was, but for the man himself. I don't know how much they knew him or of him, but they all felt drawn to him because they liked him as a man. Subhas [...] did not inspire any awe although his [...] perfect naturalness won the hearts of even those who did not agree with him. We sat down later in front of a long table beautifully decorated with flowers with a birthday cake in the middle and then someone asked me to say something.[35]

An embarrassed Mookerjee mumbled something praising Bose's work although he wondered precisely what that work was. He had an opportunity to find out the following day with Nambiar. 26 January, now marked annually by the Indian National Congress as 'Independence Day', was celebrated with much fanfare at the Kaiserhof Hotel. Mookerjee was surprised to see a 'good cross-section of German society', from senior governmental officials to high-ranking officers, businessmen, diplomats and journalists.[36] The ballroom was draped with Congress and Nazi flags while a German orchestra struck up *Jana Gana Mana*, the anthem selected by the Free India Centre. 'A meeting on India in Europe, whether it was in London, Paris or anywhere else' Mookerjee noted 'used always and invariably to be attended by the same types of people, namely, the vegetarians, the theosophists, the cranks and the spinsters'.[37] Berlin offered a striking contrast.

Two days later, Bose met Mookerjee again for an extensive conversation as, unlike Nambiar, the latter was still trying to decipher what had brought him to Berlin and the precise nature of his involvement with the Germans. This conversation ended up being intimately revealing as Bose opened up in the presence of a trusted compatriot in a manner denied to him when dealing with the Germans. He patiently explained his actions in detail. His main motivation in escaping from India, he claimed, had been a growing conviction that Germany was going to win the war. England would have to sue for peace sooner or later. Mookerjee noticed that he was silent regarding the invasion of Russia and how this had altered his plans. Realising that Mookerjee was an even more pro-Soviet left-winger than himself, Bose chose not to delve into the matter. Still, Mookerjee was disturbed by the omission.[38]

Bose was more interested in criticising Gandhi, describing his leadership as 'hesitant'. Instead of wavering, India should have seized the opportunity from the start of the war to align itself with the Axis camp. Bose left no doubt that the attitude of Gandhi had been central to his leaving India.

This was all very well with Mookerjee but at one point he interrupted to ask bluntly: 'But how could the Nazis be our friends?' A rather surprised Bose assured him that it was not a question of friendship; rather it was about tactical alliances. Why should Indian nationalists not accept foreign assistance, even from a dubious regime? After all, had not England forged an alliance with the Soviet Union despite ideological enmity? 'Why couldn't we do the same?' Bose asked rather naively. 'We have nothing in common with the Nazis, it is true. But why should that prevent us from taking some help from them, provided they do not try to interfere with our work or influence us ideologically?' The least Indians could do was exploit the German airwaves. 'We won't say anything either in favour of or against the Germans for what they do in Europe does not strictly concern us' he assured Mookerjee.[39]

Bose was satisfied with his own explanations not realising that Mookerjee was still troubled by the prospect of collaborating

TRIPLING THE EFFECT: BERLIN, ROME, TOKYO

with the Nazis and struggling to convince himself that Bose was right. It required considerable effort before he gradually and reluctantly came to accept some of Bose's views. Even then he never fully understood Bose's optimism regarding the Nazi regime, remaining fervently anti-Nazi throughout.

After his meeting with Mookerjee, Bose rushed off to attend the first of two *Abwehr* meetings on India scheduled for that day and 6 February. The Japanese assistant military attaché, Colonel Bin Yamamoto, was also present. This proved to be a mistake as the meetings ended up becoming little more than exchanges between Yamamoto and Bose, leaving the Germans as passive spectators. It was an acknowledgment at the same time that Japan now held the trump card on India when it came to determining Tripartite policy. First and foremost on Bose's mind was concern that Japanese aircraft would attack Calcutta. He first wanted the population prepared psychologically with leaflets dropped from the air explaining that bombing would only be directed at British military installations. British propaganda might otherwise portray the Japanese as aggressors. Yamamoto assured him that the necessary precautions would be taken.[40]

It was in Bose's interest to play up the Japanese 'aggressor' card as it gave him an opportunity to plea—yet again—for the Tripartite declaration. Yamamoto revealed that his government was divided between those who were prepared to issue the declaration immediately and those who preferred to wait for military operations to have a greater impact on India. What Bose did not know—and what Yamamoto did not tell him—was that although the Germans had been pushing for the declaration throughout the month, Tokyo had already decided on the second alternative.[41]

Another matter of concern was the manner in which Indian and Japanese troops would react to each other on the battlefield. Bose argued that it was imperative for the Japanese to avoid military engagements and win over as many Indian troops as possible. Yamamoto would soon reveal the existence of an 'Indian National Army' already fighting alongside Japanese troops in Malaya. It was constituted of Indian troops who had defected to the Japanese. Details were imprecise but what was certain was that this rapidly expanding army had committed itself to liberate India.

Bose was flabbergasted. What he had tried to precipitate all along in Germany without much success had already been achieved within weeks of the conflict in Southeast Asia. It was nearly too good to believe. Was this a Japanese propaganda stunt? Or could it be that Indian POWs in Southeast Asia had done what their counterparts in Germany had failed to do? Was there really an Indian army preparing to liberate India? Bose would soon find out that Yamamoto was hardly exaggerating.

Throughout the meetings, Bose emphatically argued that Japanese victories would create widespread panic in India, causing a second 'Dunkirk'. That would be the perfect opportunity to attack, with the British on the defensive and Indian troops ready to defect.[42] Indeed at the time there was only one British division to defend the whole of India.[43] If the six Indian divisions revolted, British rule would be over in a matter of days. Had the participants known this they would have undoubtedly pushed their governments to concentrate their joint efforts against India.

Nevertheless, Yamamoto carefully noted down Bose's proposals, promising to pass them on to Imperial General Headquarters in Tokyo. At the same time he warned that Tokyo remained undecided as to whether it should turn next to India, Australia or Russia. An invasion of Australia would play a critical role in annihilating British power, while an invasion of Russia, while it was still engaged in fighting Germany, might bring about a quick victory in the war. India was the third alternative. It was nevertheless agreed that the Forward Bloc should launch a major sabotage and fifth column campaign across India in anticipation of a Japanese invasion.[44]

TRIPLING THE EFFECT: BERLIN, ROME, TOKYO

The meetings ended with Bose feeling satisfied that his views would at least be known in Tokyo. The Germans were left to draw up the minutes. Nevertheless, the High Command did not abandon its own plan of launching an offensive in India. Proof of this was the dispatch of a few dozen POW volunteers to a special military training camp in Regenwurm, near Meseritz. There they received commando training for operations in the North-West Frontier. This Special India Detachment was to spearhead the German offensive into India. The soldiers received training in mountaineering, parachuting, sharp-shooting, explosives, demolition, sabotage, horse-riding and operating wireless sets. Captain Harbich, who had established liaison with Bose upon his arrival in Berlin, was appointed commander. He took on his commission with enthusiasm.[45]

Chiang Kai-shek, Tojo and the Impact of Singapore, February–March 1942

Bose was soon engrossed observing an unusual political development in India which was not to his liking at all. The Chinese leader, Chiang Kai-shek, had taken it upon himself to visit India and meet the Congress leaders and the British in the hope of securing a political compromise.[46] If India genuinely rallied round the Allied war effort, it would be of great help to China.

When Chiang Kai-shek met the Congress president, Abul Kalam Azad, and Nehru, on 11 February, he asked them bluntly: 'Where does India rightly belong? Is its place with Nazi Germany or with the democracies?'[47] Azad and Nehru assured him that India would join the democracies as soon as democracy itself was applied to India. There could be no compromise before.[48] Chiang Kai-shek was not so easily deterred and pursued his efforts for several days, trying to convince the Congress leaders of their moral obligation to support the Allied cause.

Chiang Kai-shek's visit caused as much consternation in Berlin as it did in London. Ribbentrop sought to uncover the motives behind the Generalissimo's self-appointed mission. The German legation in Bangkok provided regular reports containing what little information it could garner. London, meanwhile, was concerned that Chiang's visit would confer international legitimacy and attention on the Congress. Churchill, in particular, disliked this business, as he put it, of 'the head of a foreign state intervening as a kind of impartial arbiter between representatives of the King-Emperor and Messrs. Gandhi and Nehru'.[49] He wrote in vain to dissuade Chiang from meeting Gandhi.[50] In the event, Chiang's visit to India failed to accomplish anything.

Bose disliked the visit as much as Churchill although for entirely different reasons. He was vexed that Chiang—a fellow Asian nationalist leader—should seek to bring about an Anglo-Indian compromise instead of displaying complete solidarity with Indian independence. It was highly ironic of Chiang to do so, Bose believed, as he was a symbol of anti-imperialist resistance—in his case against the Japanese. Had Bose not as Congress president sent a medical mission to assist Chiang?[51] When he was able to make his voice heard in Asia, Bose targeted Chiang, denouncing him as a 'tool of the Anglo-Americans'.[52] The sentiment was reciprocal—Chiang in turn considered Bose to be an Axis puppet.

Chiang's visit to India was followed by better news. On 15 February, the Japanese captured Singapore in what Churchill described as the 'worst disaster and largest capitulation of British history'.[53] The Indian National Army had also participated in the attack. The fall of Singapore was one of the most momentous events of the war for Bose. He was absolutely convinced that it signalled the collapse of British power in Asia. Looking at events as they unfolded there was little indication that he was wrong. But Bose was more optimistic than most in believing that the repercussions would be swift in India.

There was more surprising news the next day as Bose read in the newspapers that the Japanese Prime Minister, Hideki Tojo, had made a speech in the Imperial Diet announcing that the fall of Singapore was a 'golden opportunity' for Indians to rise up in revolt and attain their freedom.⁵⁴ Japan would do everything in its power to help. This practically amounted to the declaration Bose so desperately sought. Tojo's statements could not have been less unequivocal. He clearly expressed support for a liberated India while the Japanese had committed themselves to be of assistance. Tojo's claim that the fall of Singapore was a turning point for India echoed Bose's sentiments perfectly.

Bose spent the entire day in an agitated state pondering what implications the announcement would have. Did it still make a Tripartite declaration necessary? Did the Japanese have a comprehensive plan to liberate India? Were they planning an offensive? How would London react? Would not the British respond by launching an anti-Japanese propaganda campaign in India?

After pondering these questions repeatedly, Bose was left with two thoughts utmost on his mind. First, the realisation that the time had come for him to speak out. As a prominent Indian he had a duty to do so on behalf of all 'freedom-loving' Indians. With Japan openly supporting Indian independence and Germany not wavering in its commitment, powerful forces had arrayed themselves against British India. Now was not the time for silence. The second realisation was that Nehru—in one of his sudden emotional outbursts—might publicly reject Tojo's offer of help. Bose feared Tokyo interpreting this as a reflection of Indian sentiment. He was determined to pre-empt Nehru by being the one to speak out first.

Accordingly, the next day, Bose wrote to Woermann outlining his concerns.⁵⁵ He had to address them taking German interests into account. The British, he warned, would react to Tojo's announcement by launching a propaganda campaign in India. They would 'manoeuvre to get prominent Indians like Nehru to issue anti-Japanese statements in reply to the Tojo declaration'. Bose was content to portray Nehru as a willing stooge. Nehru was quite capable, however, of making such statements on his own without British prompting. Bose's central argument was that an 'anti-Japanese attitude in India' would 'mean automatically an anti-German attitude'. It was therefore imperative for 'freedom-loving Indians' to declare before the 'whole world' that they were ready to align themselves fully with the Tripartite powers. Accordingly, Bose asked Woermann to make the necessary press and radio arrangements to publicise a statement he was preparing. 'In propaganda, as in war', he added, 'those who take the initiative have always an advantage over the others'.[56] Having been taken in so much by Tojo's announcement, he did not even bring up the Tripartite declaration.

Tojo's announcement took the Foreign Office by surprise as well as it had after all specifically requested the Japanese government not to make any declaration without first consulting Berlin and Rome. The Japanese had apparently 'forgotten'. The diplomatic *faux pas* created utter confusion within the Foreign Office. A perplexed Ribbentrop instructed the German embassy in Tokyo to try to find out whether Tojo's announcement implied a change in policy.[57] With Chiang's visit still on his mind, he also instructed the embassy to emphasise the importance of countering any Anglo-Indian political rapprochement with a concerted Tripartite propaganda campaign. In this connection the Japanese were asked to confirm whether they were prepared to publicise Bose's statement.[58] Ribbentrop, fully appreciating the importance it would have, wanted to exploit it to the maximum.

As a result, Bose was asked to postpone his statement for a few days pending a response from Tokyo. For its part, the Italian government made enquiries as to whether Bose was prepared to speak out, suspecting correctly that the fall of Singapore would not leave him indifferent.[59] The Foreign Office brushed the Italians aside, waiting instead for a response from Tokyo.

The Special India Bureau, meanwhile, responded to Tojo's announcement by drafting a Tripartite declaration on 22 February, hoping it would be released shortly. Copies were forwarded to Hitler, Tokyo and Rome. It differed significantly from Bose's original draft in that it addressed independence from a Tripartite perspective while adopting a more populist quasi-left-wing sounding approach intended to appeal to the Indian masses:

Germany, Italy and Japan are fighting. [...] for the freedom of all the peoples that have been outraged by British imperialism. [...] Among the nations which have had to suffer longest and most cruelly under British domination is numbered the ancient Indian people, a nation which during its great past has conferred such rich cultural benefits on humanity. In the endeavour to open the gate of freedom to the Indian people [...] the German, Italian and Japanese governments hereby solemnly declare that they recognise the inalienable right of the Indian people to independence and self-determination. India for the Indians! [...] The Tripartite Powers are concerned to end—on a basis of social justice—the misery and poverty of the Indian people, and to see the exploited masses assisted to a proper standard of living as well as to employment and prosperity.[60]

Reinvigorated by Japanese successes and with an increasingly stable eastern front, the High Command meanwhile, decided the time was approaching to implement Operation Tiger. Accordingly, a third *Abwehr* meeting was convened on 26 February. Bose again dominated the proceedings. Much had changed since the last conference. The Japanese were now approaching Rangoon and shortly after the talks concluded they launched their first air strike on India, attacking the sparsely inhabited but strategic Andaman islands in the Bay of Bengal.[61] Thailand, meanwhile, aligned itself with the Axis powers, sending troops to march alongside the Japanese in Burma and declaring war on Britain and the United States.

Bose for the first time openly expressed his desire to proceed to Asia. He advocated turning Rangoon into a base for joint Indian nationalist and Tripartite operations against India.[62] After Rangoon, the next major city in the path of Japanese troops was

Calcutta. If Japanese troops—ideally alongside the Indian National Army—managed to get there, Indians would welcome them as liberators, Bose argued. The Indian army would then rally round the Free India banner and the gates of India would be open, making further Japanese incursions unnecessary.[63] Bose emphasised, however, that this military surge had to be carried out with the approval of Indian nationalists. Nevertheless he urged quick action so that Nehru could not influence public opinion against Japan.

With a Japanese offensive in the northeast and a German one in the northwest, combined with an internal revolt orchestrated by the Forward Bloc, Bose was confident that British rule would collapse. Few questioned his conclusions and optimism now ran high. Bose's views were passed on to Hitler's closest military advisor, the Chief of the High Command, Field Marshall Wilhelm Keitel.[64]

Inspired by the meeting and the rapid pace of events, the Foreign Office stepped up its own efforts, preparing an elaborate scheme whereby once Bose's statement had been publicised, he was to be received by Hitler and the declaration issued with much fanfare.[65]

A few days after Ribbentrop's initial request, the green light arrived from Tokyo. The Japanese, in a concerted effort with Berlin and Rome, were ready to publicise Bose's statement. Given less than twenty four hours to prepare himself, on 28 February Bose finally broadcast his statement on the radio:

This is Subhas Chandra Bose speaking to you over the Free India Radio. [...] now that the hour has struck, I come forward to speak. The fall of Singapore means the collapse of the British Empire. [...] and the dawn of a new era in Indian history. The Indian people who have [...] been ruined spiritually, culturally, politically and economically while under British domination—must now offer their humble thanks to the Almighty for the auspicious event. [...] one fifth of the human race has been ruthlessly suppressed and persecuted. For other nations, British imperialism maybe the enemy of today, but for India, it is the eternal foe. [...] Standing at one of the cross-roads of world-history, I solemnly declare on behalf of all freedom-loving Indians in India and abroad, that we shall continue to fight British imperialism till India is once again the mistress of her own destiny. During this struggle, and in the reconstruction that will follow, we shall heartily co-operate with all those who will help us in overthrowing the common enemy. [...] The hour of India's salvation is at hand.[66]

Bose's statement was very much in tune with the world conflagration and he left no doubt as to where Free India stood. The 'enemies of British imperialism are the natural allies of India—just as the allies of British imperialism are today our natural enemies' he said half-way through his broadcast.[67] His use of the term 'Anglo-American imperialism'—which soon marked his public utterances and exonerated the Soviets—was a clear indication that Bose perceived the United States as much of a threat to India as Britain was. He failed to make any distinction, as events were to prove.[68]

Bose's fight therefore was not just a fight for independence but also one for the destiny of the world. Free India had a crucial stake and a role to play in this struggle. Bose's statement amounted in essence to a declaration of war on the 'Anglo-Americans'. In denouncing 'voices coming from India, claiming to speak either in the name of the Indian National Congress or of the Indian people' and of conspiracies by 'agents of Anglo-American imperialism' to 'throw dust in the eyes of the Indian people', Bose was indirectly referring to Nehru and those Congressmen still inclined to reach a compromise with the British.[69] Nevertheless, Bose was not prepared to tackle Nehru head on by attacking him directly; nor did he mention Gandhi.

Bose's broadcast caused an international sensation. There was no need for speculation as to where he was or what his views were. 'Bose's appeal has made a deep impression on world public opinion' Goebbels commented delightedly in his diary.[70] The speech was extensively reported in both the Axis and Allied press and was also rebroadcast repeatedly in several languages on Axis radio stations around the world. Azad, the Congress president, suspected that it would only enhance the growing admiration Gandhi now, ironically, felt for Bose since he had escaped from India.[71] Even Hitler spoke of Nehru, the—'man of compromise'—as having been 'eclipsed' by Bose.[72] Goebbels invited the entire staff of the Free India Centre to the Ministry of Public Enlightenment and Propaganda for a celebratory tea party.[73]

On 1 March, Goebbels noted in his diary: 'We shall now begin our official fight on behalf of India'.[74] On 2 March, still excited by the impact of Bose's broadcast on the world, he wrote: 'The crisis in India can no longer be denied. We are doing everything possible to pour oil on the fire'.[75] 'In London there is boundless wrath about the appeal of Bose' he wrote gleefully two days later.[76]

While the Germans, Japanese and Italians relished the effects of Bose's statement, it left him, in contrast, strangely dissatisfied. Despite its success, there was no green light from Tokyo regarding the Tripartite declaration and his meeting with Hitler did not materialise as a result. The political disappointment—from governments Bose had just proclaimed to be allies—left him profoundly dejected. In protest, and to escape what has been described as the increasingly 'suffocating atmosphere of empty promises', Bose returned to Bad Gastein for a cure.[77] On this occasion events on the international scene quickly propelled him back to Berlin.

4

OFFENSIVE FROM BERLIN

THE CRIPPS MISSION

Bose's Propaganda Campaign and Japanese Intervention, March–April 1942

On 11 March, the British government announced that it was sending the Lord Privy Seal, Sir Stafford Cripps, to India to reach a political compromise. The fall of Rangoon a few days earlier—in the face of what seemed to be an unstoppable Japanese advance—had finally convinced the British cabinet (however reluctantly—particularly in the case of Churchill) that the time had come to gain Indian support if there was to be any chance of mounting an effective defence of India. British troops had hastily abandoned Rangoon and withdrawn into central Burma without putting up much of a fight. The consensus was that it was now only a matter of time before the Japanese reached India itself. In these circumstances, the British government felt compelled to secure a political agreement, if only to secure its rear, stuck as it was between the advancing Japanese and an increasingly hostile Indian population. Although it did not reveal by what means it hoped to reach an agreement, it was widely speculated at the time that the government was prepared to grant India dominion status.

'Cripps' mission to India is a world sensation' Goebbels noted in his diary on 13 March.[1] Indeed, it was to dominate international headlines for weeks to come, leaving one country resorting to military action in response. Both Washington and Chungking put much store in what came to be known as the 'Cripps Mission', afraid that failure to reach an agreement would take away from the claim that the Allies were fighting for freedom in the world. In contrast, Berlin, Tokyo and Rome placed much hope in a breakdown in negotiations, knowing this would intensify the crisis in India.

In such circumstances, Bose could hardly remain idle in Bad Gastein. Within days he was back in Berlin ready to launch an aggressive political offensive on the airwaves. Sceptical that Cripps would succeed in achieving a compromise, Bose reacted in a stoic, calm and confident manner, seeing in the Mission an opportunity to denounce British policy. He was completely unaware, or unwilling, to appreciate how great the desire was in India to reach a compromise. Many, if not most Congressmen, were confident of success. Azad and Nehru would work particularly hard with Cripps to achieve this. Although Bose expected as much from them his venom was reserved for the British.

On 13 March, even before Cripps reached India, Bose launched his campaign on the radio. It began with a long broadcast denouncing British policy in general. Bose claimed that the fall of Rangoon was symbolic of the manner in which Britain was 'losing her positions one after another'. There was nothing 'visible on the horizon' which would 'arrest the collapse and break-up of her vast empire'. He could hardly contain his satisfaction. Bose expressed regret that the British had not responded earlier to requests for the 'principles of freedom and democracy' to be applied to India—even hinting that India might have otherwise voluntarily participated in the war. Instead, the British had responded with a 'refusal,—not plain and blunt, as we would have preferred—but perfidious and hypocritical'. This was partly due to the very nature of British imperialism, he explained. Throughout their time in India, the British had encouraged disunity. These 'artificially engineered dissensions' were now being used as an excuse to deny India 'self-determination'.[2]

Bose insisted that it made no difference whether the empire was governed by a Conservative or a Labour cabinet. In the end, the result was the same. Emulating Churchillian oratory, he denounced British hopes that Indians would sacrifice their 'blood, toil, tears and sweat' in a last ditch effort to save the empire—ironic in his view considering that India had 'no enemy outside her own frontiers'. Bose accused the British of bringing the war to India. Had they not forced India into declaring war in 1939? Had they not converted the entire country into a massive military base? Had they not exploited by 'fair and foul' means Indian resources? If India were neutral, like Ireland, the Japanese would not be about to invade. Bose squarely placed the blame on the British.

Bose also went further than in his previous broadcast in warning against those Indians who were sympathetic towards Britain. He was unequivocal this time, stating: 'any Indian who now works for Britain acts against the best interests of his country and is a traitor to the cause of liberty'. Bose was determined that such strong language should serve as a warning. The 'lackeys of British imperialism' were as much a target as the British were. As for the notion of any compromise with an empire about to 'disappear', Bose dismissed this as 'futile' and 'ridiculous'. It was only towards the end of his broadcast that Bose directly referred to the Cripps Mission:

The British Prime Minister, Mr Churchill, has in his recent utterance before Parliament promised Dominion Status to India. [...] after the war. [...] Under his mandate, Sir Stafford Cripps, is to visit India in order to bring about an agreement between the different sections of the people. [...] Only one who lives in a fool's paradise could imagine that India still cares for Dominion Status within the Empire and that a single Indian could be found who still has the least faith in British promises. [...] People in India know fully well that. [...] as long as the British remain in India they will continue their nefarious policy of 'divide and rule'. Mr Churchill and his Cabinet will soon realise that political crumbs thrown at the Indian people from Westminster will not bring them over to the British side. The British Empire is going the way of all other empires of the past and out of its ashes will rise a free and united India.[3]

Bose concluded that there was one side fighting to maintain the Versailles status quo and the other struggling for a new world order. In such a context India had 'nothing to lose but her chains'.[4]

A few days after Bose's broadcast a delegation of Indian civilian and military dignitaries set off by air from Singapore to Tokyo to attend an important conference on Indian independence. The aircraft they were travelling in, however, was caught in a violent storm and crashed. The BBC announced that Bose had been onboard. Not certain of the precise whereabouts of Bose, the BBC picked up a report emanating from a Vichy news agency.[5] The next day shops, bazaars and offices across India closed in a spontaneous expression of national grief. Gandhi sent a condolence telegram to Bose's mother stating: 'THE WHOLE NATION MOURNS WITH YOU THE DEATH OF YOUR AND HER BRAVE SON. I SHARE YOUR SORROW TO THE FULL'.[6] Azad issued a sorrowful statement on behalf of the Congress claiming that Bose's death would 'cause deep sorrow to all those who knew him' as 'he lived and died for the cause to which he had dedicated his life'.[7]

If Bose had any doubts about his popularity in India, they dissipated quickly. It was clear that he remained an immensely important and revered figure. His presence in Germany—and more importantly his endorsement of the Axis powers—had done little to change this. Equally significant, Bose's political position (despite hardening considerably since the late 1930s) was neither criticised nor even questioned by the Congress. He was still considered very much part of the Congress, regardless of internal differences. Nothing could have been more reassuring to Bose. He could proceed with his plans now knowing that neither the Congress nor his countrymen were likely to stand in his way. The report of his death in a strange way served as a great morale boost to Bose. It also brought him more publicity than his broadcasts had.

On 25 March, Bose returned to the airwaves to inform the world that he was not dead:

This is Subhas Chandra Bose [...] speaking to you over the Free India radio. British news agencies have spread all over the world the report that I had died in an aeroplane crash on my way to Tokyo. [...] Ever since I left India last year, British propaganda agencies have from time to time given contradictory reports of my whereabouts, while newspapers in England have not hesitated to use uncomplimentary language about me. The latest report about my death is perhaps an instance of wishful thinking, I can imagine that the British government would, at this critical hour in India's history, like to see me dead.[8]

Bose used the broadcast to launch one more diatribe against the Cripps Mission. While admitting that he had considered the Cripps Mission 'very carefully', he insisted that Cripps was pursuing the 'age-long policy of British imperialism—'divide and rule'. He denounced Cripps' emphasis on the need to find a solution acceptable to all the different races, castes and religions of India as well as the Indian Princely States, insisting that the real intention was to 'split India into a number of states'. Bose accused Cripps of 'living in a fool's paradise'. The time to gain freedom through 'discussion or argument, propaganda and passive resistance' was over. Now was the time to act decisively. Bose left few in doubt as to what he meant by this. The era of Gandhian civil disobedience was over. Despite what had been agreed to at the Italo-German conference of 8 and 9 December, Bose went on a rampage against the Muslim League denouncing it as a tool of British imperialism and dismissing claims that it represented Muslims. He rejected any attempt to portray it as the Muslim equivalent of the Congress.[9]

Bose's broadcast received more attention for its confirmation that he was alive than for his criticism of Cripps. Two days later, the Viceroy, Lord Linlithgow, dismissed the possibility of any serious threat arising from Bose's broadcasts in a telegram to the British Ambassador in Washington, Halifax, although he did concede that they might 'have some effect' on the Cripps Mission.[10] This was in response to concern over attention Bose was receiving in the United States.[11]

Bose's broadcast was not without political consequence. Gandhi and Azad (Nehru declined to join them)[12] reacted by sending Bose's mother a telegram, stating: 'THANK GOD WHAT PURPORTED AUTHENTIC HAS PROVED WRONG. WE CONGRATULATE YOU AND NATION'.[13] The British were furious. It was in this political context that Cripps arrived in New Delhi. The timing could not have been worse.

Nevertheless, Cripps optimistically got down to work, even hoping to bring about an agreement within days. He had good reason to be optimistic. Congress leaders responded positively to his proposals. Azad and Nehru worked hard to reach an agreement with him—the only difficulty being that the British wanted to retain control of defence for the duration of the war.[14] Even Jinnah, a man certainly not known for his ability to compromise, responded positively to Cripps' proposal, surprised at how far it went in meeting an eventual Muslim state.[15]

Bose's broadcasts from Berlin, now constantly re-broadcast to India on at least a dozen Axis stations, suddenly seemed out of tune with political developments in India. There was, however, one prominent politician who shared Bose's opposition to the Cripps Mission. When Cripps met Gandhi on 27 March, the latter—after glancing over his proposals—responded by snapping: 'If this is your entire proposal to India, I would advise you to take the next plane home'.[16] When a stunned Cripps (who had always maintained friendly relations with Gandhi) reminded him that the proposal was based on one they had informally agreed to before the war, Gandhi replied that he only remembered discussing vegetarianism.[17] Whether or not this was an unorthodox political tactic employed by the Mahatma, it understandably left Cripps fuming. Having been particularly offended by the vegetarian remark, he now accused Gandhi of being 'desirous to bring about a state of chaos while he sits at Wardha [ashram] eating vegetables'.[18] Cripps had already been annoyed with Gandhi over his handling of the Bose affair complaining to Azad about the 'glowing terms' he had used in describing him.[19]

As if this was not enough, Bose broadcast a particularly witty 'open letter' to Cripps on 31 March. It was his most effective propaganda yet:

Dear Stafford Cripps. [...] In the days when you fought [...] in vindication of your own principles and convictions, you commanded the admiration of many people including myself. [...] in London in January 1938, I had the pleasure of making your acquaintance. But today you appear to be quite a different man. You may perhaps say that your task is to bring about a reconciliation between India and England. But your Cabinet has made it perfectly clear that the offer to India is not one of independence [...] knowing as you do that the Indian National Congress stands for undiluted independence is it not an insult to India that a man of your position and reputation should go out there with such an offer in his pocket?. [...] If British politicians really believe in democracy why don't they apply the democratic solution to India and solve the Indian problem?[20]

Needless to say, Cripps did not respond. 'Bose's propaganda, conducted from Berlin, is extremely embarrassing to the English' Goebbels noted with satisfaction in his diary on 26 March.[21] Cripps fired off a telegram to Churchill on 1 April, warning that the failure of his Mission might worsen an already difficult situation in India. 'Anti-British feeling is running very strong' he warned 'and our prestige is lower than it has ever been owing to events in Burma and more particularly in Singapore'. 'The outlook so far as the internal situation goes is exceedingly bad' he continued 'and if we cannot persuade the Indian leaders to come in now and help us we shall have to resort to suppression which may develop to such a scale that it may well get out of hand'.[22]

To make matters worse, Japanese aircraft attacked and bombed the eastern coast of India forcing hundreds of thousands to flee into the interior and leaving entire coastal villages abandoned. The army prepared for what it assumed was a Japanese invasion. In reality, this was only a psychological offensive intended to remind Indians of Japan's presence in the region—hardly necessary in a country anxiously aware that the Japanese were at the gate. The bombing campaign was reinforced by a statement by Tojo on 6 April, in which he urged Indians not to be 'deceived any more by the sweet words of Britain' while warning that Japan would be 'compelled to carry the war to India' if the British remained.[23] It was a not very subtle warning to Indians to get rid of the British before the Japanese marched into India and did it for them.

Bose observed these rapidly unfolding events from far away in Berlin with growing excitement. Tojo's statement perfectly echoed one of his key arguments—namely that Indians had nothing to gain by compromising with a crumbling empire. Gandhi had implied as much when he was quoted by the press comparing the Cripps Mission to a 'post-dated cheque on a bank that is failing'.[24] Bose's conviction that Japan was the one power in Asia which India had to deal with appeared vindicated; his gamble on the Axis appeared to be paying off. For the first time an Axis state had struck militarily and challenged British rule in India. If mass evacuations and panic were the price to pay, then so be it. Indians would have to earn freedom with their own blood and the sooner they aligned themselves to the Axis the better. Bose took comfort in knowing the Japanese had caused more panic than actual human loss, confining themselves essentially to military targets.

Bose responded to Tojo's statement the same day with a short radio broadcast.[25] His last three speeches had focused on the Cripps Mission and British policy. This one addressed Japan and the war from a larger perspective. While expressing gratitude for his pledge of support, Bose assured Tojo that Indians would not miss this 'golden opportunity' to liberate India. He went further than before in denouncing 'Anglo-American imperialism', this time describing it as a menace to all of Asia. Until its eradication, Asia would remain in 'perpetual danger' and Indians therefore welcomed Anglo-American defeats with 'joy and satisfaction'. Bose concluded on an idealistic note, expressing hope that India and Japan would co-operate in the 'noble task of creating a great Asia that will be free, happy and prosperous' although it was clear that his main intention had been to express solidarity with Japan.[26] He was successful. Tokyo would not remain indifferent to this gesture; it was after all Bose's most aggressively anti-British and anti-Allied broadcast to date.

Bose, Gandhi, Churchill and Nehru: Convergence and Collision, April 1942

A few days after Bose's broadcast the Cripps Mission broke down when the Congress formally rejected the British proposal. There was much finger pointing between Cripps and the Congress and even among the British themselves. At one point, Cripps had even threatened London with his resignation only to be stopped at the last moment by Churchill.[27] Such a resignation would have revealed the Cripps Mission for what it had become—a political farce. The Viceroy in particular was happy to see a disgraced Cripps—or 'Sir Stifford Crapps' as he preferred to call him[28]—leave, assured now that his imperial prerogative was safeguarded.

In public, the British maintained a united front, placing the blame squarely on the Congress. 'The British are now making earnest attempts', Goebbels noted, 'to unload the blame for the breakdown of negotiations on the Indians themselves. That is childish and absurd'.[29] While resenting this and hurling accusations back, Azad and Nehru nevertheless regretted the failure to reach an agreement realising, that apart from British intransigence, Gandhi's opposition had played a key role in ensuring a break down.[30] What particularly appalled Azad was the manner in which he believed Gandhi had allowed himself to be influenced by Bose.[31] Although they differed ideologically, Bose's daring escape to Berlin, his continued defiance of the British, combined with his broadcast offensive, left an indelible impression on the Mahatma. He now saw in Bose a kindred spirit who fought with equal determination for his convictions. Gandhi and Bose—in contrast to their Congress colleagues—shared a belief that the British would probably be defeated or at least badly mauled and that it was therefore quite pointless to reach an agreement. The essential difference was that Gandhi did not want India to participate in the war. He advocated total neutrality. Nevertheless, Azad believed that Gandhi's 'admiration for Subhas Bose unconsciously coloured his view about the whole war situation'.[32] This admiration was particularly evident during the Cripps Mission.

There was much rejoicing in Berlin. Ribbentrop believed that the failure of the Cripps Mission was Churchill's greatest political defeat yet.[33] There was even talk of resignation. What Ribbentrop and the Foreign Office did not understand was that the failure of the Cripps Mission suited Churchill perfectly.[34] He had never been fully sincere about it, stuck as he was—to the astonishment even of his cabinet colleagues—in the early glory days of the British Empire.[35] The Secretary of State for India, Leopold Amery,—by no means a liberal himself when it came to India— confided to the Viceroy that Churchill's political outlook was mid-Victorian, that he did not really sympathise with Dominion self-government, and when it came to India, that he had hardly gone 'beyond the early Kipling stage'.[36] For Churchill, the Cripps Mission had accomplished one of its most important aims, namely impressing American public opinion.[37] As he informed Cripps the day his Mission collapsed: 'The effect throughout Britain and in the United States has been wholly beneficial'.[38] He was not particularly bothered by the mess it left behind in India. There was good reason for this. Churchill preferred just about anything to the 'rule of the Congress and Hindoo Priesthood machine' as he put it.[39] He would soon be hurling wild accusations against Gandhi, including, in a letter to Roosevelt, falsely accusing him of being 'prepared to negotiate with the Japanese on the basis of a free passage for Japanese troops through India' so that they could join 'hands with Hitler'.[40]

While Churchill derived much satisfaction from the collapse of the Cripps Mission, Bose and Nehru did not. Bose was worried that his Congress colleagues—Nehru in particular—might still succeed in reversing the political stalemate and achieve a last minute compromise. He could hardly conceive the extent of Churchill's duplicity in the matter. As for Nehru, he was embittered by the outcome of events. It had become evident during the Cripps Mission that he was willing, if not enthusiastic, to have India fight alongside the great democracies and contribute to the defeat of the Axis, in stark contrast to Bose who hoped to fight with the Axis. They were now in opposing camps with Gandhi in the middle still advocating neutrality. The collapse of the Cripps Mission was a relief for Gandhi—as it had been for Churchill, albeit in a different way—as it meant that India would not participate in the war. While Nehru could not challenge Gandhi directly, it was easier for him to go after Bose. Nehru got his chance to do so on 12 April, during a press conference. He revealed his thoughts as diplomatically as he could when asked to comment on Bose:

I do not [...] doubt the *bona fides* of Mr. Bose. I think he has come to a certain conclusion which I think is wrong, but nevertheless a conclusion which he thinks is good for India. We parted company with him many years ago. Since then we have drifted further apart and today we are very far from each other. It is not good enough for me, because of my past friendship and because I do not challenge his motives, to say anything against him. But I do realise that the way he has chosen is utterly wrong, a way which I not only cannot accept but must oppose, if it takes shape. [...] It is a bad thing psychologically for the Indian masses to think in terms of being liberated by an outside agency.[41]

Nehru followed this up a few days later by denouncing the Forward Bloc in a speech in Calcutta,[42] but he carefully refrained from attacking Bose. Nehru's statements were part of a pro-Allied campaign emphasising the importance of not hampering the British war effort so as not indirectly to assist the Axis.[43] The British were unimpressed, suspecting that these speeches were designed primarily to impress American public opinion.[44] Everyone except Bose it seemed was now trying at the time to win over the American public. The latter made this evident in a broadcast on 13 April, urging his countrymen to abandon all hopes of reaching a compromise and for the first time explicitly attacking the United States. Bose dismissed the notion that the American government could end political stalemate in India by guaranteeing an agreement reached with Britain.[45] This was a notion gathering momentum in India as it was seen as the last hope of salvaging something from the debris of the Cripps Mission.

Bose referred to Roosevelt as the 'all-promising president' who had left numerous countries in the lurch. This was his first denunciation of Roosevelt. Bose accused his administration of 'playing a role of an agent provocateur' in the world while seeking to inherit the remnants of the British Empire. He vigorously denounced American political interference in India, singling out in particular Roosevelt's 'Personal Representative', Colonel Louis Johnson, who—the moment it became apparent that the

Cripps Mission was crumbling—pushed Cripps aside and took over much of the negotiations himself.[46] At the last moment he even came up with a 'Cripps-Johnson formula'[47] which seemed close to bringing about an agreement.[48] Churchill was forced to intervene to remind Cripps that an American—even Roosevelt's 'Personal Representative'—had no business conducting imperial negotiations on behalf of the King-Emperor.[49] Johnson, in turn, suspected that the reaction over his attempt to mediate reflected London's real desire for a failure in negotiations.[50]

None of this was of much concern to Bose who simply denounced Americans as the 'latest converts to imperialism'. He condemned their attempt to secure an Anglo-Indian compromise, claiming that the motive was to get India to participate in the war. Indians could therefore spurn all 'offers and threats' emanating from 'Whitehall or from the White House' or 'go down' with the British Empire. By resorting to such language, Bose clearly equated the United States with Britain. No longer was his venom reserved for British politicians as he warned against walking into a 'trap' laid by 'Allied' politicians.[51] He also launched a thinly veiled attack on Nehru and his followers while being careful to refrain from mentioning names:

> It is no less comical that the Indian saviours of British imperialism are the men who regard themselves as international democrats. These estimable gentlemen shut their eyes to the fact that India's one and only enemy is British imperialism [...] they conveniently forget that India today lies under the heel of Britain and [...] talk of lining up with the progressive forces of the world. They do not talk frankly of co-operating with Britain but camouflage their real motives by asking the Indian people to co-operate with China or Russia or America. But such camouflage cannot deceive the Indian people who are fully aware that the British Empire does not represent a progressive force in this world and is in fact the citadel of reaction.[52]

Finally fed up, Nehru returned the compliment a few days later:

SUBHAS CHANDRA BOSE IN NAZI GERMANY

Hitler and Japan must go to hell. I shall fight them to the end and this is my policy. I shall also fight Mr Subhas Chandra Bose and his party along with Japan if he comes to India. Mr Bose acted very wrongly. [...] Hitler and Japan represent the reactionary forces and their victory means the victory of the reactionary forces in the world.[53]

5

SUSTAINING THE OFFENSIVE

POLITICS, INTELLIGENCE AND PROPAGANDA

Hitler, Mussolini and Bose, April–June 1942

While Nehru and Bose exchanged insults, Berlin received welcome news from Tokyo. With the failure of the Cripps Mission, the Japanese government was now prepared to issue the Tripartite declaration.[1] It also extended a formal invitation to Bose. Indian nationalists clamouring for his presence in Southeast Asia had long suspected that Japanese hesitation stemmed from hope of reaching an agreement instead with Gandhi and Nehru. The Cripps Mission had ensured that this would not happen. Nehru was still making a daily ritual of denouncing Japan. Japanese policymakers gradually realised that Bose was the only Congressman with whom they could work. His broadcast of 6 April, in response to Tojo's statement, had not gone unheard.

The Japanese sent their own Tripartite draft declaration to Berlin and Rome as they had not been impressed by the German one. The Germans were in turn appalled by the Japanese draft, dismissing it as 'journalistic'.[2] They seemed to think—not without irony—that they were more qualified when it came to matters pertaining to national sovereignty and independence. The Special India Bureau immediately revised the draft.

Ribbentrop, who was still committed to the declaration, decided not to inform Bose, lest he interfere with the drafting process, thereby causing further delay. He was determined that nothing—not even Bose—should now come in the way. Neither was Bose initially informed of Tokyo's formal invitation as the Germans did not want to agitate him. After all they had a major logistical problem on their hands: how was Bose to be transferred half-way across the world? The only feasible methods—by air or sea—presented huge challenges. It was one thing to resolve that he should leave, another to put this into effect.

Ribbentrop sent the revised draft, along with the Japanese original, to Hitler on 16 April, emphasising Italian acquiescence and the breakdown of the Cripps Mission. He advised immediate acceptance.[3] Hitler was very irritated that the Japanese had not responded earlier to the German initiative. He replied that he saw 'no point in adhering to such a declaration just when the Japanese want it [...] after they had needed months to examine earlier German proposals'. He merely agreed to discuss the matter with Mussolini during a conference scheduled at the end of the month. Hitler only responded positively to Bose's departure hoping it would be 'as soon as possible' fully realising that he would be of more use in Tokyo than Berlin.[4]

Within days, it was the Japanese who were annoyed. On 23 April, the Foreign Minister, Shigenori Togo, summoned the German Ambassador and instructed him to inform his government to come to a quick decision regarding the declaration.[5] That this only further antagonised Hitler became evident during his meeting with Mussolini on 29 April, in Salzburg. Ciano, who was also present, described the atmosphere in his diary:

> Hitler talks, talks, talks. Mussolini suffers. [...] Hitler talked uninterruptedly. [...] He omitted absolutely no argument: war and peace, religion and philosophy, art, and history. Mussolini automatically looked at his wristwatch, I had my mind on my own business, and only Cavallero, who is a phenomenon of servility, pretended he was

listening in ecstasy, continually nodding his head in approval. [...] General Jodl, after an epic struggle, finally went to sleep [...] Keitel was reeling, but he succeeded in keeping his head up. He was too close to Hitler to let himself go.[6]

When it came to the declaration, Hitler was negative, arguing that it was useless to issue a 'platonic declaration to grant freedom to peoples as long as the military situation does not allow the enforcement of this guarantee, if necessary even with arms'.[7] It would only be possible once German troops had reached the Caucasus. Hitler nevertheless conceded the right of the Japanese to do so on their own since they were in such a military position. This revealed the extent to which Hitler perceived the Tripartite alliance as a loose political entity as opposed to one working in close co-ordination. He was also willing to impose more generous terms on himself as to when Germany would be in a military position to issue the declaration—that is as soon as German troops reached the Caucasus—as opposed to the Japanese who had already reached India.

Ribbentrop tried to change Hitler's mind, arguing that further postponement might arouse Japanese suspicions and exclude German and Italian participation from Japanese policymaking on India. Hitler was more worried that a declaration might not even elicit much enthusiasm from Indians thereby embarrassing the Tripartite powers. Even if Indians responded enthusiastically—which Hitler realised was unlikely—the danger was that the British might use the declaration as a pretext for internal repression. There was the added risk that a declaration would reinforce British determination to wage war.[8] Throughout the discussion, Mussolini and Ciano sat passively, agreeing with everything the Führer said. Hitler had his way with the Japanese as well who—although by no means subservient to him—agreed to drop the matter as soon as they were informed of the German and 'Italian' desire to postpone the declaration.[9]

Bose, in the meantime, travelled to Rome for a much needed change of air. It was a poor substitute for Tokyo. The Germans were delighted to see him leave as it fell on the Italians to inform Bose that the declaration had been postponed. By now he had come to suspect that the Japanese were prepared to issue the declaration. In the aftermath of the Cripps Mission and taking into account Tojo's statements, this was hardly surprising. Neither could he have failed to notice the sudden flurry of diplomatic traffic at the Special India Bureau. Bose was therefore confident of obtaining Italian support for the declaration.

It fell on Ciano to inform Bose, on 4 May, that the declaration had been postponed *sine die*.[10] Bose was appalled and insisted that this was a grave mistake. How could Germany and Italy fail to do so when British rule was on the verge of collapse? Now, surely, was the time for action. Failure to do so only reflected a lack of foresight. Would not Japan seize control of Indian policymaking to the detriment of German and Italian interests? Bose made his arguments forcefully this time feeling freer, no doubt, in being critical of Axis policies in Rome than he was in Berlin.

Nevertheless, Ciano was not impressed, commenting that evening in his diary: 'We must take these declarations by Bose for what they are, because he is trying to bring grist to his mill'.[11] Ciano believed that the moment to act would come 'only if and when the armies of the Axis have reached a point where they can impose the declaration of independence with armed force'.[12] He had imbibed Hitler's views perfectly.

Nevertheless, Mussolini saw Bose the following day in Ciano's presence. The Duce was trying to make up for his earlier failure to receive Bose, the two men not having met for several years. Much had changed since then. Although they had agreed before the war that the British Empire constituted a mutual threat, they could have never imagined that their interests would become so intertwined. The efforts Mussolini made to cultivate Bose in the 1930s appeared to be paying off although it was the Germans who were reaping the benefits. Mussolini was delighted to see

Bose as it also reminded him of those happier days when he was still the strongman of Europe. Bose was equally pleased, particularly with the opportunity to bring about a reversal over the declaration.

As they discussed the situation in India, Mussolini admitted that he had been impressed by Gandhi during the Cripps Mission.[13] He agreed with Bose that the failure to reach a compromise was a turning point in Indian politics. Ciano watched with growing distress as Bose gradually convinced Mussolini that the declaration should be issued. Having finally gotten himself excited and worked up—to a large extent at the thought of defying the Germans—Mussolini ordered Ciano to instruct Berlin that the declaration should be issued without further delay.[14] A sceptical Ciano wrote prophetically that night in his diary: 'I feel that Hitler will not agree to it very willingly'.[15]

Nevertheless, by having convinced Mussolini and persuaded him to cable the Germans—'contrary to the Salzburg decisions'[16]—as Ciano put it, Bose had won an important victory. The Nazis were now in a difficult situation faced with Italian and Japanese opposition to their stance. Bose rushed back to Berlin and wrote a letter to Ribbentrop urging him to accept the 'Italian' initiative.[17] Ribbentrop was won over. He sent a memorandum to Hitler on 14 May, advising acceptance while quoting extracts from Bose's letter and recent statements by Gandhi to bolster his argument. Hitler remained firm and did not respond. Ribbentrop therefore sent him another memorandum, on 25 May, again insisting on acceptance. This time he used a German offensive in Egypt as justification.[18] The Foreign Office, in the meantime, prepared a meeting between Bose and Hitler, realising that only the latter could explain why he was so adamant about postponing the declaration. By now Hitler was completely isolated, opposed as he was not only by Bose, the Japanese and the Italians but also by Ribbentrop and the Foreign Office. Bose would be given his chance of doing with Hitler what he had succeeded in doing with Mussolini. In essence, the Foreign Office, having done all it could to obtain the declaration, washed its hands of the affair.

The meeting was scheduled for the end of May. In the meantime, the situation became increasingly complicated as rumours circulated that Bose had obtained Italian support to set-up an Indian government. Goebbels noted in his diary that, according to a confidential source, Mussolini 'had a talk with the Indian nationalist leader Bose, in the course of which he pleaded for Bose to appear more conspicuously and especially to set up a counter-government'.[19] Goebbels revealed the German line on this: 'We don't like this idea very much, since we do not think the time has yet come for such a political manoeuvre. It does appear, though, that the Japanese are very eager for some such step. However émigré governments must not live too long in a vacuum. Unless they have some actuality to support them, they only really exist in the realm of theory'.[20]

In reality, Bose had never discussed the issue with Mussolini, having given up hope of establishing a government in Europe. The rumours were symptomatic of how German policy was increasingly at odds with Japan and Italy when it came to Bose. That the latter had carefully refrained from divulging the contents of his discussions with Mussolini and Ciano hardly helped matters. He had by now developed a cautious nature in Berlin, never revealing more than was necessary.

In any case, Bose was little bothered by these rumours. He was more concerned with growing portrayals of him in the Allied press as an Axis stooge. Shortly upon his return to Berlin, he responded with a long broadcast—the first in weeks. Complaining that it was a 'moral tragedy' that some of his compatriots were still being 'duped by British propaganda', Bose insisted on setting the record straight. He complained of 'misguided people' who spoke of 'aggression by Japan or Germany or Italy, without knowing at first hand what policy these powers have with regard to India'. Bose assured his listeners—'in all seriousness and sincerity'—that they only wanted to 'see India fully independent' and the 'mistress of her own destiny' again. He clarified his position on this delicate issue:

> I am not an apologist of the Tripartite Powers and it is not my task to defend what they have done. [...] My concern [...] is with India and it is my duty [...] to inform my countrymen as to how best we can achieve the liberation of India in the present world crisis. [...] Friends, I have laughed whenever I have heard Britain's paid propagandists calling me an enemy agent. I need no credentials when I speak to my own people. My whole life, which has been one long, consistent and continuous record of uncompromising struggle against British imperialism, is the best guarantee of my bona fides. [...] If the British, who are the past masters in the art of diplomacy and political seduction, have, in spite of their best efforts, failed to tempt, corrupt or mislead me, no other power on earth can do so.[21]

Bose insisted that there was nothing wrong in seeking foreign assistance, especially as the British had 'been going round the world with the begging-bowl, asking for men, money and munitions, not only from the free nations of the world, but also from enslaved countries like India'. If the British allowed American troops entry into India, then Indians had every right to grant the same rights to their allies. 'American diplomats, American businessmen and American Army units are now overrunning India' Bose complained, warning that this amounted to a 'new peril'. Instead of preoccupying themselves with an imaginary Axis threat, Indians should respond to the actual American threat.[22]

Bose mocked a recent broadcast by the Viceroy in which he had asked Indians to set up a national war front in anticipation of an Axis attack. Bose encouraged his listeners to do just that but direct it instead at the British, stating sarcastically that the Viceroy was 'right when he told you that you must rouse the will to unite and the will to act'.[23]

Bose also attacked Chiang Kai-shek, fiercely rejecting the notion that the Axis powers constituted a threat to India because of past events in China. Reminding his listeners that he had sent a medical mission to assist the Generalissimo, Bose denounced him for attempting to drag India into the war. Chiang Kai-shek was a 'different man' now, actually a 'puppet of the Anglo-American Powers'. In contrast, Japan had changed drastically. It was fighting to eradicate 'Anglo-American imperialism' from Asia. Bose claimed that Chiang Kai-shek could even come to an 'honourable understanding' with the Japanese if only he could 'emancipate himself from the grips of his Anglo-American masters'.[24] The abuse Bose hurled at the Chinese leader reflected the manner in which he was himself portrayed by the Allied press.

Bose ended his broadcast assuring his countrymen that the final phase of India's liberation was about to begin and that Indians outside India were doing everything to help. He concluded on a positive note for the first time referring to 'post-war reconstruction' and the need for a 'social order' based on the 'principles of justice, equality and brotherhood'.[25]

This was Bose's most rabidly anti-American broadcast to date. He was addressing the issue of Indian independence increasingly through the prism of the world conflict and was convinced that India could not emerge as a liberated entity until the British Empire was crushed. It had a crucial stake therefore in the creation of a new world order, something that would transpire only after an Axis victory. Bose fully appreciated the empire's dependence on the United States. American power therefore also had to be curtailed, if not destroyed. In the process Bose became not just a fighter for Indian independence, but also one for the Axis cause.

While Bose waited to meet Hitler, there were encouraging developments in Afghanistan. German intelligence reported that the Fakir of Ipi had launched the long awaited attack on the British. Much to everyone's surprise—particularly the British—it was a resounding success. Hundreds of tribesmen attacked a heavily fortified British position at Datta Khel. The British sent in reinforcements—supported by aircraft and tanks—but they were unable to reach their objective. The British then in sent two additional infantry brigades but it took several weeks of fierce fighting before they actually reached Datta Khel.[26] With the Japanese threatening the northeast of India, the last thing the British needed was trouble in the northwest. The High Command in India, suspecting that the Germans were planning to attack the Frontier, was already hastily constructing numerous airfields in Baluchistan and eastern Iran.[27]

Bose had already instructed Talwar to launch a widespread subversion campaign via the Forward Bloc across India. This was to include an intensification of propaganda to weaken confidence in British rule and gradually prepare the public for the entry of Axis troops. Indian agents were to position themselves along strategic points on the eastern coast of India to assist disembarking Japanese troops. A 'go-slow' campaign was to be launched in factories to paralyse the British war effort. Indian troops prepared to defect in Burma and North Africa were to use the code word 'Silver Moon'. Finally, Bose envisaged deploying the Legion in the North-West Frontier where it would co-operate with the local tribes.[28] Bose's instructions reflected his firm conviction that it was only a matter of time before the Axis attacked India and a revolution broke out. As events proved Bose was actually not off the mark when it came to predicting an explosive situation in India, one bordering on revolution. Bose's instructions might have created serious problems for the British had not Talwar passed them on to Soviet intelligence.[29]

Bose also decided to pressure the Germans into speeding up his transfer to Tokyo. On 22 May, he wrote to Ribbentrop informing him that conditions were 'now ripe for a revolution' in India and that it was 'absolutely essential' that he reached the Indian frontier. 'Our common goal' he wrote, 'the final defeat of Anglo-American imperialism—demands that I should now go to the east and, from close quarters, guide the Indian revolution towards that goal'. Bose was confident that Hitler would 'appreciate this imperative and objective requirement'.[30] He knew that this letter and the urgent manner in which he presented it—he did not even bring up the declaration—would help set the agenda for his meeting with Hitler.

Bose had reason to be impatient. Although he did not mention it in the letter, Mussolini had offered him the use of a Savoia-Marchetti S. M. 75 aircraft for a flight from Europe to East Asia.[31] It would be an *experimental* flight—the first of its kind—and therefore extremely dangerous. It was also not scheduled to leave for several weeks. Nevertheless, for the first time, Tokyo appeared within reach. Bose's departure became his new obsession, now in effect, replacing the declaration.

While handing his letter to Woermann the next day, the latter responded in his usual defensive manner, reminding Bose of the difficulties in reaching Tokyo and suggesting that the Japanese might not be all that eager to receive him after all. Bose revealed the Italian offer leaving Woermann fumbling for words. As for Japanese intentions, Bose refused to get into a drawn-out discussion now that he had access to Ribbentrop and Hitler. Nevertheless, Woermann's attitude reflected a sentiment within the Foreign Office that Bose's departure was not necessarily in Germany's best interests.[32]

By the final week of May, Hitler was ready to receive Bose. An embarrassed Ribbentrop first met the latter, apologised for not having answered his letters and admitted that he no longer knew what to do about the declaration. The reality was that Ribbentrop had given up in the absence of a response from Hitler. Bose listened contemptuously. The two then set off to see Hitler.

A photograph commemorating the meeting shows a beaming Bose firmly extending his hand to Hitler while the Führer appeared carefully to scrutinise his facial features. Bose, addressing Hitler as an 'old revolutionary', expressed gratitude for the 'hospitality and kindness' he had received in Germany, adding that this day would forever remain engraved in his memory. Hitler, slightly taken aback by the 'old revolutionary' remark, immediately proceeded to expose his views on India. The gist of his argument was that Germany and India had the same 'merciless opponents'. They were 'fighting the same battle against the same enemies, absolutely irrespective of where they met them'. For good measure, he threw in the Soviets as well, convinced that they also posed a threat to India. 'Certain friendly views of Pandit Nehru regarding the Russians' therefore appeared 'extremely dangerous' he added.[33] While Bose was not averse to criticism of Nehru, he was naturally far from convinced by Hitler's Soviet thesis.

When it came to the declaration, Hitler explained that he was waging war as a soldier, not a politician. He could not guarantee anything 'beyond the range of his own effectiveness' nor would he make 'false prophecies'. He referred for example to the ongoing German offensive in Egypt where a declaration guaranteeing Egyptian independence would be issued only when it was clear that the offensive had succeeded. He was 'no Englishman' working for the 'defeat of Egypt and the revolutionary Arabs' but rather to help them achieve 'real success'. It was for this reason that he did not want 'a diversionary operation carried out by them as Englishmen would do'.[34]

Referring to himself now as an 'old revolutionary' Hitler advised Bose to 'bank on the Japanese' and get as close to India as possible. An internal revolt, combined with external pressure would ensure Indian liberation. Hitler was sceptical that Gandhi's tactics would accomplish anything. He termed 'Japan's astonishingly rapid advance' a major 'historical event', while admitting that he did not know what his ally was planning next. ('They had not mentioned anything positive to Germany'.) Nevertheless, Hitler advised Bose—again as an 'old revolutionary'—quickly to reach an agreement with the Japanese so that no 'psychological mistakes' would be made. He did not elaborate as to what he meant by 'psychological mistakes'.[35]

Although he encouraged Bose to leave for Tokyo, Hitler ruled out going by air—thinly concealing his contempt for the Italians in the process—claiming that he was 'too important a personality to let his life be endangered by such an experiment'. Instead, Hitler proposed Bose board *I-30*, a Japanese submarine scheduled to reach German-occupied France that summer. If this was not feasible he proposed placing a German submarine at Bose's 'disposal'. With the help of a map, Hitler traced the likely route through the Atlantic Ocean, around the Cape of Good Hope and into the Indian Ocean.[36]

Bose only brought up two issues in the course of the meeting. First, the need for Hitler's views on India to be clarified in the absence of a declaration, particularly as passages of *Mein Kampf* were still being exploited by the British in India. Secondly, the need for continued German assistance after the war so that India would not depend exclusively on Japan. Hitler was dismissive of his remarks in *Mein Kampf* suggesting that they belonged to the past. As for the future, he only promised economic assistance as 'the power of a country could only be exercised within the range of its sword'. Hitler then got up, presented Bose with a precious stone cigar case and wished him the best in his endeavours to liberate India. With that the meeting ended.[37]

For Bose it resolved his two most important concerns, namely the declaration and his transfer to Tokyo. Although Hitler indefinitely postponed the declaration, he did make clear his willingness to arrange a transfer to Tokyo. This had now become Bose's overriding preoccupation—more so than the declaration. It was Hitler, not Bose, who made a central issue of it during the discussion. Bose was already developing greater ambitions which included setting up a fully-fledged government in Southeast Asia, thus making the declaration irrelevant.

Bose had also come to be more understanding of Hitler's rationale for postponing the declaration, confiding in Nambiar that Hitler did have a 'sense of realism', although he admitted that he did not know whether it was matched by any 'real feeling for Indian independence'.[38] Hitler's remarks on the danger posed by Nehru, the need to get as close to India as possible and an internal revolt combined with outside pressure inevitably struck deep chords.

In spite of his imminent departure, Bose carried on with his work. On 11 June, he outlined a plan to open a branch of the Free India Centre in Paris.[39] Ever since arriving in Berlin, Nambiar and Mookerjee had been pushing for such a branch, aware that there was much scope for anti-British propaganda in France. Bose himself noticed that his broadcasts had renewed interest for India in France. He was also anxious to forestall any attempt by outside agencies—particularly Shedai—to set-up an Indian office in Paris. Bose assigned several tasks to the Paris centre. It would:

Distribute, for propaganda purposes, such anti-British material as we publish in Berlin […] try to place in the French press articles which we shall send […] try to do as much anti-British propaganda […] as possible […] to influence French writers and journalists in the non-occupied zone […] cultivate contacts with the Indian colony in France and try to influence them in an anti-British direction.[40]

Having waited nearly two weeks for his meeting with Hitler to have an impact in the international press—as hostile as it was sympathetic depending on which camp was reporting—[41] Bose held his first press conference, on 12 June. He was not to be disappointed. Axis and neutral journalists converged to hear him speak, while photographers jostled with one another to get the best shot. Bose knew that his statements would be picked up by the world's press and he was determined not to disappoint either friend or foe.

Bose only briefly alluded to his meetings with Hitler and Mussolini, without delving into their contents, although he did describe the two dictators as the 'best friends that the Indian people have, outside India'. While it was widely speculated that

Tokyo was his next destination, Bose would only say—for obvious reasons—that the 'plans of a revolutionary must always be adapted to the circumstances of the moment and to the needs of the situation'. Portraying himself as a revolutionary was very much in keeping with the image he wished to convey. He urged the press not to be misled by British propaganda, insisting that India was on the verge of revolt.[42]

Assuring his audience that the 'vast majority' of Indians opposed British rule and were eager to 'break the chains of bondage', Bose insisted that it was impossible for him now to 'regard any Indian nationalist as a political opponent'. This was a conciliatory gesture in response to Nehru's public statements. Nevertheless, Bose left no illusion that while some nationalists might resort to passive resistance others would 'not hesitate to draw the sword'.[43]

Bose dismissed claims that he was an Axis puppet, stating 'abuse is only a sign of weakness'. He also emphasised the need for Indians to decide what form of government they wanted and who would lead them after the war. 'I certainly have my own ideas regarding post-war reconstruction' he admitted, but affirmed that it would be for 'India to decide upon them'.[44] Significantly then, Bose remained committed to democratic principles—at least in public.

Bangkok, Regenwurm and Rome, June–July 1942

While Bose addressed the press, Indian nationalists in Bangkok prepared for a major conference on Indian independence. Bose had received an invitation but had to content himself in joining Axis statesmen, including Ribbentrop, in sending messages of support.[45] Bose's message took on a somewhat precautionary note as he warned his compatriots that while the Axis powers were 'our best friends and allies' and would 'gladly render us such assistance as we may need', the 'emancipation of India must be the work primarily of Indians themselves'.⁴⁶ He again reiterated that it was for the Indian people to decide what form of government they wanted. Not knowing the precise nature of their activities, Bose feared that his compatriots might have already compromised themselves by making too many concessions to the Japanese.

On 17 June, after an absence of five weeks, Bose felt that it was time to broadcast on the rapidly changing political situation in India. In the aftermath of the Cripps Mission, the British only made minor political concessions. These essentially revolved around an expansion of the Viceroy's Executive Council—a largely symbolic advisory body—to include a few more Indians. This was combined with a smear campaign by the Viceroy to portray the Congress as pro-Nazi.⁴⁷ Not surprisingly it achieved little, only hastening the divide between British and Indians.

Bose's broadcasts also appeared to have influenced the political landscape as Gandhi now suddenly launched a campaign demanding the immediate withdrawal of British and American troops from India.⁴⁸ Whether this was a coincidence or whether Gandhi had indeed been influenced by Bose remains a matter of conjecture, but what is certain is that it left many Congressmen deeply shocked and embarrassed.⁴⁹ Gandhi and Bose's radical positions set them apart although their political importance ensured there was little Congressmen could do to oppose them. Nehru kept his counsel, refraining from directly challenging Gandhi although he remained hopeful that India would still eventually fight alongside the Allies. An increasingly despairing Azad considered asking Roosevelt to act as mediator between London and the Congress until an infuriated Gandhi threatened to throw him out⁵⁰ much in a manner he had once threatened Bose.

British officials responded hysterically, denouncing Gandhi with words such as 'fifth columnist' and 'quisling'.⁵¹ The language was very similar to that used to describe Bose. Churchill also became increasingly abusive, eventually describing Gandhi as a 'rascal' and a 'thoroughly evil force'.[52] 'I hate Indians' he finally admitted to the Secretary of State for India, Amery, claiming they were 'a beastly people with a beastly religion'.[53]

Bose, not surprisingly, lauded Gandhi in his broadcast. Referring to him now as 'Mahatma', Bose welcomed his campaign to expel British and American troops from India. He went so far as to state that he would report in person to Gandhi as soon as India was liberated, thereby implying that he still recognised his leadership. Nevertheless, in the course of the broadcast, which was to a large extent a repetition of many points already raised, Bose claimed that it would be an 'act of political suicide' for India to 'remain inactive or neutral' in the war. India had to 'play a dynamic role' and 'contribute materially' to defeating the British so as to ensure it would not remain subdued or receive liberation as a 'gift from the victorious Tripartite Powers'. 'We want neither' Bose asserted. 'The Indian people' had to 'fight for and win their own liberty'.[54]

Bose was adamant that an alliance with the Tripartite powers did not imply 'acceptance of their domination or even of their ideology in our internal affairs'. He assured his listeners that his socioeconomic views were 'exactly what they were when I was at home'—namely anti-imperialist, radical and socialist. Bose urged his countrymen not to be 'carried away by ideological considerations alone'. 'The internal polices of Germany or Italy or Japan do not concern us' he argued. Only independence was what mattered.[55]

Apart from its positive portrayal of Gandhi, Bose's broadcast was noteworthy for the distinctly independent line it advocated *vis-à-vis* the Axis powers. While acknowledging them as allies, Bose for the first time set specific limitations. Given the growing attention and criticism over his association with the Axis, Bose had little choice. His meetings with Mussolini and Hitler—combined with his departure for Tokyo—gave him the confidence to do so.

SUSTAINING THE OFFENSIVE

A few days after the broadcast, the Italians once more offered Bose a seat on board their experimental aircraft.[56] Bose was inclined to accept, despite the risks, realising that he could be in Asia within weeks. The Germans sabotaged any such possibility, fearing for his safety. They responded to the Italian initiative with a mixture of contempt and irritation at what was perceived as interference in German affairs. Ribbentrop cabled Rome dismissively.[57] Bose was not so easily deterred. He resolved to go to Rome and decide for himself. Before leaving he completed two important tasks in the event he should not return.

First, Bose visited the Special India Detachment in Regenwurm.[58] The unit had expanded and made significant progress. The Legionaries, attired in standard German field grey uniforms with the exception of the Sikhs, who were allowed to retain their turbans, appeared fit and invigorated. Bose asked them a few questions about their daily routine and praised their efforts. He was visibly pleased. His satisfaction was not confined to military matters. In the course of a discussion with the training staff, the German officers proudly affirmed having succeeded in surmounting the greatest difficulty of all—religious differences. Bose had insisted, despite the initial scepticism of the Germans, that Hindus, Muslims and Sikhs be mixed into a common formation unlike in the Indian army where they had been segregated, not only on a basis of caste and religion, but even ethnicity.[59] The Germans confirmed that the experiment was a success, instilling in the troops for the first time a sense of nationality.[60] Politically, this is what mattered most to Bose.[61] There could be no Indian military formation worth speaking of if it was not unified politically. Bose did not visit Frankenberg as he was annoyed by the still low level of recruitment there. This was a matter he also wanted to raise in Rome as thousands of Indian POWs were still stranded in Italian POW camps in North Africa.

Before leaving, Bose also sent a long telegram to Rash Behari Bose, the leader of the Indian independence movement in Southeast Asia, via the German embassy in Tokyo. Rash Behari had risen to prominence following his involvement in a failed assassination attempt on a Viceroy, Lord Hardinge, in 1912. During the First World War, he pursued his anti-British activities in collaboration with Germany only to end up afterwards exiled in Japan. Bose assumed that he was addressing a fellow radical, not realising that Rash Behari Bose had long since moderated his views. Bose's telegram was one of the most important documents he wrote during the war as it revealed his inner thoughts on his Congress colleagues—in striking contrast to his public rhetoric.

Bose claimed that 'Gandhi's epoch in India's history' had ended as early as 1939. While acknowledging that he had 'imparted political consciousness to the Indian masses' and 'built up an All-India political organisation', Bose criticised Gandhi's commitment to non-violence and civil disobedience. 'With such methods you can never expel the British' he affirmed. Using language similar to that used when first meeting Ribbentrop, Bose accused Gandhi of keeping the 'door open for a compromise with the British'.[62] He therefore dismissed any compromise with Gandhian ideology. It had outlived its purpose and Indian nationalists had to resort to other, more practical, means of liberating India. Bose outlined three principles constituting as he put it, the 'correct strategy' to pursue. These were:

(1) Alliance with all powers hostile to Britain.
(2) Launching of a revolution now in India, when British power is collapsing.
(3) Seeking such military aid from outside as is necessary.

'I have worked under Mahatma Gandhi for twenty years' Bose continued 'and I know him thoroughly. I do not underestimate his strength and influence, nor do I overestimate it'. Claiming that Gandhi was 'no longer a dynamic and revolutionary figure', Bose contended that it was the Forward Bloc which had forced him to adopt a more radical agenda. He dismissed Gandhi's campaign for the expulsion of Allied troops from India, for example, as a result of 'our propaganda'. Nevertheless, Gandhi would never 'advocate the use of arms' nor adopt a 'pro-Axis' policy. 'Consequently' there could be 'no room for co-operation' with him. Bose also insisted that it would be a 'fatal mistake' to 'lionise Gandhi or praise him too much' as this would amount to 'political suicide'. He only conceded the occasional 'compliment' thereby revealing the manipulative nature of his 17 June broadcast in which he had enthusiastically praised Gandhi.[63]

The extent of the contempt Bose felt for Nehru and Azad is evident in the manner in which he dismissed them with a sentence each: 'Nehru is fanatically anti-Axis and he is much worse than Gandhi. Azad is a blind follower of Gandhi now'.[64] Bose's contempt for his Congress colleagues remained carefully concealed for the duration of the war.

By the time Bose reached Rome, the experimental aircraft had already taken off and landed safely in Tokyo. The Italians were less inclined to put him on board another flight as a result of German and Japanese pressure. While waiting for things to be sorted out, Bose concluded some useful political business. First, he protested vigorously to the Italian military authorities—with the backing of the Foreign Office in Berlin—over its failure to transfer the thousands of Indian POWs still stranded in North Africa.[65] Bose was also very annoyed to learn that a Free India Battalion, modelled on the Special India Detachment, was being organised by the Italian army. This partly helped explain Italian reluctance to transfer Indian POWs. Shedai of course was behind this but this time Bose had had enough. He launched an open campaign against Shedai with the help of the German embassy in Rome. Bose told anyone who cared to listen that—apart from gross political incompetence—Shedai was not only sabotaging the Indian Legion but engaging in sectarian politics as well by supporting the Muslim League. These were serious accusations and they received their due attention if not in Rome, then in Berlin and Tokyo. The Germans and Japanese promptly joined hands with Bose in trying to oust Shedai but as the German embassy in Rome reported to Berlin, Shedai was one of 'those unpleasant types who once thrown out from the main staircase, reappear untroubled from the back staircase'.[66] Nevertheless, Shedai had made powerful enemies and he would soon bear the consequences.[67]

6

TRANSITION TO TOKYO

I-30 TO *U-180*

Interactions with the Nazi Leadership: Bose, Himmler and Goebbels, July 1942

With no immediate flight plans in sight, Bose returned to Berlin shortly before mid-July hoping to board *I-30*, the Japanese submarine now scheduled to reach France in early August. In the meantime he cultivated the Nazi leadership. This included an extended visit to the headquarters of the *Reichsführer-SS*, Heinrich Himmler, who administered the concentration camps. As Bose had established cordial relations with the army, he now hoped to do so with the powerful *SS*. Himmler had his own reasons for meeting Bose, ranging from the theoretical (racial and spiritual fascination with India) to curiosity (aroused by the international press attention Bose had garnered). Bose presented an opportunity of discussing various issues on Himmler's peculiar mind, Aryans, Hinduism—particularly the caste system— subjects which his guest would have preferred to avoid altogether. Nevertheless, it came as quite a surprise for Bose to learn that Himmler was deeply versed in Hindu scripture, including the *Upanishads*, *Vedas* and the *Bhagavad-Gita*.[1] This made obtaining

Himmler's support for Indian independence all the more easy. One statement that baffled Bose, leaving him in something of a quandary, was Himmler's assertion that he could not understand how Aryan warrior tribes like the Rajputs, Marathas and Sikhs had allowed themselves to become enslaved by the British.[2] Bose's nationalist sensitivities were inevitably aroused by this question, all the more so as he had no adequate explanation to offer, implying validation to some extent of Himmler's question. Nevertheless, according to one senior SS official, Bose's 'outstanding intelligence' made a 'deep impression' on Himmler.[3] Himmler certainly proved to be an ardent supporter of Free India.[4] One Free India official who met Himmler on several occasions would recall that he was the 'only man of consequence in the Third Reich who seemed to accept India's right to independence as a matter of fact, rather than a mere exigency' and that 'his interest in our affairs did not remain restricted to expressions of sympathy in words'.[5] Certainly, one of the outcomes of the talks was plans for the SS to train Indians.[6]

On 21 July, a week after the meeting with Himmler, Goebbels received Bose. This time the discussion revolved primarily around politics and propaganda. Bose severely criticised Gandhi, comparing him unflatteringly to the ultra-conservative president of the Weimar Republic, Paul von Hindenburg.[7] He claimed that Gandhi's tactics had delayed independence and insisted that Indian nationalism needed to be modernised through a 'revolution of action'.[8] Goebbels could not have agreed more. He privately considered Gandhi to be a 'fool' who had 'brought nothing but misfortune to India'.[9] In contrast, Goebbels thought highly of Bose, confiding to an aide after he left that 'the right man' was 'being used in the right way'. He issued instructions so that 'careful attention should continue to be paid to the Indian question' while warning that 'no mention should be made of actions in India until these are in fact imminent'. Goebbels wanted to ensure as much credibility as possible when it came to India. The central theme of German propaganda was straightforward: 'we want to make India free'.[10] It was a message that was to be repeated endlessly so that Germany would be associated with freedom in the minds of Indians. A paradox of sorts.[11]

I-30, *August 1942*

Two days after his meeting with Goebbels, frustrated to learn that *I-30* was still lingering in the Atlantic, Bose wrote to Ribbentrop. He now wanted to proceed by air only, claiming that a submarine journey was too unpredictable and perilous. Bose suggested that the Italian government would 'gladly make the necessary arrangements for another flight to the Far East, if requested by the German government'.[12] 'In view of the internal developments in India, I should like to be in the Far East in the first week of August' Bose ended with excessive optimism.[13]

Ribbentrop was still opposed to the aerial route. He cabled Tokyo hoping it would acquiesce in Bose boarding *I-30* as it slowly approached the French coast.[14] It was a dangerous affair, involving as it did, navigation through heavily mined waters while facing the threat of aerial and naval attacks. The German navy had to send several minesweepers, supported by eight *Luftwaffe* Junkers Ju-88 bombers, simply to escort *I-30* safely into the naval base at Lorient. The arrival of the submarine on 5 August, was a naval and propaganda feat for the Axis powers. The entire German Naval High Command was present to welcome the Japanese, while Hitler waited to decorate the Japanese commander in Berlin.

Bose happily packed his suitcases until an embarrassed Foreign Office official informed him that Tokyo had refused him permission to board *I-30*. Apart from not wanting to assume responsibility for his safety, the Japanese Naval High Command had rigid regulations prohibiting civilians from boarding its vessels.[15] Bose was so taken aback that he did not protest for fear of antagonising the Japanese even before he reached Tokyo.

The Japanese attitude was certainly most unhelpful. After refusing Bose permission to board the submarine, Tokyo took another two weeks before it finally approved the aerial route, only to suddenly reverse this decision, citing concern with possible violations of Soviet air space.[16] The Germans now finally resolved to take matters into their hands. Hitler was forced to make good on his promise to place a submarine at Bose's 'disposal' and the Naval High Command began making the necessary arrangements.

Congress Compulsions and Post-War Plans

With an abundance of time on his hands, Bose wrote two important articles for the *Free India* journal. The first, 'The Situation in India' was essentially a reaction to a Congress Working Committee resolution which had been passed in July after nine days of deliberations. While threatening a massive civil disobedience campaign if immediate independence was not granted, it nevertheless made an important concession by granting Allied troops permission to remain in India. The resolution—yet to be ratified by the All India Congress Committee—was an uneasy compromise between Gandhi and Nehru as well as the Congress Working Committee.[17]

Bose had little doubt that it would be ratified. Referring directly for the first time to Nehru, Bose described him as a 'lone figure' and an 'ideological fanatic' who had become 'the favourite of the Anglo-Americans'. Of the resolution, Bose dismissed it as nothing but a demand for independence—'on paper'. By allowing Allied troops to remain in India, British rule would only be reinforced. He was also concerned with Gandhi's leadership, suggesting that he was prone to begin a 'campaign brilliantly' but end it in a 'muddle'. Nevertheless, Bose advocated giving Gandhi full support in his efforts to obtain immediate independence while stressing the need to be 'very careful'. The Forward Bloc would support Gandhi but also continue agitating against the presence of Allied troops in India. 'Under no circumstances' should India obtain independence in return for participation in the war. The most that could be expected was neutrality.[18]

Comparing Nehru with Gandhi, Bose claimed that the former would go to 'any length in order to fight the Tripartite Powers' as this was his primary ideological preoccupation while for Gandhi it was non-violence. The realisation that non-violence might not bring about an independent India had made Gandhi prone to compromise, which in turn forced him into an anti-Axis position. Nevertheless, Bose suggested that it was possible to influence Gandhi as the Forward Bloc had succeeded in doing in the past.[19] His article was the most transparent and personality-driven analysis he had yet made of the Indian political context in Berlin. It was for this reason that he chose to have it published in a journal that was not easily accessible as opposed to broadcasting his opinions.

Bose's second article was an even greater exposé of his views which he realised would be best not to air on the radio. In one of the most important articles he wrote in the war it outlined his vision of the 'New State' he hoped to see emerge in India. Entitled 'Free India and her Problems', it argued that the first national priority would be to reorganise the armed forces as soon as a new civil administration was set up. 'The dearth of Indian officers of high rank remains and will present some difficulty' Bose conceded although he asserted that it would be possible to train a new officer corps within a few years.[20]

While the 'New State' would be inspired by various political experiments, 'one thing however, is clear' Bose insisted. It would have a 'strong central government' responsible for ensuring public safety and order. This would ensure a 'well organised' and 'disciplined' one party state. Nevertheless, the state would 'guarantee complete religious' freedom for 'individuals and groups' as well as political and economic rights for all. It would eliminate poverty and unemployment through state-subsidised agriculture and industrialisation. Workers would be entitled to a 'living wage, sickness insurance' and 'compensation for accident'. Peasants in turn would be relieved of heavy taxation and the burden of debt.[21] The gold standard would be abandoned while foreign trade would be state controlled and subject to a barter system.

One of the principal objectives of the New State would be 'national unity' achieved through the various means at its disposal including—'press, radio, cinema, theatre etc'. Hindustani, written in the Roman script, would be the national language of India.[22] Attempts to sabotage the state and national unity would be 'punished heavily'. Bose rejected the notion that Muslims could not be assimilated into the New State claiming that the religious problem was a consequence of British rule akin to the situation in Ireland and the 'Jewish problem' in Palestine. It would simply 'disappear' with the collapse of British rule. Over time, power would be gradually decentralised and transferred to provincial governments.[23] Bose also dismissed the Indian Princely States as an 'anachronism' to be 'abolished'. The Maharajas would 'disappear along with British rule'. In foreign affairs, India would maintain close relations with the Axis powers in the expectation that they would contribute to the development of the new Indian state.[24]

Although Bose tried to be as restrained as possible, his article was particularly revealing. It combined a peculiar blend of nationalist and socialist ideology, using a democratic façade, to mask its authoritarian character. A strong secular state ostensibly giving way to a more democratic one in the future. Although the article did not derive much attention due to its limited circulation, Bose was satisfied that he had at least made his vision of the future clear.

A new difficulty suddenly emerged in early August, leaving Bose preoccupied for days. The High Command decided to attach the Indian Legion to a German-Arab unit in Greece. It was a poor compromise for its inability to deploy the Legion further east owing to a stagnant front. Bose was not impressed by this attempt to bring the Legion 'closer' to India. He also feared that attaching the Legion to the unit would subordinate it to Arab interests. He could not see in what way Indian interests would be served by such a deployment. Bose was therefore adamant that the Legion remain in Germany.

Accordingly on 11 August, Bose wrote an irritated letter to Ribbentrop formally objecting to the High Command's decision.[25] He used the occasion also to protest the slow pace of POW recruitment, indirectly blaming the Italians. While handing his letter to Woermann the next day, Bose reiterated his views more crudely, suggesting that elements within the High Command were insincere in regard to Free India.[26] The angry and disillusioned tone of Bose's letter and statement—a disillusionment reflecting his frustration at still being in Berlin—were not expressed in vain; three days later the High Command backed down and cancelled plans to transfer the Legion to Greece. Bose's complaints were now being taken seriously as he was treated increasingly as a genuine ally.

'Quit India', August–September 1942

On 7 August, the All India Congress Committee convened in Bombay to vote on the July resolution demanding immediate independence in return for granting Allied troops permission to remain in India. The gravity of the situation was made evident when Gandhi ended his speech with the slogan 'Do or Die', implying that the time had come to launch the final battle for freedom. 'We shall either free India or die in the attempt' he assured his countrymen.[27] Bose could not have agreed more with his choice of words.[28]

The resolution—in spite of last minute reservations by Azad and Nehru as well as opposition from communist Congressmen—was passed by an overwhelming majority. It came to be known as the 'Quit India' resolution. Before it even had a chance of being implemented, the British launched countermeasures. The next morning the entire Congress leadership including Gandhi, Azad and Nehru, were arrested and imprisoned for what turned out to be much of the war.[29] The British had initially considered deporting them to Africa but in the end realised that this would only further inflame public opinion.[30] Nevertheless by launching what was supposed to be a pre-emptive measure, the colonial authorities ignited the very reaction they sought to avoid. For several weeks India erupted into endemic revolt.[31] Protests, rallies and demonstrations were countered with lathi charges and police firings giving way to even more unrest and mob violence which spread across urban and rural parts of India and even into the Princely States.[32] The Congress tricolour was defiantly raised on top of countless government buildings and the British 'V' for victory sign systematically erased.[33] For the first time since the 'Sepoy Mutiny' British soldiers were attacked and killed.[34] In view of the gravity of the situation, President Roosevelt ordered American troops in India to remain inconspicuous.[35]

The British responded to the revolt with increasing large-scale repression including more police firings, public whippings, collective fines as well as setting entire villages on fire and even machine gunning mobs from the air.[36] The director of military operations at the War Office, Major-General, Sir John Kennedy, described the prospect of machine-gunning as an 'exhilarating departure from precedent'.[37] Thousands were killed and tens of thousands imprisoned—often in hastily improvised conditions. Many British battalions were engaged in the massive repression effort, leaving India's frontiers dangerously unguarded. On 31 August, the Viceroy, Linlithgow, warned Churchill:

I am engaged here in meeting by far the most serious rebellion since that of 1857, the gravity and extent of which we have so far concealed from the world for reasons of military security. Mob violence remains rampant over large tracts of the countryside and I am by no means confident that we may not see in September a formidable attempt to renew this widespread sabotage of our war effort. [...] If we bungle this business we shall damage India irretrievably as a base for future allied operations.[38]

One worried British official concluded in a note on 'subversive activity' that the Axis did 'not need to set up a fifth column in India' as it already existed '*par excellence*'.[39] Atrocities were committed on both sides. A senior British official in Nagpur enjoyed boasting that he had 'jolly good fun having shot down twenty-four niggers' himself.[40] Policemen were caught by angry mobs, doused with kerosene and set alight.[41] Two RAF officers were pulled out of a train in Fatwah by an angry mob and paraded through town after having their limbs hacked off before finally being thrown into a river.[42] Churchill was not perturbed by events in India. On the contrary, he was rather pleased to finally see Indians 'on the run' as he put it.[43]

The intensity of the uprising caught Bose by surprise as he had never expected anything of this magnitude.[44] He responded in a calm manner making a number of suggestions to the Foreign Office as how best to respond—suggestions which were immediately passed on to Ribbentrop. First on his mind was adding to the confusion by creating two new radio stations. The first—National Congress Radio—would as its name implied broadcast in the name of the Congress. The second, Waziristan Radio, would incite tribesmen along the Indo-Afghan border to attack British India. German paratroopers would then be dropped to apply additional pressure. Bose also proposed going himself to North Africa and touring POW camps on a recruitment drive. Finally, more branches of the Free India Centre were to be opened in Europe.[45]

Nevertheless, for the most part Bose reacted to the 'Quit India' revolt in a rather subdued manner, never exploiting it to the maximum. He responded essentially with two mild and restrained broadcasts. This contrasted significantly with the relentless campaign he had launched during the Cripps Mission. It quickly became apparent that Bose considered 'Quit India' premature—as events would prove—and that he feared it would simply fizzle out. He would have much preferred to see it launched in co-ordination with an Axis offensive. Bose also feared that British counter-measures would thwart a more important uprising in the future. He hoped that 'Quit India' would develop into a long term campaign gradually spreading from one region to another over several months. He certainly did not envisage immediate success—only a long drawn out affair ultimately culminating with an Axis offensive.

This became evident in his first broadcast aired shortly after the outbreak of 'Quit India', and in the second, aired in early September.[46] Bose surprised many by calling for a Gandhian style civil disobedience campaign or as he preferred to put it a 'guerrilla war without arms'. He laid out two fundamental aims. First, the paralysis of British administrative machinery and secondly the destruction of war production. But even then Bose's immediate proposals were mild. He called only for 'small acts of sabotage' in factories such as removing bolts and nuts from machinery rather than challenging management and production through strikes and shutdowns. Bose even suggested that sabotage should be carried out without 'bringing too much trouble on the workers themselves'. Similarly, when it came to disrupting public transport, Bose emphasised the importance of causing as little inconvenience to passengers as possible. He seemed content with ticketless travelling. As for servants, on whom the British were so dependent, Bose merely advised them to demand wage increases and at the most cook bad food so that 'living in India will be impossible for Englishmen'.[47] Nowhere in his broadcasts or in his public statements of the time did he extol the use of violence.

While acknowledging that India had powerful allies, Bose again warned of the dangers of receiving independence as a gift from foreign powers insisting that Indians had to accomplish this themselves. If freedom was obtained without paying the proper price, it would not be worth having at all, he argued. 'It is the baptism of blood, which gives a nation the strength to achieve liberty and to preserve it' he affirmed. In a typically Gandhian manner the blood Bose wanted was Indian, not British.[48]

With the entire Congress leadership imprisoned, Bose reminded his listeners that he was the only Congress leader still free of British clutches and that it was therefore his duty to utilise the international situation to India's advantage. He called on Indian political parties, including the Muslim League, to join the 'Quit India' movement emphasising that Indians had to be united in this last critical phase of the struggle for liberty. This was not the time for divisive politics: internal differences would be resolved after India was freed.

The extent of British repression allowed Bose to exploit it for propaganda purposes in a way bound to generate sympathy in other parts of the world. He denounced the British for 'freely indulging in shooting' on 'unarmed and defenceless' people, claiming that they considered Indian lives to be 'cheap'. Referring to the thousands of wounded and killed, Bose reminded his listeners that Indians only had 'stones and soda-water bottles' to respond with in the face of police firings, armoured cars, tanks, tear gas explosions and aerial bombing. It made for eloquent propaganda, all the more so as Bose was hardly exaggerating. While denouncing the British, for the first time he attacked Churchill, denouncing him as the 'high priest of imperialism, the arch-enemy of Indian nationalism' and—as if that were not enough—'the sworn opponent of all forms of socialism'.[49]

Significantly Bose ended the first of his two broadcasts with the phrase 'victory or death', strongly reminiscent of the words 'do or die' that Gandhi had used in his 'Quit India' speech. After months of suggesting that Gandhi was imitating him, it was now Bose who was doing so. From then on, divergences between the two would be few and far between, improving their relationship dramatically to the extent that they would eventually praise each other in public.[50] It was clear that when it came to launching the final assault on British rule, Indian nationalists were as one.

After the broadcasts, Bose continued keeping himself busy. On 11 September, he inaugurated an Indo-German cultural organisation in Hamburg.[51] Three days later he was in Königsbrück where the Legion had been transferred on what was now one of his regular visits. Bose was pleased with the changes.[52] With India in political turmoil, the number of recruits had doubled. 'Quit India' legitimised enlistment in the Legion, ensuring expansion remained consistent and eventually went into the thousands.[53] What seemed like a political embarrassment and military failure only weeks earlier was suddenly transformed into a resounding success. Bose's perseverance, combined with events in India, brought about this change. By the autumn, the Legion had reached battalion strength. An oath-swearing ceremony was held in the presence of Bose, the Assistant Japanese Military Attaché, Yamamoto, and high-ranking German officers in Königsbrück.[54] After much wrangling between the High Command and the Free India Centre over the wording,[55] the soldiers swore their oaths in groups of six, touching an officer's sword:

> I swear by God this holy oath, that I will obey the leader of the German state and people, Adolf Hitler, Commander of the German Armed Forces, in the fight for the freedom of India, in which fight the leader is Subhas Chandra Bose, and that as a brave soldier, I am willing to lay down my life for this oath.[56]

This was followed by field manoeuvres. On Bose's next visit, the battalion marched through the streets of Königsbrück drawing cheers from the local townspeople impressed by the unusual sight of colonial turbaned troops in German uniform.[57]

Reinvigorated by 'Quit India' and the Legion's expansion, Bose also sought to intensify activities in the Tribal Territory. On 16 September, he instructed Talwar to gather more intelligence on India while urging him to be generally more active.[58] The Germans, however, remained reluctant to undertake anything decisive in the Tribal Territory until Axis troops were closer to India.[59]

'On the Path of Danger', October 1942–February 1943

On 10 October the German embassy in Rome reported that another Italian aircraft was scheduled to take off in the near future. Bose decided to leave and take that flight, come what may. There was nothing Ribbentrop or the Foreign Office could do to stop him as the Naval High Command was still in the planning phases of arranging his transfer. Ribbentrop succeeded only in delaying the departure for a few days so that he could host a proper farewell ceremony at the Foreign Office, on 14 October. This was the last time Ribbentrop and Bose would meet.

With little choice other than to make the best of a bad situation, Ribbentrop expressed confidence in the Italian flight.[60] When it came to events in India, he expressed concern over reports that there were now 170,000 American troops in the country in addition to 1,000,000 Indian troops. He cited these figures as though he hoped that Bose would prove him wrong. The latter, while not entirely refuting these figures, was dismissive, claiming that most Indian soldiers were ready to defect.

Bose was more preoccupied with long-term Japanese aims—something he now brought up, realising this was his last chance to do so. Ribbentrop assured him that the 'conquest of India was not the intention of the Japanese'. He was instead optimistic that Axis operations in the Near East and the Indian Ocean would soon have a powerful impact and that 'the liberation of

India would follow without any problems'. The sensitive issue of Muslim separatism was also raised. Ribbentrop brought the issue up knowing it would have to be resolved sooner or later. Bose resorted to his standard line, namely that it was a problem caused by the 'English and their propaganda'. He dismissed the Muslim League as a 'backward looking clique' with 'plutocratic and special interests' and portrayed plans to partition India as nothing but a 'British manoeuvre' akin to the partition of Ireland. Wanting to put Ribbentrop's mind at ease, he assured him that Muslims would be guaranteed 'absolute and complete cultural freedom' as well as 'economic and social equality' in a liberated India.

More concerned with events on the Indo-Afghan border, Bose proposed the 'immediate deployment' by parachute of German agents in the North-West Frontier. Ribbentrop proved evasive, claiming that nothing could be accomplished until German troops first reached the Caucasus. The 'march to India could not be expected yet' as he put it.[61]

Bose also brought up the issue of German police training for Indians.[62] He had disloyal elements, religious fundamentalists and other state enemies in mind. Again, Ribbentrop was non-committal, agreeing only to 'examine this question'. In any case it was not for Ribbentrop but Himmler to 'examine' the question, which he did eagerly, ensuring that arrangements were eventually made so that between two to three hundred Indians would be trained by the Gestapo.[63]

Finally, it was agreed that Bose would maintain liaison through the German embassies in Tokyo and Bangkok. Ribbentrop hoped that Bose's presence in Southeast Asia might even bring about greater co-operation with Tokyo. The meeting was considered sufficiently important for Hitler to be sent the official minutes to go through.

That evening, Bose visited Königsbrück one last time. Since his previous visit a month earlier, hundreds more of POWs had enlisted.⁶⁴ There were even reports from North Africa of Indian troops defecting specifically to join the Legion⁶⁵ now designated *Infanterie Regiment (ind) IR 950*.⁶⁶

While Bose was pleased with these developments, he was less than delighted when informed a few days later by the Foreign Office that the flight to Asia might be postponed as the British were already aware of its imminent departure, the Germans suspecting an Italian leak.⁶⁷ The Italians had already infuriated the Japanese by making the experimental Rome to Tokyo flight public.

Nevertheless, on 6 November, Bose set off for Rome, hoping the flight would still take off. 'No news' should be 'good news' he wrote to Emilie Schenkl before leaving, hoping that he would not return.⁶⁸ There was no news for more than a week but it was not 'good news'. Italian and Japanese failure to reach an agreement, combined with technical difficulties, left Bose stranded in Rome. He had some cause for satisfaction though. A few days after his arrival, the Free India Battalion organised by the Italian army was disbanded. The soldiers had ripped off their insignia, defiantly thrown down their arms and demanded reinstatement as POWs upon being ordered to fight the British in North Africa, insisting they would only do so in India.⁶⁹

It was not the military failure that gave Bose satisfaction, but rather the political consequences. Shedai was now fully discredited and the Italians forced to dismiss him. The previous month his political credibility had already come into question as a result of the persistent campaign waged by Bose, the Germans and the Japanese. It proved fatal. In a letter to the Italian Foreign Ministry, full of loathing, recrimination and self-pity, Shedai lashed out at the man he held responsible for his downfall:

Bose [...] is an opportunist and for his selfish ends he will sacrifice even his country [...] Knowing Mr Bose through and through it was impossible for me to co-operate with him. [...] My propaganda in India was a blow to him. People [...] prefer to hear me [...] I was putting Gandhi

[...] Azad, Nehru [...] as the chief Indian leaders [...] The chief blow to him was that in Italy I was making a small Indian legion [...] the Germans, too, believe [...] I am the mischief maker [...] Bose [...] excited the Germans to do everything in their power to bundle me out. He is successful. [...] The blow which has been dealt to me is a cruel one. I am stopped to do any service to India and my adopted country—Italy. [...] After this blow Bose will try to eliminate me altogether. [...] He will soon arrive here to get hold of Radio Himalaya. [...] I am sure my Italian friends will not be a party to establish Bose as [...] Führer of India [...] the Muslims of India will never bow down before this cruel policy of Hindu domination.[70]

That was the last that was heard of Shedai until he resurfaced again in Pakistan.

Upon his return to Berlin, Bose wrote to Ribbentrop asking him to resume German naval preparations to transfer him to Asia, recognising that he could no longer depend on the Italians. Bose emphasised in elaborate detail the urgent necessity of his departure. While claiming that recent Axis reversals in North Africa (including an Anglo-American invasion of Vichy Algeria and a British counter-offensive in Libya) had not diminished Indian determination to resist the British, Bose nevertheless wrote of the need for a 'common struggle' against a 'common enemy' through a 'common strategy'. 'Viewed' from this 'standpoint' it was 'imperatively necessary' for him to reach Asia. 'I could do much more' he wrote 'if I could be somewhere near India'. He brushed aside persistent German concerns over his safety insisting that he would 'gladly' and 'voluntarily' take the necessary risk. 'I believe in my destiny' he concluded.[71]

Bose's letter ensured the Naval High Command immediately resumed its plans. Bose was to be transferred from a German submarine onto a Japanese one in the middle of the Indian Ocean. This time the Japanese navy was forced to allow Bose onboard. By now even the Japanese government was prepared to do the necessary.[72]

Shortly after submitting his letter, Bose made his last major political broadcast from Germany. He downplayed recent Axis defeats claiming that 'the war has reached a stage when time is working definitely for the Tripartite Powers' and 'against our common enemy'. While nothing further could have been from the truth he nevertheless reaffirmed his faith in an Axis victory, even ridiculing important Allied victories in Africa. As for a 'Second Front' or an Allied invasion of Europe, Bose dismissed this as 'childish dreams' destined to end in failure. Yet, at the same time, Bose was forced to acknowledge American might. He warned of an emerging 'American world-empire' which had already reduced Britain to a subservient status. In a mocking manner he denounced Churchill as Roosevelt's 'junior partner'. Picking up on his theme of a 'common world strategy', Bose argued that one side was fighting for the 'perpetuation of the old order with all the injustice on which it was based' while the other was fighting for the 'creation of a new one'. He left no doubt as to where he stood. Above all, Bose warned his countrymen not to expect help from 'the so-called United Nations in their struggle for liberty'. He sought to coin a new catchphrase: 'Between British Imperialism and Indian Nationalism no compromise is possible'. One of them had to perish.[73]

By now it was clear that Bose identified strongly with the Axis powers and was no longer apologetic about doing so. He was also increasingly preoccupied with American power. This contributed in part to his devoting the greater part of his broadcast to world events rather than to India. He had developed a firm conviction that its fate was intricately linked to the outcome of the war and he was therefore increasingly inclined to look at events from a larger perspective. Bose spoke as an active participant with a stake, not just in India's future, but also in the war.

Bose made his last public appearance in Berlin on 26 January 1943, at the Kaiserhof Hotel to celebrate Indian 'Independence Day'. It was a solemn affair with the entire 'Who's Who' of

SUBHAS CHANDRA BOSE IN NAZI GERMANY

Berlin present. Indian and Nazi flags draped the walls side by side. Axis diplomats, along with hundreds of representatives and officials of the Foreign Office, the High Command and the Nazi party were in attendance. The event was relayed live on German radio by a commentator who described the atmosphere in vivid detail:

We are at present at a big meeting in Berlin on the occasion of the Independence Day of India. Many hundreds of guests have assembled to hear an address by Subhas Chandra Bose. There are a great many Indians here, and representatives of many other nations of Europe [...] There are many Germans, Italians, Japanese and many high officials [...] officers of the Wehrmacht and members of the National Socialist Party. Among the guests are the Grand Mufti of Jerusalem and the Prime Minister of Iraq, Rashid Ali al-Gaylani—a very colourful and eminent gathering. The hall is decorated with beautiful flower arrangements—red tulips and white lilacs. Now, Subhas Chandra Bose—the great leader of independent India, gets up and walks towards the speaker's chair. He is dressed in a black sherwani. There is thunderous applause and cheering as he comes up. [...] Now here is Subhas Bose speaking to you.[74]

Bose's address was a long philosophical, cultural, historical and political condemnation of British rule in India, reiterating many points already made in his broadcasts. Inevitably, his words were received with thunderous applause. It was an appropriate end to Bose's two year stay in Germany and symbolised how far he had come since arriving in April 1941 as the marginalised renegade of Indian politics.

On 8 February, Bose left behind a letter for his brother, Sarat, realising that he might never return to India:

Today once again I am embarking on the path of danger. [...] I may not see the end of the road. If I meet with any such danger, I will not be able to send you any further news in this life. That is why today I am leaving my news here—it will reach you in due time. I have married here and I have a daughter. In my absence please show my wife and daughter the love that you have given me throughout your life.[75]

That evening Bose boarded *U-180* at the naval base in Kiel.[76] With some difficulty he was transferred onto a Japanese submarine in April 1943 in the Indian Ocean. It eventually reached Sabang, on We, a small island off the northern tip of Sumatra. Much to his surprise, Bose was received at the Japanese naval base by the former assistant military attaché in Berlin, Colonel Yamamoto, who had since been transferred, via the Soviet Union, to Southeast Asia. Bose, escorted by Yamamoto, flew to Tokyo where he was enthusiastically received by Tojo, ministers and high-ranking representatives of the army and the navy—in stark contrast to his initial reception in Berlin. Bose essentially had two aims: first, securing Japanese recognition for an Indian government he still planned to establish and second, military support for an offensive into India which he was convinced would accelerate the timetable for independence. He never once mentioned the declaration in Tokyo, confident that the establishment of a government made this obsolete.

In Southeast Asia, Bose donned a military uniform and was acclaimed with adulation by Indians in his new role as Supreme Commander of the Indian National Army. Mass rallies and meetings were organised throughout the region as Bose drummed up support and sought recruits in preparation for the offensive into India. In October 1943 he established a 'Provisional Government of Free India' in Singapore. Bose assumed the positions of Head of State, Prime Minster, Minister of War and Minister of Foreign Affairs, while the remaining portfolios were mostly assigned to high-ranking officers of the Indian National Army. The first act of the new cabinet was to declare war on Britain and the United States. The government was promptly recognised by Japan, Germany, Italy, Croatia, Thailand, Burma, Manchukuo, China (Nanking) and the Philippines. For increased legitimacy, the Japanese transferred the Indian Andaman Islands in the Bay of Bengal to the government in December 1943.

SUBHAS CHANDRA BOSE IN NAZI GERMANY

In March 1944, Japanese and Indian National Army troops finally launched a joint offensive into northeastern India from Burma. The tide of war, however, had already turned against the Axis and they were decimated before reaching Bengal.[77] In Berlin, Hitler ridiculed their efforts claiming that they had 'dispersed like a flock of sheep'.[78]

The Indian Legion, meanwhile, positioned on the Atlantic Wall along the southwest coast of France in anticipation of an American or British landing, was forced to retreat once Allied forces landed in Normandy. When the Third Reich collapsed, the Indian Legionaries were treated by the British as POWs and interned in camps along with the civilians of the Free India Centre before being repatriated to India and eventually released.

As for Bose, he remained defiant to the very end, refusing ever to envisage freedom as a 'gift' from Britain. He died during the closing days of the Second World War in an air crash, although few of his countrymen ever came to believe that so great and mythical had his reputation become by then.[79] His wife, Emilie, along with the baby he left behind, survived the war and were welcomed afterwards into the Bose family in India.

7

EPILOGUE

INDO-NAZI COLLABORATION

Post-War Legacy

Bose's departure for Berlin was the greatest political gamble of his career. From then on he would be perceived outside India as little more than an Axis collaborator, or, at best, a highly controversial figure. In India, where the sincerity of his patriotism was never questioned after the war—quite the contrary—he was quickly rehabilitated into Congress ranks. Gandhi publicly extolled the fallen 'Netaji'[1] (leader) while Nehru put on his barrister's robe for the first time in a quarter of a century and defended Bose's troops in court.[2] These trials—arguably little more than show trials at the time—galvanised the nation on behalf of Bose and the Indian National Army. Bose's Congress colleagues could be generous in their praise now that he was out of the way[3] while his death ensured that Nehru emerged as the uncontested leader of independent India.[4] The Gandhi-Nehru vision of what India should become was firmly set in stone, to the detriment of Bose's inevitably more radical agenda.[5] Nevertheless, Bose gradually found a central place of honour in Nehruvian India over the next few decades.

SUBHAS CHANDRA BOSE IN NAZI GERMANY

By the time of his hundredth birth anniversary in 1997, the government in New Delhi had issued stamps and coins bearing Bose's name and image while his portrait and statue decorated the Indian parliament. He was more popular, it seemed, dead than alive. This was partly a side effect of disillusionment with the Nehru-Gandhi legacy and the revolt against the non-aligned, socialist and secular vision they had imposed on what was now a more centrist, capitalist yet assertive and fundamentalist India. The time had come to search for new heroes.

Bose's involvement with Nazi Germany was for the most part ignored[6] by Indian historians and emphasis placed instead on the campaign he waged as head of an Indian government-in-exile to liberate India in concert with his Japanese allies. After all Japan, for all the atrocities and horrors it perpetrated in China and Southeast Asia, was not quite Nazi Germany. When Bose's activities in Germany were alluded to obliquely, it was usually done with astounding levels of historical revisionism and distortion, even to the extent of portraying him as an 'anti-fascist resistance leader'.[7] Nothing further could have been from the truth.[8]

While Bose was not a Nazi (although he did advocate a synthesis of Nazism and Communism as the political solution to India's problems as late as 1944 in a major ideological speech at Tokyo University)[9] neither was he an 'anti-fascist leader' nor in any way a political dupe of the Nazis. Bose knew what he was doing and had few regrets. While the Congress embraced Bose in the post-war years (largely in response to popular sentiments) it never was (and is still not) quite at ease with this enigmatic figure. He was and would remain the most controversial president of the Indian National Congress. Nevertheless the relationship was always an ambivalent one. When Nehru's daughter, Indira Gandhi, became prime minister, she recruited at least one former *Waffen-SS* veteran as her bodyguard.[10] It was not without irony that such a staunch anti-fascist leftist should do so.[11] This in no way implied sympathy for the Nazis, rather that Indians shared a common anti-British nationalist legacy. Past differences were conveniently forgotten.

While politicians may be selective about the past, history is not. One service the Nazis did to history was leaving behind hundreds of documents meticulously recording what were more often than not their repulsive activities. This made reconstructing Bose's activities in Nazi Germany not only feasible, but historically necessary. The documents speak for themselves to the extent that sources can. While there may be no spectacular 'revelations' or 'discoveries', they do allow for a better understanding of Bose and his political outlook during the Second World War. They also offer a fascinating and alternative perspective of Nazi racial attitudes and political policies when applied to India. From the historical record it is possible to draw a number of conclusions that transcend conventional wartime, and even contemporary, perceptions of Bose.

Misconceptions and Political Divergences

Not without good reason, much emphasis has been laid on the central role of ideology in the functioning of the Nazi state,[12] but one of the more surprising aspects of Bose's involvement with Nazi Germany was that policy for the most part evolved in response to the initiative provided by Bose, not vice versa. If there is a case for dismissing the facile Allied wartime and in some cases post-war portrayals[13] of Bose as a Nazi Quisling this is one. Bose did not do the bidding of the Nazis. He certainly served their interests—at times—but it was a complimentary relationship. It never seemed to have occurred to the Germans to treat Bose as a puppet issuing him with *diktats*. Considering the nature of the Nazi state, Bose acted with remarkable independence, at times even contempt for Nazi policy. This was a state, after all, that violently eradicated all forms of dissent, whether internal or external, and often turned on its allies after generally exploiting them cynically and reducing them to a status little better than servility.

It was Bose who consistently provided the Germans with advice on how to formulate policy in the form of 'proposals', many of which were implemented, the notable exception being the famous declaration on India, which acquired additional importance as Bose turned it into a personal obsession. Nevertheless, this did not imply the two sides were always in agreement or had a common perspective—rather that Bose provided the initiative and German policy followed accordingly.

It became apparent that there were significant differences between the two sides the moment Bose arrived in Berlin. He brought with him a number of misconceptions, among which was an erroneous belief that Germany was out to defeat Britain. It was not. During the initial stages, the Nazis hoped that the British would sue for peace although it eventually became evident that 'England' was as much of a foe as the Soviet Union and United States were to become. There was no escaping this and Bose was always there to remind the Germans of the fact. He himself quickly developed doubts as to the extent of German sincerity in fighting Britain, as he made repeatedly clear—in a rather frantic manner—to Ribbentrop during their first meeting in April 1941.[14] The latter of course resorted to his 'the Führer is determined to defeat England' argument and if he sounded convincing it was only because Ribbentrop was genuinely sincere. He was then after all trying to deter Hitler from attacking Russia, preferring to see the emergence of a German-Italian-Japanese-Soviet 'Continental Four-Power Bloc' or 'Quadruple Alliance' which would smash the British Empire.[15] Ribbentrop's foreign policy aims and the manner in which they contrasted with those of Hitler typically reflected the chaotic, cross-purpose functioning of the Nazi regime.

Another matter which did not concur with German realities was Bose's facile, if not naive, assumption that the Germans would oblige him in setting-up an Indian provisional government in Berlin. Why should they have done so? Working with Indian nationalists against the British was one thing but setting up an entire government, on the flimsiest of pretexts, another. After all, Bose never revealed with whom he intended to constitute such a government. The truth was that he had no one but himself. At least in Southeast Asia he had a credible entourage and his government was essentially a military one, constituted of high-ranking officers of the Indian National Army, so the problem never presented itself. This was not the case in Berlin. His proposed government would have been a sham and an object of speedy and justified attack, if not ridicule. In denying Bose the possibility, the Germans inadvertently helped his cause and spared him much political embarrassment. Nevertheless, it was surprising that a man of Bose's political experience should have made such a proposal in the first place and expected the Germans to respond to it positively.

Bose also naively assumed that his rejection of Gandhi and Nehru would reinforce German prejudices against them. On the contrary, they realised only too well that should German troops ever penetrate the sub-continent they could ill afford to antagonise these two men—at least until Bose proved to be a viable alternative, which was not the case in 1941. As for the Japanese, they did not give up on Gandhi and Nehru until the middle of 1942, despite repeated agitation by Indian nationalist organisations in Southeast Asia.[16]

Another factor which Bose overlooked was the divergence of views between Hitler and the German Foreign Office. In two significant areas, Hitler departed from the stance of the latter. First, he was prepared initially to set up an Indian government, in opposition to the cautious bureaucrats of the Foreign Office, few of whom knew at the time of his plan to invade Soviet Russia (April–May 1941). Hitler realised that setting up an Indian government in Berlin might serve as a last attempt to persuade the British to sue for peace before he turned his attention to the east. After his expected victory, under the delusion that all he had to do was 'kick in the door' and the 'whole rotten structure' would 'come crashing down',[17] Hitler would not be so benevolent with England. At some level he recognised the risk of turning east when his rear remained threatened. An Indian government could have acted as the necessary pinprick to bring about a change in British policy—in the Führer's mind at least. At the same time it is difficult to evaluate how serious Hitler was about this. He mentioned the possibility of setting up a government only once, and this too in private to his trusted confidant Goebbels.[18] Hitler brought the issue up while discussing Iraq, realising that a successful anti-British rising there would change the entire political dynamic of the Middle East and ultimately affect India too. He had reason to be optimistic as he prepared to intervene militarily in Iraq, recognising that the reinforcement of a pro-German regime would seriously challenge British interests in the region. This too when he had difficulty in thinking beyond continental strategy.[19] A significant change of political orientation and loyalties in the Middle East was a necessary prerequisite to playing the Indian card. Hitler eventually dropped the matter, however, allowing the Foreign Office to sabotage Bose's proposal.

It was less successful, though when it found itself in opposition again to Hitler this time over Bose's proposal for a declaration on India. Hitler reacted positively by approving the declaration on 10 May, although this should be seen as connected with his initial willingness to establish an Indian government.[20] Yet, what is peculiar is that while he approved the declaration—at a time when the Foreign Office ridiculed the notion—he soon changed his mind (proving to be very obstinate) even when the Foreign Office reverted from its own position and began promoting the declaration. Bose found himself increasingly frustrated, stuck between the two. Inevitably, in the

EPILOGUE: INDO-NAZI COLLABORATION

end, Hitler had the last word. He matched Bose's obsession with his own obstinacy despite mounting opposition not only from Ribbentrop and the Foreign Office, but the Italians and Japanese as well. Tokyo's opinion Hitler was inclined at least to take more seriously than Rome's.

Military Intervention and Soviet Sabotage

There was one area where Indian and German (or Hitlerian) aims perfectly converged: a military operation in India. This was the most controversial aspect of Bose's agenda in Berlin. Even if one ignores the predominantly pacifist inclinations of Gandhi and the Congress, Bose's proposal presented serious ethical and political dilemmas. Here was a nationalist asking an aggressive, expansionist and brutal regime to invade his homeland in order to expel one set of foreign troops with another. Undeniably there was something politically perverse about assigning Nazi troops the role of liberators. Yet Bose realised that such extreme measures were a fundamental form of *realpolitik*, particularly in the midst of a conflagration in which nothing less than the destiny of the world was at stake. In his mind, the end justified the means.

If Indians welcomed German troops they would do so only in the belief that they were liberators. What Bose hoped for was not a German invasion of India as much as a military spark which would incite Indian troops to revolt. The entire edifice of British rule in India rested on the loyalty of the Indian army. Bose hoped Indian soldiers would do the actual work of liberating the country (even if this was wishful thinking) while the Germans would provide, at most, military support. German intervention was to be confined primarily to the northwest. Penetrating the frontier was one thing; occupying the entire subcontinent, another. Bose's plan for German military intervention in India was therefore not quite the dangerous gamble it initially appeared to be. Rather it was a desperate attempt to bring about a quick end to British rule. Gandhi, Nehru and their cohorts might voice their opposition but once India was liberated they would be silenced.

That Hitler was also prone to such flights of fantasy—seeing his initially spectacular victories as the beginning of a brave new world in which German troops would simply march into India—made a convergence of views possible. It is a fitting coincidence that Hitler issued his order for an invasion at the same time that Bose escaped to Berlin with a similar idea in his head. Both men were guilty of excessive over-confidence.[21] Naturally it is easy to state this in retrospect when subsequent events proved them wrong, but there is no denying a general lack of realism and failure to appreciate the enemy's resources. Hitler, after all, was about to get mired in and then defeated by Soviet Russia. His fantasies of marching into India were a gross overestimation of his abilities.[22] As for Bose, he at least had the excuse of not being a military expert, but if anything this should have made him more cautious and less reluctant to fantasise about the course of events.

Nevertheless, the convergence of these aims—as unrealistic as they were—allowed for some kind of joint Indo-German policy to emerge. Politics and propaganda, which in themselves could have provided sufficient basis for Indo-German collaboration, proved subservient to the greater military aim. This is why intelligence planning quickly occupied such a central place in Indo-German policymaking. Bose had brought this up at the very beginning in his 'Plan for Co-operation between the Axis Powers and India', unaware that the Germans were already planning a major operation along India's frontier.

As such there was hardly any disagreement over intelligence matters. What there was in abundance was a shared sense of dejection over the lack of achievements in the Tribal Territory and the North-West Frontier Province. This was Bose's fault. His presence in Berlin strengthened the intelligence card the

EPILOGUE: INDO-NAZI COLLABORATION

Soviet Union had to play against Germany. Ignorant that Bhagat Ram Talwar was a communist, Bose never suspected that he was a Soviet agent as well. Not only did he expose Bose's plans to the Soviets, who took particular delight in sabotaging them, but he also gathered as much intelligence as he could from the German and Italian legations in Kabul regarding Axis plans, information which ended up in both Moscow and London.[23] It is difficult to estimate to what extent Bose's agent damaged German interests but what is undeniable is that his activities were not without impact. Moscow fed misleading intelligence, via Talwar, to German intelligence agencies in Berlin. In return, it obtained valuable intelligence from these same agencies. The initial concerns over Bose's leftist inclinations, indirectly expressed by Woermann in an April 1941 memorandum,[24] were not without justification and proved damaging in the end.

The question inevitably arises as to what might have been accomplished had Talwar not been a Soviet agent. No doubt considerably more, but certainly not enough to turn the tide of events along the Indo-Afghan frontier. What 'Quit India' failed to accomplish, Axis fifth column activity could hardly substitute.[25] A lasting impact could only be achieved through military means—something the Japanese were overall more apt to appreciate than the Germans were with their 'Lawrence of Arabia' fantasies, which actually included a solitary *Abwehr* agent riding on horseback across the Afghan desert.[26] On this point Hitler proved more realistic, realising that propaganda and intelligence activities had their limitations and what mattered ultimately was military action, as he told Mussolini and Ciano in April 1942—and Bose the following month—while postponing the declaration on India.[27]

Nazi Realpolitik

The pursuit of a German declaration on Indian independence was by far the most persistent aim Bose pursued in Berlin and—

ironically—the one he completely failed to achieve. The Nazi foreign policy specialist, Gerhard L. Weinberg, has written contemptuously of Bose's efforts: 'It is difficult to believe, but there were still those who thought Hitler's word when given in public and in written form might prove useful outside the toilet'.[28] What is particularly significant is that the issue did not occur to Bose before he left for Berlin. Why did it suddenly assume such importance? If he omitted it from his 'Plan for Co-operation between the Axis Powers and India', there was good reason for his doing so. His request for an Indian government and an Indo-Axis treaty guaranteeing Indian independence made a declaration unnecessary. It was only when the Foreign Office rejected an Indian government that Bose began clamouring for a declaration. As long as Germany refrained from making a commitment or expressing support for Indian independence, Bose's presence in Berlin remained awkward. Why should he be seen to collaborate with a regime that could not express solidarity with India? This only served to bolster the arguments of his critics that he was a Nazi Quisling. While Bose cared little for what the British had to say, he knew that such accusations carried more weight in India. When it came to Gandhi, Nehru and the Congress there was no sympathy for Nazi Germany. If Germany at least publicly displayed an inclination to recognise Indian aspirations, Bose's presence in Berlin would be more legitimised, his actions justified—at least somewhat—and Indian public opinion mollified.

What Bose failed to realise was that a declaration was not a simple matter. A propaganda gesture of this sort had important implications. First, apart from providing short-lived political capital, there was the question of credibility. Any German and—particularly Italian—guarantee to liberate the entire sub-continent would be open to ridicule. This was something Hitler genuinely feared. When Germany was in no position to defeat the Soviet Union, let alone reach Afghanistan, a guarantee on Indian independence would have been an exercise in political

EPILOGUE: INDO-NAZI COLLABORATION

futility. Military realities had to determine political actions. Hitler was correct in stating that a declaration only had validity if backed by military force. This reflected a sense of realism he could on occasion indulge in, particularly when it suited his purposes, in this case to postpone the declaration.

Even Bose eventually came round to appreciating—albeit reluctantly—this point of view.[29] If the aim was to score a few propaganda points then a declaration would have been useful, but in the long run it was detrimental to German interests. Naturally, Bose initially looked at the question from an Indian perspective only. Nevertheless, he should have taken German interests into consideration earlier and been more realistic. While a declaration would have provided him with relief and political capital, it was unrealistic on his part to expect Germany to issue one in view of its strategic situation. It had after all failed to occupy England in 1940. Invading India and guaranteeing its independence only existed within the realm of military speculation. Even a militarily presumptuous and incompetent regime like Fascist Italy realised that it was in no position for the most part to issue declarations regarding distant countries like India.

Had conditions changed in the Middle East as a result of events in Iraq, German penetration in the region would have been all too real; and had the *Afrika Korps* succeeded in breaking through the Suez Canal and linking up with German troops from the Near East or Caucasus, a genuine and lasting impact on India might have been realised. Ribbentrop himself assured Bose that the declaration would be issued the moment German troops advanced beyond the Caucasus.[30] It is interesting to note that Hitler, Ribbentrop and the Foreign Office concurred for once in regard to postponing the declaration at the end of May 1941, as Iraqi resistance petered out. A few days later, the British overthrew the Iraqi government and marched into Syria. The political dynamics of the entire region were suddenly transformed, making a declaration on India absurd at this point. Of course, Bose was not concerned with German strategic considerations, rather the political benefits he would accrue from the declaration. But as a politician, Bose should have been able to assess both sides of the equation and arrive at a more realistic conclusion.

The declaration assumed obsessive proportions in Bose's mind following the German invasion of Russia which proved a devastating blow for him. Having naively overestimated the German desire to defeat England, Bose overlooked the fact that the Soviet Union was the real focus of Germany's determination to wage a fanatical war of annihilation. The invasion placed him in an awkward position and made the declaration all the more relevant. The Foreign Office was still prepared to consider the matter, particularly with German troops advancing closer to India, but when it became clear that victory was not in sight that summer and that the war might drag on for a long time, it was permanently shelved.

The only time Bose lost his temper over the matter was when Woermann casually urged him to be patient during their meeting in July 1941. It then dawned on Bose that he was not about to get the declaration and that the Germans attached little importance to it. Bose's letter to Ribbentrop a few weeks later was an effort in self-restraint and politeness. But, yet again, it failed to accomplish anything. Neither did it help that Ribbentrop was not on speaking terms with Hitler at this point and had resolved never to contradict him again following a very unpleasant scene between the two men in which an enraged and exasperated Hitler accused his subordinate of 'killing' him with his 'contradictions' before slumping into a chair and nearly having a seizure.[31] There remained much tension between the two men over the invasion of Russia, which Ribbentrop opposed. Under these circumstances, Bose's letter was ignored. When the matter was presented to Hitler in the autumn, he postponed it again—not unjustifia-

EPILOGUE: INDO-NAZI COLLABORATION

bly—from fear that the British (and Soviets) might invade Afghanistan as a follow-up to the successful invasion of Iran.

Bose's hopes were resurrected by Japan's entry into the war as it initially at least appeared to be in a military position to enforce the declaration. As Hitler stressed to Mussolini and Ciano in April 1942, while there was no military justification for German and Italian involvement the Japanese could issue a declaration on their own. This at least gave Bose a new direction in which to vent his frustrations as it became increasingly apparent that the Japanese were hardly any more forthcoming either. Although they briefly showed interest in the declaration, shortly after the Cripps Mission, they quickly dropped the matter, putting into question the extent of their sincerity in the first place.

It is significant that when Bose arrived in Tokyo and was granted access to civilian ministers as well as army and navy commanders, he never once brought up the declaration. Having obtained support for a provisional government, he saw no purpose in doing so. He had also gained enough political experience by now to realise there was no point in begging for something he would not get. Instead he became increasingly statesmanlike in Southeast Asia, not hesitating to lodge strong protests—always through the correct diplomatic channels—when dissatisfied with Japanese policy but willing to then drop the matter if nothing could be achieved. There was nothing to be gained by making a fuss, sulking, blowing up at officials or over-emphasising a point already made. In Germany, Bose had been guided by a sense of insecurity and hypersensitivity as though he wanted the Nazi regime to reassure him that it was not the cynical, racist and opportunistic regime he suspected it to be.

Bose eventually found a new substitute to replace his obsession with the declaration, one that was more justified. His desire to leave for Asia became apparent as soon as Japan entered the war. Even the Germans appreciated this reasoning, recognising that their own interests would be better served as well by having him in Southeast Asia. This was an example of Nazi *realpolitik* at work, as was its opposition to an Indian government and to a declaration. The Germans went out of their way, after all, to make the necessary arrangements. Bose's transfer from a German to Japanese submarine in the Indian Ocean was an important logistical and technical feat of the Second World War. This too at a time when Germany had insufficient submarines to fight the war at sea it was already losing. When Bose made his disillusionment with the Italians clear and asked the German government to arrange his transfer, the response was immediate. The mistake the Germans made was relying excessively on their allies. If there were endless delays, these were primarily the making of the Italians and Japanese. Had the Japanese navy not been so rigid and allowed Bose to board submarine *I-30*, he would have reached Tokyo six months earlier. Bose's greatest accomplishments during the Second World War were attained in Southeast Asia and possible, in part, because of Nazi *realpolitik*.

Political Realities and Renewal

Bose arrived in Berlin in 1941 a bruised and marginalised politician but left in 1943 with a burnished political reputation. His broadcasts and the worldwide attention they derived helped achieve this, as did his fervent obsession with securing independence. For a relatively unknown exile, Bose rapidly earned the trust and the respect of the Nazi leadership. Hitler thought highly of him, as is attested to by a private conversation he had with his entourage in early 1942, in which he described Bose as having 'eclipsed' Nehru.[32] Ribbentrop always behaved in an uncharacteristically cordial manner with Bose, never revealing the more arrogant and abusive side to his personality as was usually his wont with foreign statesmen and diplomats.[33] Goebbels, a fanatical Nazi, eulogised Bose, while finally, the most dangerous of them all Himmler, acted as though trying to woo

EPILOGUE: INDO-NAZI COLLABORATION

him. By the time Bose left, he had more or less obtained what he wanted: a submarine to go off to Asia, limitations as to how and where the Legion could be used[34] (the only one in fact not directed at the Soviet Union), *Luftwaffe* training[35] at a time when Germany suffered a serious dearth in aircraft, acceptance of left-wing Indians in high-ranking positions and even racial exemptions to marry German women.[36] Bose himself was the prime example, living and conceiving a child openly as he did with Emilie Schenkl, in complete defiance of Nazi racial laws. No Gestapo official ever discreetly advised her to abandon her liaison. Instead the Gestapo was busy training hundreds of Indians in Nazi police techniques![37]

Indians were treated with consideration by Nazi standards and increasingly as genuine allies in spite of their non-European ethnicity at a time when the regime was mercilessly killing millions of European Jews on ethnic grounds. A peculiar form of race politics formed the core of Nazi ideology. The case of Free India, moreover, contradicts some general perceptions of Nazi racial attitudes and policies.

That the Germans adopted so 'benevolent' an attitude with Indians is to be attributed more to their political, rather than ethnic, value and to the fact that their interests converged rather than collided. As long as their relationship was based on mutual hostility to Britain, there was little cause for friction. Had German troops penetrated India, Nazi racism would have become all too evident. It was easy enough to handle a few quasi-Marxist Indian intellectuals at the Free India Centre in Berlin. The Germans looked the other way and the Indians did the same when it came to the more unsavoury aspects of the regime. As for the Legionaries, they were encouraged to vent their frustrations on the French while manning defences on the Atlantic Wall, to the extent even at one point—during the retreat of German forces in the summer of 1944—of raping and pillaging, in some cases more or less at will.[38] Racial tension, if it existed in the Legion, was not between Germans and Indians, but rather, between Indians and the French. The Indian Legion quickly acquired a notorious reputation and became one of the most despised 'German' formations in occupied France. Dozens of captured Legionaries were executed by the resistance. A racist resentment against subject colonial, turbaned troops in German uniform exercising control over a 'civilised' population, played a crucial role in this.

Shedai was the prime example of an Indian who pushed the boundaries of Nazi leniency. While he openly mocked Nazi policy, junior officials practically grovelled in their efforts to win him over. If the Germans eventually turned on Shedai, it was not because of his anti-German sentiments but only because Bose convinced them that his actions were counter-productive. This was also a convenient means of embarrassing the Italians. Nevertheless, in the first place, it is surprising that a political charlatan such as Shedai should have been treated with such consideration during—and even after—his August 1941 visit to Berlin.

One particularly important explanation for German indulgence towards Free India was that supporting Indian independence was one of the more 'noble' cards Germany had to play to bolster its own moral justifications for waging war. For once this aggressive and expansionist regime was taking up a popular cause. It certainly put the Americans, Chinese and Soviets in a peculiar position. Why were they restrained when Germany was assertive in promoting Indian freedom? It was not only Bose who raised this point but also Gandhi, Nehru, Azad and the Congress, being genuinely perplexed by the Allied coalition's reluctance to ensure the introduction of democratic principles in India. Was this war not being fought for freedom and democracy? If so, why was it denied to India? It was a valid question and one that the Germans were only too happy to answer. Of course, this was purely opportunistic but propaganda did matter

EPILOGUE: INDO-NAZI COLLABORATION

and the increasingly hostile and angry mood of the Indian public was a factor that could have affected the course of the war. Germany, whether it liked it or not, had little choice but to support Indian independence. It certainly was a peculiar paradox.

Bose had come a long way since his unsuccessful visits to Germany in the 1930s. At the time he was a hyper-sensitive nationalist and the slightest remark critical of Gandhi, the Congress or India, would prompt him to write letters of protest to German officials or denounce Nazi racism at press conferences. A decade on and Bose was keen to vent his criticisms of Gandhi before the Nazi leadership. It therefore came as a surprise to him, when first meeting Ribbentrop in April 1941, to hear the latter speak rather positively of Gandhi and his tactics. In fact, it was only Bose who was critical.[39] His attempts to disseminate such views within the Foreign Office were a total failure.

Bose found a more sympathetic audience when he met Goebbels more than a year later and launched into one of his now standard diatribes against Gandhi. Nevertheless, some decorum was maintained. Goebbels did not actually cross the line and tell Bose that he considered Gandhi to be a 'fool'.[40] It was one thing for Bose to be critical of his compatriots, another for the Germans. Yet, the fact that Bose could now comfortably criticise his compatriots with the Nazis shows a dramatic shift from his position in the 1930s.

The Germans found it easier to look on more favourably towards Gandhi and the Congress now that they were at war with the British. Even Hitler spoke of Gandhi and Nehru in a restrained and polite manner, which was unusual for a man who loved pouring scorn on others and laughing at them, but nevertheless making it clear to Bose in May 1942 that he did not expect much from their tactics. Yet there was a certain level of respect, when compared to the 1930s, for Gandhi which reflected a recognition that India was a factor of growing importance in the war. With British aircraft pounding German cities nightly, it was not surprising that the Germans now found it easier to sympathise with India: political opportunism was wrapped up in a mutual, if not imaginary, sense of victimisation by the British. Indian independence also served as a partially useful alibi for a guilty Nazi conscience.[41]

In the end, Bose obtained more from Germany than it did from him. The propaganda effects of supporting Indian freedom—if it deceived anyone—were minimal. It did nothing to change the essentially negative manner in which the world perceived Nazi Germany. Those who had made the mistake of initially looking to the Germans as liberators (Ukrainians, Byelorussians, Russians) were quickly stripped of their delusions. Bose would have undoubtedly served a greater purpose had Germany been successful in the Middle East or Russia but the reality was that for all its ideological pronouncements on 'inferiority' and 'superiority', the Nazi regime was itself too militarily inferior to achieve even this.

That Germany once supported Indian freedom is forgotten in India today. If it is recalled, it is usually done with indifference, if not embarrassment. One or two minor German bureaucrats made a literary post-war career in India rambling away about Bose but besides that, Germany got little in return for its efforts.[42] A few thousand Indian Legionaries could not alter the course of the war, neither could Bose's propaganda.

For Bose, however, it was a different matter. Having arrived in Berlin a bruised politician, his broadcasts brought him—and India—renewed world notice. The attention devoted to him in the American, British, Indian and even Canadian press—not to mention German, Italian and Japanese—was impressive even if half of it was vitriol. This publicity not only reaffirmed Bose's political credibility *vis-à-vis* the Germans but also had an impact where it mattered most—in India. Azad, the Congress president, was appalled by the impact his broadcasts had on Gandhi and believed that they contributed to Gandhi's impossible attitude

EPILOGUE: INDO-NAZI COLLABORATION

during the Cripps Mission.[43] It has also been suggested that his broadcasts motivated the Mahatma to launch his campaign for the expulsion of Allied troops from India just as the Japanese were threatening to invade.

In sum, Bose's broadcasts were a success. The failure was in his refusal to broadcast earlier. Had he done so a year beforehand, their impact would have been even greater. Bose also had an unfortunate tendency to repeat himself. Certainly, there were limits as to the number of ways he could denounce British rule and praise the Tripartite powers but his broadcasts nevertheless suffered from excessive monotony.

Still, the radio speeches allowed Bose to re-establish his political credentials as the defiant figure of Indian nationalism, thereby generating interest in Tokyo and more importantly among the millions of Indians in Southeast Asia. His radicalism allowed them to break free from the compulsions of non-violent politics and justify their status as allies of Japan. By the time Bose reached Southeast Asia in 1943, he had acquired a reputation of near mythical proportions and Indian mass adulation was the reaction to his arrival. He was certainly one of the most popular national leaders of his time. This reaction was achieved not through totalitarian means but was entirely genuine, strangely so, because Bose mobilised all Indians on behalf of independence and insisted they spill their blood for freedom. 'Men, money and material' became his rallying call in Southeast Asia. Even women were recruited as soldiers, much to the bewilderment of the Japanese. Such measures only increased Bose's popularity though. Soon, even British intelligence reports assessing Axis collaboration with Indian nationalists referred to Bose in a more respectful, if not a slightly admiring, manner than had been the case when he had been in Germany. By then, the simplistic notion of Bose being a 'Nazi Quisling' was already outdated.

Bose's presence in Berlin, as embarrassing as it was in retrospect, allowed him to establish his credentials *vis-à-vis* the Axis and acquire sufficient credibility to establish his Free Indian government upon reaching Southeast Asia. This was certainly not the case in 1941, and it is very doubtful that the Japanese would have acceded to such a request at the time. By 1943, everything had changed: Bose had succeeded in establishing himself in Berlin, Rome and Tokyo. He had been received by Hitler and Mussolini and so it was inevitable that he should be received by Tojo and the Emperor, Hirohito, as well. If anything, the Japanese leadership proved even more accommodating than the Germans or the Italians had been. If Bose gradually obtained respect in Berlin, in Tokyo he earned fervent admiration and was seen very much as an 'Indian samurai'.[44] He had come a long way since arriving in Berlin in April 1941.

While Bose's actions during the Second World War ensured his entry into the pantheon of Indian nationalist heroes, not so much because of his presence in Berlin as for his attempt to liberate India from Southeast Asia, it also proved to be his undoing. Had Bose chosen a more moderate path akin to that of his less temperamental colleagues such as Azad and Nehru and remained in India he would have played an important role, even a possibly decisive one, in the post-war period, opposing not only Partition, but the emergence of the Gandhi-Nehru regime. Bose derived great attention and accomplished much in a few short years in Nazi Germany but all this would have been put to better use in the post-war period. His fundamental mistake was being on the wrong side of history.

Bose's going to Germany was a gamble. He overestimated German abilities, as Hitler did, always falling victim to wishful thinking. It came as a terrible surprise to him also to see his seemingly once invincible Japanese allies invade India in 1944, only to lie prostrate the following year, following an Allied counter-offensive. Inevitably, his fortunes were linked with those of the Axis and their defeat became his defeat.

EPILOGUE: INDO-NAZI COLLABORATION

Bose and the 'Jewish Question'

The most troubling aspect of Bose's presence in Nazi Germany is not military or political but rather ethical. His alliance with the most genocidal regime in history poses serious dilemmas precisely because of his popularity and his having made a lifelong career of fighting the 'good cause'. How did a man who started his political career at the feet of Gandhi end up with Hitler, Mussolini and Tojo? Even in the case of Tojo and Mussolini, the gravity of the dilemma pales in comparison to that posed by his association with Hitler and the Nazi leadership. The most disturbing issue, all too often ignored, is that in the many articles, minutes, memorandums, telegrams, letters, plans and broadcasts Bose left behind in Germany, he did not express the slightest concern or sympathy for the millions who died in the concentration camps. Not one of his Berlin wartime associates or colleagues ever quotes him expressing any indignation. Not even when the horrors of Auschwitz and its satellite camps were exposed to the world upon being liberated by Soviet troops in early 1945, revealing publicly for the first time the genocidal nature of the Nazi regime, did Bose react.[45] Not that this should have come as a surprise to Bose as before the war he had already prophetically written to a friend: 'I have a feeling that both at present and in the near future the condition of the Jews of Central Europe will not be good at all'.[46] Yet in the end Bose only expressed—not necessarily unjustified—gratitude and sympathy to a fallen Germany. When it came to the legacy of the Nazi regime, the most he would offer in the way of criticism and reproach was that it should have never made the mistake of fighting a two-front war.[47]

One can argue that Bose was an Indian nationalist, not a Jewish one, and that the fate of European Jewry was not his concern, but such an argument has its limits. History will not ultimately absolve Bose so easily for his alliance with Nazi Germany. The question that inevitably arises is what was his attitude to the greatest act of large scale industrial mass murder in history, one that was committed in his presence? That Bose chose to be silent is a testimony in itself. Would it have made any difference had he spoken out, if not to the Jews, then at least to his historical legacy? His biographer even implies that Bose wrote a partially anti-Semitic article for Goebbels' newspaper *Der Angriff*.[48] Interestingly, the article in question has never been found but it certainly did elicit a hostile reaction from *The Jewish Chronicle* which denounced Bose as 'India's Anti-Jewish Quisling'.[49] There seemed to be a precedent for this insensitivity towards the 'Jewish question'. Already, before the war, Bose had not particularly welcomed attempts to grant Jewish refugees asylum in India.[50] Typically, he got into an argument over this with Nehru who was more open to this at least.[51]

In some ways, though, this was inevitable. Bose was a radical nationalist and such a perspective inevitably narrows one's view and concerns. He was bothered with little more than India throughout his life. Had he been exposed to German atrocities, there is no doubt that he would have reacted with revulsion and that all of his former reservations regarding Nazi ideology and racism would have come to the fore. Bose was not exposed, however, to the darker side of the Nazi regime. He lived a protected existence in the luxury of his villa. Of course, nationalism is not, and never will be, an excuse for political apathy and blindness. But in 1945, having placed all his cards on the Axis, Bose would have made a fool of himself by suddenly condemning Germany. It would have put into question his reasons for having gone there in the first place. Bose was a nationalist politician, not a Gandhian idealist. He had chosen to back the Axis and he was merely carrying out that policy to the bitter end.

It was easier for Bose to focus on the thousands of Indians who had sacrificed their lives fighting for freedom, American and British aircraft mercilessly pounding him and his allies day and night causing the deaths of hundreds of thousands of innocent civilians—not to mention millions alone in Bengal as a result of a famine aggravated by Churchill's decision to prioritise military supplies instead of grain.[52] It was easier to focus on these horrors than on the fate of unknown peoples in Europe. Yet, Bose would have emerged from this phase of history a far 'better man' and certainly a less controversial and morally enigmatic figure, had he done so, even if only in private. Racism was fundamentally contrary to everything he stood for and this is what makes not only his presence but his silence in Germany—and afterwards—so problematic. It was perhaps an inevitable consequence of Bose's decision to ally himself with Germany. It is, of course, not for historians to pass moral judgements. Time will do so but it is undeniable that Bose's years in Nazi Germany do not make for the most inspiring chapter of his life. Nevertheless, it was a crucial period which cannot be ignored.

APPENDICES

APPENDICES

1

PLAN FOR CO-OPERATION BETWEEN THE AXIS POWERS AND INDIA

9 APRIL 1941

As in the World War, England in the present war again attempted to exploit India for her war aims. Since the beginning of the war England has not relaxed either her political or her economic pressures on India, despite the numerous defeats inflicted on her by Germany. To us in India it is therefore quite plain that England, even though she is gradually collapsing, will increasingly tighten her stranglehold upon India, up to the very last. It is just as evident from England's present policy in India that if she should survive the war, England will try to restore her power by the exploitation of India's rich resources, in order to resume the fight against the new order a few years later.

India is naturally interested in seeing England totally defeated in this war and the British Empire completely broken up so that India would recover her freedom as a nation. The British Empire is the greatest obstacle, not merely to India's advance towards her freedom as a nation but also in the path of human progress.

As the Indian people's attitude towards Britain is very hostile in the present war, it is able to render material assistance to bring about Great Britain's downfall.

SUBHAS CHANDRA BOSE IN NAZI GERMANY

To achieve full cooperation between the Axis Powers and India for the achievement of the common aim, the destruction of Great Britain, I am proposing the following plan. It will involve work in Europe, in Afghanistan, in the tribal area (independent zone) situated between Afghanistan and India, and last but not least, in India itself.

I. Work in Europe

1) A free India government should be established in Europe, if possible in Berlin.
2) A treaty between the Axis Powers and the free India government should be drawn up which, among other things, would provide for India's liberation in the event of an Axis victory. Special privileges for the Axis Powers in India when a free government takes over, etc., etc.
3) Establishment of Legations of the free India government with, as far as possible, all the friendly countries in Europe. (nota bene: The steps mentioned above will convince the Indian people that in the event of an Axis victory its freedom would be guaranteed by the Axis Powers and that the fact of India's independence is already being recognised.)
4) Thereafter propaganda should be started, especially over the radio, calling on the Indian people to rise up for their freedom and launch a revolt against the British authorities. The broadcasts would have to be made in the name of Radio Free India.
5) Arrangements should be made for sending the necessary materials via Afghanistan to India in support of the rebellion.

II. Work in Afghanistan (Kabul)

1) In Kabul a headquarters should be set up to maintain communications between Europe and. India. The existing Lega-

tions could be expanded to cope with the work; or special committees would have to be set up to do the necessary work.
2) These headquarters should have the necessary equipment, automobiles, trucks, couriers, etc., to maintain communications between India and Europe.

III. Work in the Independent Zone

1) Our agents are already at work in this independent zone, which is situated between Afghanistan and India. Their activity would have to be co-ordinated and a plan drawn up for large-scale raids on British military bases. Offensive action by isolated anti-British elements, such as the Fakir of Ipi, could be integrated into this big plan.
2) A few military experts would have to be dispatched from Europe to this region.
3) A powerful centre of propaganda should also be set up in this zone and the necessary equipment for a printing shop should be procured.
4) Arrangements should also be made to set up a radio transmitter in this region.
5) Agents from the independent zone should be recruited who would select the necessary scouts from the [Northwest] Frontier Province. (This is the province adjoining the independent zone.)

IV. The Activity in India

1) Broadcasts to India ought to be made in grand style. At first they could be transmitted from a station in Europe, later from transmitters in the independent zone.
2) The printing shops in the independent zone will have to turn out the propaganda material for India as well.

3) Our agents and party members in the various Indian provinces will have to be instructed to hamper the activities of the British authorities in India as much as possible. They should work along the following lines:

   (a) Intensive propaganda among the Indian population against service in the Army and payment of even a single rupee in taxes;
   (b) Inducing the civilian population by propaganda to refrain from paying taxes to the authorities or obeying the laws of the British Government, etc.
   (c) Secret action among the Indian units of the Army towards inducing the Indian soldiers to engage in a military rebellion.
   (d) Organizing strikes in those factories which support the British war effort.
   (e) Acts of sabotage against strategic railway lines, bridges, factories, etc. The required material for this would have to be shipped to India.
   (f) Organizing insurrections among the civilian population in various parts of the country, which could then be used as a spring-board for the revolution of the masses.

V. Financial Matters

The funds required for the aforementioned activities would have to be provided by the Axis Powers in the form of a loan to the free India government, which has its seat in Europe. After the termination of the war, when an independent government has been installed in India, this loan would be repaid in full.

For disbursements in Europe the mark currency might be used. For expenditures incurred in Afghanistan marks can be converted into afghanis. For payments in India afghanis can be converted into rupees, although this might encounter some difficulties at this time. But it might be considered whether 10-rupee notes could not be printed in Europe, in order to be taken to India through Afghanistan.

VI. Military Aid in the Annihilation of British Power in India

The British Government has in India a maximum of 70,000 British troops and auxiliary forces which are loyal to the Government. Therefore it will be difficult for England to hold India with British troops alone, if the Indian troops should rebel. If at that time a small contingent of 50,000 soldiers, equipped with the most up-to-date weapons, would be dispatched to India, the English could be completely driven out of India. The Axis Powers should in any event take this important fact into consideration.

2

MOHAMMED IQBAL SHEDAI LETTER TO THE GERMAN EMBASSY (ROME)

ROME, 21 SEPTEMBER 1941

The following lines are not being written with any ill will or a complaint against anyone. I simply inform you about my impressions I have had during my short sojourn in Berlin. I am sorry I could not meet any of the chiefs [...] Probably some people did not like that I should meet them [...] well it is nothing. I am not an ambitious man and I have never worked for my country in the hope of any reward or honour.

[...] I stayed there in Berlin for two weeks [...] A young gentleman, Herr von Trott, met me several times and every time told me to stay in Germany instead of Italy [...] He told me that [...] he will put everything at my disposal i.e. propaganda machine, to prepare a Free Indian Legion etc. I told him that before giving any reply in the affirmative, I have two conditions which the German Government should accept. The first condition is the declaration for Indian independence signed by Germany, Italy, Japan, Hungary, Slovakia, Romania and Bulgaria. The second condition was that my Italian friends should allow me to come to Berlin. Before these two conditions were fulfilled it was not possible for me to accept the invitation. Herr von Trott always said that I should start the work and the conditions would be fulfilled afterwards.

My compatriot Mr. Bose—now dubbed by Herr von Trott as 'His Excellency' Mr. Mazzotta–also pressed me to come to Berlin without any condition. I gave him the same answer. [...] On the very first day I told 'His Excellency' Mr. Mazzotta that it would be much better if an Italo-German-Indian committee should be made which should start the work. 'Excellency' Mazzotta did not like the idea that Italy should join in the business. He also told me not to mention it to any of the Germans who were interested in Indian affairs. I refused to accept this 'advice'. Probably it was the reason that I could not approach [...] Woermann and [...] Keppler.

I being the friend of the Axis powers could not admit that any kind of bad blood should be created between two friends who were fighting for the same cause [...] with their failure and success lies India's future, and perhaps the future of [...] humanity. [...] on the day of my departure 'Excellency' Mazzotta told me that I should tell my Italian friends that they should apply to join the committee. A committee is to be made in Berlin without the knowledge of Italy and she is required by 'Excellency' Mazzotta to apply to join it. It looks quite childish. It must be the duty of that Committee to request Italy to take part in it. I think this is the proper way to do business.

Indian Prisoners in Germany

'Excellency' Mazzotta proposed to the German Foreign Office that a Free Indian Legion should be formed which shall fight side by side with German soldiers against the British. The idea was splendid. The German Government accepted it and got some 1500 Indian war prisoners to Germany from Libya. They have been put in a camp in Annaburg. I was sent [...] to see them. I found out that they were all discontented and requested me to help them to go back to Italy where they were being treated very well. The most important question was of food. It was bad rather awful. When I told the Commander of the camp that the food question should be remanded at once he [...] replied that it was not in his power. I impressed upon him that these soldiers were not ordinary prisoners. They were to be used for propaganda work, and therefore they must have special treatment. 1000 soldiers will not be a heavy burden on German finance.

I was told by the soldiers that in the beginning while they were in Libya, they were quite willing to fight against the British but now after seeing the treatment in Germany they could not think of any such adventure.

The German military authorities did another mistake. They left the Indian officers with the soldiers. Indian officers are generally very loyal to the British Government. They are also taken from the most loyal families. [...] The Indian officers told these soldiers that Germany wanted to occupy India. Every one of the prisoners now believes this story. They told me quite plainly that they would prefer to remain under the British than to change masters. I had to explain to them that it was quite false propaganda. Germany had not the least design to occupy India. She wanted our complete freedom. But it was very difficult to make them believe contrary to what their officers had told them. [...]

Another silly mistake is being done. Every week or fortnightly the prisoners receive red cross packets from England. They believe that these packets are being sent by the British Government. I told the commanding officer that these packets should be changed. Everything German should be given to them so that they should know that it is Germany which looks after their welfare. The officer told me that it was against the law. [...]

Another big mistake has been done by the German Foreign Office. When 'Excellency' Mazzotta proposed to make a Free

Indian Legion they, the Foreign Office officials, ought to have asked him who was to select good men out of these Indian prisoners. He himself is quite unfit to do any such work. Firstly he is not from the province of these soldiers. He does not understand them. [...] Secondly Mr. Mazzotta belongs to a class which has nothing in common with the soldiers. He cannot understand their needs because he is not one of them. I don't like to dwell on these personal qualities, but still one has to take into account all things.

I am of the opinion that a committee should be made which should select good men from among the Indian prisoners. This committee must have full powers to allot work to prisoners. [...] Now to sum the whole affair, I would like to propose the following things:

(1) An Italo-German-Japanese-Indian committee should be made for the Indian work. If Afghans and Persians will be included in it so much the better. India and Afghanistan go together and therefore there should be an Afghan member also.
(2) There should be different centres in different countries. That is to say in Berlin, Rome and Tokyo. [...]
(3) The smaller powers, too must be associated in the Oriental work. It will give international value to the movement and an answer to the Churchill-Roosevelt and Stalin declarations. Indians, Afghans and Persians will have more respect for this committee.
(4) Germany alone must not, in my opinion, conduct the whole Oriental work. Instead of some good it will be rather harmful.
(5) A declaration for the Independence of India must be signed by all the powers mentioned above.

As regards Indian prisoners I would suggest the following things:

MOHAMMED IQBAL SHEDAI LETTER

(1) The food question must be at once arranged according to their wishes.
(2) Good and revolutionary spirited men should be selected and taken out of the whole lot.
(3) People who should work among them must be [...] from the Punjab province [...]
(4) Two or more radio sets must be installed in the Annaburg camp and if necessary with loudspeakers. They must hear everyday Berlin and Rome transmissions in Hindustani [...] It will have a splendid effect on them.
(5) Educated young men among the prisoners must be given military training as the future officers of the Free Indian Legion. They must be taught guerrilla war tactics, sabotage work etc. [...]
(6) A committee has already been made in Berlin of some intelligent prisoners. The secretary of this committee is Sardar Gurbachan Singh and its presidents are Sardar Sant Singh and Mr. Alimullah. The joint secretary is Mr. Mohammed Jamil Khan. [...] All these men have sworn on my hands to die for India when I shall give them orders. [...]

As regards myself I should say that I am always ready to cooperate with Germany provided the above mentioned conditions are agreed upon [...] I can travel from home to Berlin to look after the prisoner's camp in Annaburg or anywhere else. Here in Italy I have made my headquarters for different reasons and I do not wish to change it.

I must also inform my German friends that I cannot and shall not work as an agent of anybody. I have not the least ambition to achieve [...] As regards my personal comfort [...] Count Ciano and [...] the Italian Foreign Office are doing their best to look after it. They have never asked me to do anything for Italy. When I was expelled from all countries they invited me to stay in Italy as their guest without putting any condition to me. It is myself who asked some work and I selected to work on the secret radio. They agreed [...] and allowed me full freedom in my work. Actually my work has been most useful for the Axis Powers and India. The German Government too have got proof [...].

I am loyal to my friends and nothing can persuade me to give up that loyalty. I am sure my German friends will appreciate my attitude and intentions.

I must also inform my German friends that I am not the least jealous of my compatriot 'Excellency' Mazzotta. He can be made anything in Germany if the German Government thinks it proper. I am not also complaining against anyone that I was not allowed to meet any of the chiefs of the German Foreign Office.

With my best and sincerest salutations I finish these lines.
Shedai.

3

BOSE-RIBBENTROP CONFERENCE MINUTES

F12/138–129

Memorandum by an Official of the Foreign Minister's Secretariat
RAM 59 g. Rs.   Berlin, November 29, 1941

Record of the Conversation of M. Bose with the
Foreign Minister on November 29, 1941, in Berlin

M. Bose began the conversation with words of thanks for the hospitality he had enjoyed in Germany and the request that his mission be supported. He congratulated the Foreign Minister on his speech and stated that the tone adopted in it had been very precisely attuned to England and America. In general he termed the situation hopeful, and believed that he could reckon Germany's prospects of winning the war at about 80 percent. He did not attribute any particular importance for the development of the war to America's entry, but said that Germany now had to take up the Oriental question, particularly as the European theatre of war would be finished within the foreseeable future.

The English had prepared a broader base in India. Whereas in the last war they had in the main procured manpower from India, the country had now been much more industrialized and especially adapted to the production of war material, so that all the fronts in the Orient could be supplied from there. England was so easy to attack in her Empire, and had enemies everywhere (Iraq, Iran, etc.). He, M. Bose, watched the English propaganda very closely; as an example he cited Colonel Britten, who was carrying on particularly realistic propaganda of subversion. Here the German propaganda ought to start its effort in a similar way; he expected this to have great success all over the Orient, which would greatly facilitate the work of the Wehrmacht.

It was a very important point that Germany should decide in time which party she wanted to cooperate with in each country. A prompt decision would then make it possible for the organization concerned to cooperate effectively. M. Bose then showed several clippings from the *Times*, the *Daily Mail*, and the *Daily Express*, which branded him a traitor. He indicated that it was rather necessary to make a reply to this so that his followers would not defect.

In his reply the Foreign Minister pointed out that the war, as he had already told him in Vienna, would result in the destruction of the English possessions everywhere in the world. Churchill knew, to be sure, that the war was lost, but could not and would not admit it; furthermore, there was no leader of stature to replace him. Thus he continued to make war. True, he could not be termed a great statesman; his sole strength lay in the fact that he was willing to take over the responsibility for continuing the war and that he succeeded in bringing about a certain agreement between the Labour Party and the Conservatives which others did not feel capable of achieving. It was improbable that Churchill would be overthrown; it was conceivable, however, in case the current operation in North Africa should lead to an English defeat.

As far as Russia was concerned, this would still require some effort, to be sure, but she would fall in the course of the coming year at the latest. The Russians had arrived at the point where they could not themselves replace their armaments adequately, while Anglo-American support was too scanty. In the meantime the English would lose one position after the other; this time the Führer wanted to have a clear decision and would no longer consider any compromise. It seemed that relations between Japan and America would reach a state of tension in the next few days which would at least result in a serious situation and perhaps also war.

In England Bevin was important in domestic policy; actually a half-Bolshevik, he was something of an English Kerensky. One could assume it to be certain that the Conservatives would no longer be in power at the end of the war. The more England lost, the more the course turned toward the left. America would be the heir to the English possessions in the Western Hemisphere, whereas the Axis would predominate in Europe. Once Germany had the Russian space before her as an area for colonization, she would hardly need colonies. Certainly the Russian area would be successfully colonized. In Africa, where the Duce would have a great influence, the English would be driven out and the peoples there would be given greater freedom. He, the Foreign Minister, had just seen the Mufti, who wanted to create a new Arab world, whereas Japan also had certain justified claims in the Far East.

In the question of India it was important to realize that the collapse of the Empire could no longer be prevented. One important point had to be taken into account, however: German policy did not think much of declarations with no force behind them, because it was possible that the opposite effect from the one desired could occur. As an example the Foreign Minister pointed to Iraq, where Germany was unable to help. The result was that the Grand Mufti and Gaylani were in Germany, the Government was forced into exile, and its friends were dead or in prison. After that the Syrian venture had occurred, with a similar outcome. Germany wanted to avoid taking a step which could again induce certain circles to ill-considered actions. Thus no open action should be taken that could endanger the situation. When we would be in a position to put pressure behind a declaration, and this time was no longer very far off, then we would take action. For the moment we intended to carry on all sorts of propaganda for the Arabs, for instance, but not to issue any declaration.

In the case of India matters were not entirely analogous. There, too, however, one should proceed cautiously and only say something concrete when a success was in view, for example when German troops had crossed the Caucasus. Then one might consider setting up an all-India committee under M. Bose in Tiflis, for example, which would make propaganda efforts with a large expenditure and with radio transmitters.

One thing was certain, that propaganda alone would never bring about a free India or Arabia; this could only be achieved through the destruction of the English positions of power by the Wehrmacht. At the moment England held all of these countries through her prestige; once this had been destroyed the Empire would fall.

Here M. Bose interjected that he hoped that this view of the Foreign Minister's also reflected the Führer's view.

The Foreign Minister said that the Führer believed in the final defeat of England; it was simply his view, however, that no action should take place until Germany had the power to support it properly. One should not risk the possibility of our propaganda's being torn to shreds by English counterpropaganda.

M. Bose pointed out that the Indian question differed from the Arab question in two points:

1. India was much further away. Therefore the English propaganda was much more effective there, for the Indians had no contact of any sort with Germany and no conception of Germany.
2. In *Mein Kampf* there were passages in regard to India which had been exploited in an unfavourable sense by English

propaganda. It was by far the most important thing to let the Indian people know what the Führer thought about India, because the Indian people did not know either Germany or the views held there. Technically such influence could probably be exerted through the radio.

The Foreign Minister stated that he had been thinking about an audience with the Führer for M. Bose; but at the moment he still hesitated to suggest this to the Führer because such a visit might become known. At the moment it was probably also too soon to undertake such decisive steps. At the proper time propaganda would be started against all the positions of the British Empire, possibly also including South Africa, so as to proceed with the strongest possible means against the Empire. However, he wanted to intensify the broadcasts to India and for this reason asked M. Bose for ideas which he might suggest.

M. Bose pointed out that there were millions of persons living in India who were anti-English, to be sure, but not for that reason pro-German. The great problem lay in the possibility of winning over these forces.

The Foreign Minister repeated his request for suggestions, and added that the moment would then have arrived when German troops were beyond the Caucasus and at Suez. The Axis could speak only when the military had a firm basis in the Near East, for otherwise any propaganda effect would come to nought. It was a guiding principle of German policy not to promise anything that could not be carried out later. As far as the English method was concerned, the Foreign Minister pointed to the concept of 'Blitzkrieg', which had been formulated in England so that one could say in the case of every German campaign, no matter how short, that it had failed as a Blitzkrieg. He imagined propaganda for India from this standpoint: The English oppress all nations, and Germany will help all those oppressed.

M. Bose asked to consider whether a secret radio transmitter for India should not be established. He would then direct the propaganda of this transmitter without himself making an appearance. Following this he asked the Foreign Minister to arrange an audience with the Führer, nevertheless, so that he would have the opportunity of personally presenting his views to him.

The Foreign Minister closed the conversation with the promise to consider this question.

4

TRIPARTITE DECLARATION ON INDIA

1942

In this defensive war which has been forced upon them, Germany, Italy and Japan are fighting against the Powers that have dominated the world up to now by means of subjugation and exploitation of other peoples. Their struggle serves a high ethic purpose. Germany, Italy and Japan are fighting at the same time for the freedom of all peoples that have been outraged by British imperialism. It is their earnest desire to see these peoples, too, once again free from the British yoke and in a position to shape unhampered their political and economic fate according to their own demands.

Among these nations which have had to suffer longest and most cruelly under British domination is numbered the ancient Indian people, a nation which during its great past has conferred such rich cultural benefits on humanity.

In the endeavour to open the gate of freedom to the Indian people also, at this historical moment when the British Empire is beginning to reel under the blows delivered by the armed might of the Tripartite Powers, the German, Italian and Japanese governments hereby solemnly declare that they recognise the inalienable right of the Indian people to independence and self-determination.

India for the Indians!

Germany, Italy and Japan convinced that the Indian nation will break the political and economic bonds of British imperialism and then as master of its own fate will carry out a sweeping transformation of its national life for the lasting benefit of its own people and as contribution to the welfare and the peace of the world. It is no concern of the Tripartite Powers what form the Indian people, after their liberation, will in future give to their interior political organisation. It is a matter to be decided upon by the Indian people themselves and their leaders what constitution is the most suitable for their country and how it is to be put into practice. The Tripartite Powers are concerned to end—on a basis of social justice—the misery and poverty of the Indian people, and to see the exploited masses assisted to a proper standard of living as well as to employment and prosperity.

Britain is the common enemy of the Indian people and of the peoples of the Tripartite Pact. The Tripartite powers have always cherished friendly feelings towards the Indian people, and the close cultural and economic relations which they enjoyed with India have helped to cement this friendship. Nevertheless, the people of India are compelled by their alien British government to consider themselves at war with Germany, Italy and Japan and to sacrifice both lives and property for the maintenance of the rule of their oppressors. As in the First World War, India's sons must again at Britain's behest, give their lives on the battlefields in the West and the East, in order that India is also in future to remain under British domination. Once more, Indian workers and peasants are compelled by their own war work, to tighten the bonds which Britain intends shall hold them in slavery. That is what the British call democracy and freedom.

TRIPARTITE DECLARATION ON INDIA: 1942

All the promises of self-government made by Britain to India have proved so far to be lies. Fresh promises will be given by Britain simply to mislead the Indian people; they, again will be broken. It will not be the victory of British imperialism that will bring true freedom to the Indian people but solely the victory of the Tripartite Powers.

India has never had a more favourable opportunity of attaining freedom; the hour has struck when the Indian people themselves must act to shape their own destiny.

The sincere wishes of the peoples and governments of Germany, Italy and Japan are with the people of India in their struggle for liberty, and the Powers declare their readiness to afford India every possible assistance. They are joyfully awaiting the day when India, at last a free country, will take up her rightful position in a community of free nations.

5

BRITISH INTELLIGENCE ASSESSMENT ON GERMAN RECRUITMENT OF INDIAN POWS

22 JUNE 1943: WAR OFFICE

1. The total number of Indian prisoners of war held by the Germans and Italians is now believed to be about 15,000 half of whom are in Italy and half in Germany and France. The largest camps are at Annaburg in Germany (Stalag IV D/Z), where there are believed to be over 4,200 prisoners, and at Rennes (Frontstalag 133) in Brittany, where there are nearly 2,000. Subordinate to Annaburg were formerly the "Work Detachments" of Koenigsbruecke, Frankenburg and Ringbaum, but the two last named now appear to have been abolished. Koenigsbruecke (which is not far from Dresden) does not exist officially: its prisoners are supposed to have been transferred to other camps. Actually it has achieved considerable notoriety as the "Legion Camp" and its inmates are still subjected to intense subversive propaganda from the anti-British organisation formed by S. C. Bose in Berlin. What is of special significance is the fact that, as already mentioned in a previous note, the Protecting Power was refused permission to visit Koenigsbruecke when it was officially still open. The Swiss Legation in Berlin requested that the reason for this refusal should be given in writing but has not yet received a reply. That

the Germans have a guilty conscience about Koenigsbruecke was further made evident by their refusal to permit representatives of the Protecting Power to hold conversations with Indian prison camp leaders at Stalag IV D/Z (Annaburg) except in the presence of witnesses. The order of the German High Command imposing this restriction is flatly at variance with a note issued in August 1942 by the German Foreign Office. The same unaccommodating attitude has been shown by the Germans at Stalag V C (Neubruck near Haguenau in Alsace) and at Stalag IV B (Muhlberg). At the former of these camps there are some eight hundred prisoners, but Stalag IV B is a transit camp where the number of prisoners constantly fluctuates.

2. There is very good evidence that the number of prisoners at Koenigsbruecke runs well into four figures. The latest estimate dated January 1943 places the number at 1,150. It was inevitable that persistent attempts by Bose and his associates to seduce these prisoners should ultimately achieve some success, though their own optimistic hopes may not have been realised. It is, in fact, now clear that those who have succumbed to persuasion or pressure and have joined the 'Indian Legion' are now no longer to be counted in scores but in hundreds. The total number is in fact reliably reported to be something over 2,000. What is far more doubtful is the quality of these recruits, for it is probable that for everyone who is genuinely converted by the utterances of propagandists at least half a dozen follow the line of least resistance and have no deep-seated intention of carrying disloyalty beyond the stage of expediency. The exact location of these large numbers of perverted prisoners is unknown, but it may be assumed that a considerable proportion of them are at Koenigsbruecke. Recent information also suggests that another large group, possibly amounting to fifty per cent of the total, is held at Zandvoort in Holland.

3. Attached is a complete list of all these Indian prisoners of war against whom reasonable evidence is available of treason-

able association with the enemy. (There are still a few names which have not been satisfactorily identified and which are therefore held over for the time being.) This list is very small when considered against the statement made above that some two thousand have gone over to the enemy. It contains, in fact, the names of only a few of those Indians who were captured in France in 1940 and in Libya in the spring of 1941. No information is forthcoming regarding the identities of any Indians captured in subsequent operations in North Africa and sent over to the Continent, but it is believed that the latter figure prominently among the considerable number of disaffected elements now under Nazi control at Zandvoort in Holland.

4. No important fresh information has been received regarding the attempts made by the Italians to make effective use of their Indian prisoners. Certain Indian civilians are believed to have been given the task of collecting Indian soldiers from prisoners of war camps and inducing them to join an Indian unit which would ultimately be used to strike a blow for Indian independence. About three hundred men were persuaded to enlist in this unit and it may be assumed that these were the men who in previous notes have been mentioned as being seen in the streets of Rome wearing national uniform and whose headquarters were at Centocele. After they had received their special training under Italian officers it was explained to them that the time was not ripe for them to be given service in India but that they would be afforded opportunity to fight the British in Egypt. This suggestion met with little enthusiasm from the volunteers, who considered that they had been misled as to the purpose of their enrolment. The unit was then disbanded and its personnel were re-interned. It may be that these were the men who in the concluding sentence of the last note on this subject were reported to have been sent to Camp 57 because their conduct did not prove satisfactory.

5. It is considered highly probable that there has been a lack of effective liaison between the two organisations in Berlin and

Rome dealing with Indian prisoners of war. There is reason to believe, however, that since the failure of the experiment at Centocele the Bose organisation has been making enquiries regarding prisoners of war in Italy and is particularly anxious to gather into its net the men whom the Italians wasted so much time in training. The appearance of S. C. Bose in the Far East does not by any means imply that in his absence from the continent attempts to win over Indian prisoners of war will cease. On the contrary he has succeeded in gathering around himself at a so-called Central Free India Bureau in Berlin, which has branches in Paris and elsewhere in Europe, a considerable number of Indian civilians who share his own anti-British outlook and who, it can readily be assumed, will carry on the work which he has begun.

6. The best known of these men is a certain A. C. N. Nambiar, a Madrasi journalist and one-time Communist, who is related by marriage to Chattopadhyaya, himself a noted Communist who was for many years the leader of the anti-British elements on the Continent. Chattopadhyaya fled from Berlin to Russia when the Nazis rose to power and Nambiar deemed it prudent to retire to Prague. With the fall of Czechoslovakia the latter took refuge in France but forgot his Communist principles and his sufferings at the hands of the Nazis when invited to join S. C. Bose in Berlin. He became the latter's Deputy and is now functioning for him during his absence in the Far East. He is not the only Communist who has swallowed his principles and gone over to assist Bose and the enemy. With such men Communism is only skin-deep and merely serves to conceal the fact that their underlying emotion is hatred of the British. In Berlin, Paris and Rome there are now several Indians of this type who at one time were wedded to Communism, but who have since discarded their allegiance to Moscow in the hope of striking a blow at the British. Some of these Indians have themselves joined the Indian Legion: others are being used to assist in various forms of propaganda. The majority of the prisoners of war enrolled in the

Legion are not fit for any form of specialised duty, but some are considered suitable for technical training. Bose even has hopes that some of his followers will be given some training in the *Luftwaffe*. As already reported in previous notes many have already undergone instruction as saboteurs or parachutists. Others also are being provided with training in the Police. Self-advertisement has, of course, not been neglected. The response of Indian prisoners of war to Bose's call to arms has been duly recorded on cinematograph films which have been shown on the Continent and will doubtless be displayed in due course to Indian audiences in the Far East.

7. What is not very clear is the immediate purpose to which Bose's hundreds of dupes can now be put. Unless the Axis can stage a successful thrust eastwards and so compensate for their loss of all their North African footholds there will be no military task to which these Indians can be usefully assigned. The hope of making use of them as advance elements of an invading army may have to be abandoned altogether: they certainly would not be relied on to assist in defending German soil against the invading forces of the United Nations. It is, therefore, reasonable to assume that sooner or later the German High Command may have to divest itself of all responsibility for their future and will have to give Bose and his associates a free hand to make such use of them as they please. There are already indications that Bose is anticipating some such decision.

Corrigendum

Since the above note was typed, information has been received that about a thousand perverted Indian prisoners of war left Koenigsbruecke for Holland on the 30 April, and that the same number are under training at Schnorkau in Saxony. The former are without doubt the prisoners who are reported to be at Zandvoort. Also it would appear that the Koenigsbruecke camp no longer exists, but this has yet to be verified.

NOTES

PROLOGUE

1. Minutes of the Bose-Woermann meeting, 3 April 1941 in *Documents on German Foreign Policy 1918–1945* (hereafter: DGFP), Series D (1937–1945), vol. XII, London, Her Majesty's Stationary Office, 1962, no. 257.
2. On Bose's escape from Calcutta to Berlin, which has become known as the 'Great Escape' in Indian nationalist historiography, see Sisir Kumar Bose, *The Great Escape*, Calcutta, Netaji Research Bureau, 1995; *Netaji Subhas Chandra Bose*, New Delhi, National Book Trust, 2005, pp. 104–112. See also Uttam Chand, *When Bose was Ziauddin*, Delhi, Rajkamal, 1946; Mian Akbar Shah, 'Netaji's Escape—An Untold Chapter', *The Oracle*, 1 (1984), 15–23; Sayed Wiqar Ali Shah, 'The Escape of Subhas Chandra Bose: Myths and Realities', *The Oracle*, 3 & 4 (1996), pp. 51–63; Bhagat Ram Talwar, *The Talwars of Pathan Land and Subhas Chandra's Great Escape*, New Delhi, People's Publishing House, 1976; Hans Pilger (German legation, Kabul) to Foreign Office (Berlin) 5 February 1941 in T. R. Sareen (ed.), *Subhas Chandra Bose and Nazi Germany* (hereafter: SCBNG), New Delhi, Mounto Publishing House, 1996, no. 5; Woermann to Ernst von Weizsäcker (Secretary of State) 8 February 1941, SCBNG, no. 6; Woermann to German embassy (Moscow) 9 February 1941, DGFP/D/XII, no. 36; Ambassador Friedrich Werner von Schulenburg (Moscow) to Foreign Office, 3 March 1941, SCBNG, no. 8; Schulenburg to Foreign Office, 31 March 1941, SCBNG, no. 9. See also the British interrogation reports of Bhagat Ram Talwar, Abad Khan and Uttam Chand who assisted Bose in Kabul in SCBNG, nos. 49–52.
3. The meeting was arranged by an Indian businessman resident in Germany. See his recollections in N. G. Ganpuley, *Netaji in Germany: A Little-Known Chapter*, Bombay, Bharatiya Vidya Bhavan, 1959, pp. 186–187. See also R. R. Diwakar and S. B. Nargundkar (eds), *Ganpuley's Memoirs*, Bombay, Bharatiya Vidya Bhavan, 1983. The minutes of the meeting are reproduced

in Milan Hauner, *India in Axis Strategy: Germany, Japan and Indian Nationalists in the Second World War*, Stuttgart, Klett-Cotta, 1981, Doc. 1: 'Conversation between S. C. Bose, President of the All-India National Congress and Dr O. Urchs, Regional Group Leader of the AO/NSDAP for British India and Ceylon on 22 December 1938 in Bombay', pp. 644–653.

4. Bose's disappointment is evident in a memorandum he prepared for the Foreign Office entitled 'Germany and India' including several letters he wrote during this period. See Bose to Foreign Office, 5 April 1934, Bose to Franz Thierfelder, 7 November 1935, Bose to Amiya Chakravarti, 11 March 1936, Bose to Thierfelder, 25 March 1936 in Sisir Kumar Bose and Sugata Bose (eds), *Netaji Collected Works* (hereafter: NCW), vol. 8 (*Letters, Articles, Speeches and Statements 1933–1937*), Calcutta, Netaji Research Bureau, 1994, pp. 61–64, 111–115, 151–153, 165–168.

5. For example see Hitler's statements to his entourage: 'It should be possible for us to control this region to the East with two hundred and fifty thousand men plus a cadre of good administrators. Let's learn from the English, who, with two hundred and fifty thousand men in all, including fifty thousand soldiers, govern four hundred million Indians (27 July 1941)... What India was for England, the territories of Russia will be for us (8 August 1941)... Our role in Russia will be analogous to that of England in India... The Russian space is our India. Like the English, we shall rule this empire with a handful of men' (17–18 September 1941) in H. R. Trevor-Roper (ed.), *Hitler's Table Talk 1941–1944: His Private Conversations*, London, Phoenix Press, 2000, nos. 11, 17, 20. The Hitlerian vision of the east has been described as 'one gigantic colony, a Germanic India directly connected with the German heartland'. See Karl Dietrich Bracher, *The German Dictatorship: The Origins, Structure, and Consequences of National Socialism*, London, Penguin, 1985, p. 504. The comparison with India is also strongly emphasised by Ian Kershaw in *Hitler 1936–45: Nemesis*, London, Penguin Press, 2000, pp. 401–402, 405, 449.

6. See Hitler's addresses to the Reichstag, 6 October 1939 and 19 July 1940 in Max Domarus (ed.), *Hitler: Speeches and Proclamations 1932–1945*, vol. III (1939–1940), Wauconda, Bolchazy-Carducci Publishers, 1990, pp. 1830–1848; 2042–2063.

7. The response was receptive at least in comparison to the lack of enthusiasm previously shown towards Bose. See Woermann to Moscow, 9 February 1941, DGFP/D/XII, no. 36. The Italians nevertheless were even more enthusiastic than the Germans. See the extensive report of the Italian minister in Kabul, Pietro Quaroni, to the Foreign Ministry (Rome), 2 April 1941 in *SCBNG*, no. 10.

8. Schulenburg to Foreign Office, 3 March 1941, *SCBNG*, no. 8.

9. Already, less than two weeks into his arrival, Bose threatened to leave if his proposals were not implemented. See Woermann to Ribbentrop, 12 April 1941, DGFP/D/XII, no. 323.
10. Peter Ward Fay, *The Forgotten Army: India's Armed Struggle for Independence 1942–1945*, New Delhi, Rupa, 1997, p. 189.

INTRODUCTION

1. Hugh Toye, *The Springing Tiger: A Study of a Revolution*, Mumbai, Jaico, 2001, p. 18.
2. Bose to Sarat Bose, 22 September 1920, NCW/1, no. 60.
3. NCW/2 (*The Indian Struggle 1920–1942*), p. 59.
4. Ibid.
5. On Hitler's complex involvement with India see Johannes H. Voigt, 'Hitler und Indien', *Vierteljahrshefte für Zeitgeschichte*, 19 (1971), 33–63.
6. Adolf Hitler, *Mein Kampf*, Mumbai, Jaico, 2010, p. 587.
7. Ibid.
8. Otto Strasser, *Hitler and I*, London, Jonathan Cape, 1940, p. 118.
9. Ibid., pp. 118–119.
10. Ibid., p. 119.
11. Domarus, p. 956.
12. NCW/2, p. 60.
13. Nirad C. Chaudhuri quoted in Leonard A. Gordon, *Brothers Against the Raj: A Biography of Sarat & Subhas Chandra Bose*, New Delhi, Viking, 1990, p. 190.
14. Ibid., p. 235.
15. Bose speech to the Calcutta Corporation, 27 September 1930, NCW/6, p. 128.
16. Churchill quoted in Arthur Herman, *Gandhi & Churchill: The Epic Rivalry that Destroyed an Empire and Forged our Age*, London, Hutchinson, 2008, p. 302.
17. NCW/2, p. 255.
18. Nehru quoted in Gordon, p. 241.
19. NCW/2, p. 225.
20. Mussolini quoted in Pierre Milza, *Mussolini*, Paris, Fayard, 1999, p. 622.
21. Herman, pp. 359, 368.
22. Gandhi to Romain Rolland, 20 December 1931 in *The Collected Works of Mahatma Gandhi* (hereafter: CWMG), vol. 48, New Delhi, Government of India, 1979, no. 275.
23. NCW/2, p. 256.

24. On Bose's pre-war relations with the Nazis see Diethelm Weidemann, 'Subhas Chandra Bose's Position *vis-à-vis* Germany before World War II', *Asien Afrika Latinamerika*, 4 (2002), 317–329.
25. Bose to Asoke Nath Bose, 5 April 1933 in Asoke Nath Bose, *Netaji's Letters*, New Delhi, Arnold, 1992, pp. 11–12.
26. Asoke Nath Bose, *My Uncle Netaji*, Bombay, Bharatiya Vidya Bhavan, 1989, p. 76.
27. Hauner, p. 57.
28. Mihir Bose, *The Lost Hero: A Biography of Subhas Bose*, Noida, Brijbasi Art Press, 2004, p. 259.
29. Sisir K. Bose (ed.), *A Beacon Across Asia: A Biography of Subhas Chandra Bose*, Hyderabad, Orient Longman, 1996, p. 42.
30. Bose to Bose, 12 August 1933, *Netaji's Letters*, p. 23.
31. Bose, *A Beacon Across Asia*, pp. 43–44.
32. Bose to Naomi C. Vetter, 12 January 1934, NCW/8, p. 45.
33. Bose to Bose, 15 January 1934, *Netaji's Letters*, p. 36.
34. Bose, *My Uncle Netaji*, p. 108.
35. Bose to Bose, 25 January 1934, *Netaji's Letters*, p. 37.
36. Bose to Foreign Office, 5 April 1934, NCW/8, p. 62.
37. Bose quoted in Toye, p. 38; Bose, *The Lost Hero*, p. 262.
38. Bose to Foreign Office, 5 April 1934, NCW/8, pp. 62–63.
39. Bose to Bose, 26 April 1934, *Netaji's Letters*, p. 46.
40. Bose to Foreign Office, 5 April 1934, NCW/8, p. 63.
41. Ibid., p. 62.
42. Bose to Bose, 26 April 1934, *Netaji's Letters*, p. 46.
43. Bose, *My Uncle Netaji*, p. 95.
44. Bose to J. T. Sunderland, 12 February 1935, NCW/8, p. 91.
45. NCW/2, pp. 351–352.
46. Ibid., p. 352.
47. Bose to Santosh Basu, 17 August 1937, NCW/8, p. 220.
48. NCW/2, p. 333.
49. Ibid., pp. 30, 254, 67.
50. Ibid., p. 201.
51. Ibid., p. 31.
52. Gordon, pp. 344–345.
53. Bose to Bose, 20 February 1935, *Netaji's Letter's*, p. 67.
54. Bose to Bose, 27 January 1935, *Netaji's Letter's*, p. 63; Bose, *My Uncle Netaji*, p. 107; NCW/8, p. 291.
55. NCW/8, p. 290.
56. Ibid.
57. Sarvepalli Gopal, *Jawaharlal Nehru: A Biography*, vol. 1 (1889–1947), New Delhi, Oxford University Press, 1975, p. 193.

58. Bose to Thierfelder, 7 November 1935, NCW/8, p. 113.
59. Ibid., pp. 113–114.
60. Ibid., p. 114.
61. Bose to Basu, 12 November 1935, NCW/8, p. 116.
62. Hauner, p. 63.
63. Bose to Thierfelder, 25 March 1936, NCW/8, p. 167.
64. Bose to Chakravarti, 11 March 1936, NCW/8, p. 152.
65. Bose press conference, Geneva, March 1936, NCW/8, p. 346.
66. Bose to Thierfelder, 25 March 1936, NCW/8 pp. 165–167.
67. Bose to Bose, 23 May 1937, *Netaji's Letters*, p. 111.
68. Gandhi to Vallabhbhai Patel, 1 November 1937, CWMG/66, no. 347.
69. Ibid.
70. Bose to J. Dharmavir, 6 December 1937, NCW/8, p. 234.
71. Bose to Maggiore Rapicavoli, 25 November 1937, NCW/8, p. 232.
72. Ibid.
73. Bose to Rapicavoli, 31 December 1937, NCW/8, p. 239.
74. Hitler quoted in Anthony Eden, *The Eden Memoirs: Facing the Dictators*, London, Cassell, 1962, p. 516.
75. Ibid.
76. Bose interview in NCW/9 (*Congress President: Speeches, Articles and Letters January 1938–May 1939*) p. 2.
77. Ibid.
78. Ibid.
79. Bose speech in Haripura, NCW/9, pp. 3–30.
80. Gandhi statement, 31 January 1939, NCW/9, p. 87.
81. Roy to Bose, 1 February 1939, NCW/9, p. 281.
82. Bose statement, 4 February 1939, NCW/9, p. 90.
83. Gandhi to C. F. Andrews, 15 January 1940, CWMG/71, no. 135.
84. Nehru to Bose, 11 July 1939, NCW/10 (*The Alternative Leadership: Speeches, Articles, Statements and Letters June 1939–January 1941*) p. 157.
85. Gordon, p. 392.
86. NCW/10, p. 12.
87. Ibid., p. 14.
88. Ibid., p. 82.
89. Ibid., p. 96.
90. Ibid., p. 102.
91. Gandhi, 'To Every Briton', 6 July 1940, CWMG/72, no. 281.
92. Gandhi to Linlithgow, 26 May 1940, CWMG/72, no. 128.
93. Bose to the Superintendent of Presidency Jail, 30 October 1940, NCW/10, p. 187.
94. Bose to Gandhi, 23 December 1940, NCW/10, pp. 153–154.

95. Gandhi to Bose, 29 December 1940, NCW/10, p. 155.
96. Ibid.
97. Bose to Bose, 24 October 1940, NCW/10, p. 159.
98. Ibid.

1. FORGING AN ALLIANCE: INDIAN NATIONALISM AND NATIONAL SOCIALISM

1. Bose-Woermann meeting minutes, 3 April 1941, DGFP/D/XII, no. 257.
2. Ibid.
3. Bose did find time to write a letter though to Emilie Schenkl in Vienna. See Bose to Schenkl, 3 April 1941, NCW/7 (*Letters to Emilie Schenkl 1934–1942*), pp. 216–217.
4. Bose 'Plan for Co-operation between the Axis Powers and India', 9 April 1941 in DGFP/D/XII, no. 300.
5. Bose 'Explanatory Note' attached to 'Plan for Co-operation between the Axis Powers and India', SCBNG, no. 12.
6. DGFP/D/XII, no. 300.
7. On the activities of the Fakir of Ipi see Milan Hauner, 'One Man against the Empire: The Faqir of Ipi and the British in Central Asia on the Eve of and during the Second World War', *Journal of Contemporary History*, 1 (1981), 183–212.
8. SCBNG, no. 12.
9. Bose's military figures were erroneous. The size of the Indian Army already surpassed 200,000 in addition to tens of thousands of new recruits each month. By the end of the year, the rate of recruitment reached 50,000 a month. See I. C. B. Dear (ed.), *The Oxford Companion to World War II*, Oxford, Oxford University Press, 2001, p. 443; Hauner, p. 125.
10. 'Explanatory Note', SCBNG, no. 12.
11. DGFP/D/XII, no. 300.
12. Ibid.
13. When the 'Provisional Government of Free India' was established in Southeast Asia in 1943, it was promptly recognised by Croatia and the Fascist rump state in northern Italy among other states. See S. A. Das and K. B. Subbaiah, *Chalo Delhi!: An Historical Account of the Indian Independence Movement in East Asia*, Kuala Lumpur, 1946, pp. 186–187.
14. DGFP/D/XII, no. 300.
15. Bose's first Indian acquaintance in Berlin, a political non-entity by the name of Kirpa Dhawan, already nurtured hopes of becoming prime minister of the new government with Bose serving as a presidential figurehead. See M. R. Vyas, *Passage through a Turbulent Era: Historical Reminis-*

cences of the Fateful Years 1937–47, Bombay: Indo-Foreign Publications, 1982, p. 322.
16. Hitler 'Directive no. 21 Case Barbarossa', 18 December 1940 in H. R. Trevor-Roper (ed.), *Hitler's War Directives 1939–1945*, London, Pan Books, 1966, pp. 93–98.
17. India did not even feature in Hitler's extensive 'Directive no. 32 Preparations for the Period after "BARBORRASSA"', 11 June 1941, *Hitler's War Directives*, pp. 130–134.
18. A 'Special India Bureau' was even set-up within the Foreign Office. See the recollections of Alexander Werth, *Der Tiger Indiens: Subhas Chandra Bose*, Munich, Bechtle, 1971, pp. 129–133; 'Planning for Revolution 1941–43', in Bose, *A Beacon Across Asia*, pp. 104–105. For the recollections of other staff members see Franz Josef Furtwängler, *Männer die Ich Sah und Kannte*, Hamburg, Auerdruck, 1951; Giselher Wirsing, *Indien: Asiens gefährliche Jahre*, Düsseldorf, Diederichs 1968.
19. Woermann to Ribbentrop, 12 April 1941, DGFP/D/XII, no. 323.
20. Ibid.
21. Mohammed Iqbal Shedai to Foreign Ministry (Rome), 1 June 1941, *SCBNG*, no. 21.
22. DGFP/D/XII, no. 323.
23. Ibid.
24. For an example of this contempt see the comments of the Minster of Public Enlightenment and Propaganda, Joseph Goebbels, on Gandhi in his diary whom he described as a 'fool whose policies seem merely calculated to drag India further and further into misfortune', 20 April 1942 in Louis P. Lochner (ed.), *The Goebbels Diaries*, London, Hamish Hamilton, 1948.
25. DGFP/D/XII, no. 323.
26. This was never explicitly stated but implied through euphemisms such as the 'focal points in the territorial aspirations of the Soviet Union' being 'centred south of the territory of the Soviet Union in the direction of the Indian Ocean' or the need of a 'turn to the south for the natural outlet to the open sea that was so important to Russia'. See DGFP/D/XI, nos. 329, 325. See also 'Secret Protocol no. 1' attached to draft 'Agreement between the States of the Three Power Pact, Germany, Italy, and Japan, on the One Side, and the Soviet Union on the Other Side', 9 November 1940, DGFP/D/XI, no. 309; Hitler-Molotov meeting minutes, 15 and 16 November 1940, nos. 326, 328; Hauner, p. 185; John Toland, *Adolf Hitler*, Hertfordshire, Wordsworth, 1997, p. 643. For a more explicit attempt to assign India to the Soviet sphere of influence see the minutes of Hitler's meetings with Mussolini and the Italian Foreign Minister, Count Galeazzo Ciano, 4 and 28 October 1940, DGFP/D/XI, nos. 149, 246.

27. Bose to Foreign Office, 3 May 1941, *SCBNG*, no. 15; Bose 'Detailed Plan of Work', 20 May 1941, *SCBNG*, no. 17.
28. Nehru was equally naive defending the German-Soviet Non-Aggression Pact as well as the Soviet invasion of Poland. See Manzoor Ahmad, *Indian Response to the Second World War*, New Delhi, Intellectual Publishing House, 1987, pp. 152–153.
29. DGFP/D/XII, no. 323.
30. Ibid.
31. Goebbels' diary, 3 May 1941 in Fred Taylor (ed.), *The Goebbels Diaries 1939–1941*, London, Sphere Books, 1983.
32. Hitler quoted in Michael Bloch, *Ribbentrop*, London, Abacus, 2003, p. 365.
33. Hitler's Table Talk, 22 August 1942, no. 297; 12–13 January 1942, no. 105; 15 January 1942, no. 108; Hitler speech in Munich, 26 January 1936 in N. Baynes, *The Speeches of Adolf Hitler 1922–1939*, vol. II, London, Oxford University Press, 1942, pp. 1258–1259. Hitler's stereotypical clichés were not only restricted to India. See Percy Ernst Schramm, *Hitler: The Man and the Military Leader*, London, Penguin Press, 1971, pp. 52–54.
34. Milan Hauner, 'India's Independence and the Axis Powers: Subhas Chandra Bose in Europe during the Strategic Initiative of the Axis Powers, 1941–1942' in Sisir K. Bose (ed.), *Netaji and India's Freedom*, Calcutta: Netaji Research Bureau, 1975, p. 269.
35. Hitler jokingly envisaged a similar role for himself among some Muslims, who he claimed, were already mingling his name with their prayers. See Hitler's Table Talk, 12–13 January 1942, no. 105.
36. This was increasingly apparent as the war dragged on. See Joachim C. Fest, *Hitler*, New York, Harcourt Brace Jovanovich, 1974, pp. 676–677.
37. Walter Warlimont, *Inside Hitler's Headquarters 1939–45*, Novato, Presidio Press, 1964, p. 132; Toland, p. 651.
38. Hauner, p. 263.
39. Ibid., p. 229.
40. 'Directive no. 24 Co-operation with Japan', 5 March 1941, *Hitler's War Directives 1939–1945*, pp. 105–106. See also 'Report on Conferences with the Führer and Supreme Commander of the Armed Forces', 8 and 9 January 1941 in *Führer Conferences on Naval Affairs 1939–1945*, London, Greenhill Books, 1990, pp. 169–172; Ernst L. Presseisen, *Germany and Japan: A Study in Totalitarian Diplomacy 1933–1941*, New York, Howard Fertig, 1969, p. 287.
41. Ibid., *Hitler's War Directives*.
42. 'Report of the C-in-C., Navy, to the Führer', 27 December 1940, 18 March 1941, 20 April 1941, in *Führer Conferences on Naval Affairs*,

pp. 160–163, 182–188, 190–194. See also Erich Raeder, *Grand Admiral*, Da Capo Press, 2001, pp. 363–364.
43. Gurbachan Singh Mangat, *The Tiger Strikes: An Unwritten Chapter of Netaji's Life History*, Ludhiana, Gagan Publishers, 1986, p. 35.
44. Walter Harbich, 'A Report on the Organisation and Training of the Free India Army in Europe 1941–42', *The Oracle*, 3 & 4 (1996), 43–50; Werth, *Der Tiger Indiens*, p. 138.
45. Ibid.
46. Bose 'Detailed Plan of Work', 20 May 1941, *SCBNG*, no. 17.
47. On Ribbentrop see his memoirs written while awaiting sentencing during the Nuremburg Trials: Joachim von Ribbentrop, *The Ribbentrop Memoirs*, London, Weidenfeld & Nicolson, 1954. See also John Weitz, *Hitler's Diplomat: The Life and Times of Joachim von Ribbentrop*, New York, Ticknor & Fields, 1992.
48. On the workings of Ribbentrop and the Foreign Office see Paul Seabury, 'Ribbentrop and the German Foreign Office', *Political Science Quarterly*, 4 (1951), 532–555.
49. Minutes of Ribbentrop-Bose meeting, 1 May 1941, DGFP/D/XII, no. 425.
50. Ibid.
51. Ibid.
52. Ibid.
53. Ribbentrop's opponents included former protégés like the *Reichsführer-SS* Heinrich Himmler and the Deputy Führer, Rudolf Hess as well as the *Reichsmarschall* Hermann Goering and Joseph Goebbels. See Bloch pp. 358, 443. See also Joachim C. Fest, *The Face of the Third Reich: Portraits of the Nazi Leadership*, New York, Pantheon, 1970, p. 179.
54. DGFP/D/XII, no. 300; *SCBNG*, no. 12.
55. Bose to Foreign Office, 3 May 1941, *SCBNG*, no. 15.
56. Ibid.
57. Ibid.
58. Winston S. Churchill, *The Second World War*, vol. 3 (*The Grand Alliance*), New York, Bantam Books, 1962, p. 224. More than six months later, even after the reassertion of British power in the Middle East, Churchill was still concerned that Hitler might reach India, this time, via Central Asia. See Martin Gilbert, *Winston S. Churchill*, vol. VII (*The Road to Victory 1941–1945*), Boston, Houghton Mifflin, 1986, p. 38.
59. *SCBNG*, no. 15.
60. Ibid.
61. Ribbentrop to Hitler, 3 May 1941, DGFP/D/XII, no. 435. Ribbentrop had other ulterior motives in making such a proposal hoping that involvement

in the Middle East might deter Hitler from launching Operation Barbarossa. See Bloch, p. 355.
62. 'Directive no. 30 Middle East', 23 May 1941, *Hitler's War Directives*, pp. 122–125.
63. DGFP/D/XII, no. 553.
64. Draft on Indian independence, *SCBNG*, no. 20.
65. Hauner, p. 253.
66. Bose 'Detailed Plan of Work', 20 May 1941, *SCBNG*, no. 17.

2. EXTENDING THE BOUNDARIES: ASPIRING FOR NAZI LIBERATION

1. Bose to Talwar, 20 May 1941, *SCBNG*, no. 16.
2. Ibid.
3. 'Detailed Plan of Work', *SCBNG*, no. 17.
4. Ibid.
5. Bose's attitude towards democracy has been described as 'insensitive'. See Anton Pelinka, *Democracy Indian Style: Subhas Chandra Bose and the Creation of India's Political Culture*, New Brunswick, Transaction, 2003, p. 183.
6. *SCBNG*, no. 17.
7. Ibid.
8. For a dubious version of events see Talwar, pp. 135–136.
9. Hauner, p. 236.
10. Ibid., p. 312.
11. Ibid., p. 229.
12. Rudolf Hartog, *The Sign of the Tiger: Subhas Chandra Bose and his Indian Legion in Germany 1941–45*, New Delhi, Rupa, 2001, pp. 36–37. See also Reimund Schnabel, *Tiger und Schakal: Deutsche Indienpolitik 1941–1943: Ein Dokumentarbericht* (hereafter: *TUJ*), Vienna, Europa Verlag, 1968, no. 1.
13. Apart from Iraqi military incompetence, Ribbentrop's concerns were not entirely unjustified as German military assistance has been described as 'insufficiently prepared and conducted with minimal forces' amounting in effect to 'improvisation'. See Heinz Magenheimer, *Hitler's War: Germany's Key Strategic Decisions 1940–1945*, London, Cassell, 2002, p. 70.
14. Woermann to Ribbentrop, 25 May 1941, DGFP/D/XII, no. 553.
15. Ibid.
16. Woermann to Rome, 28 May 1941, DGFP/D/XII, no. 561.
17. Shedai to Foreign Ministry, 1 June 1941, *SCNBG*, no. 21.
18. Ibid.

19. Shedai to Renato Prunas, 11 June 1941, *SCBNG*, no. 24.
20. Shedai to Blasco Lanza d'Ajeta, 4 June 1941, *SCBNG*, no. 22.
21. Ibid.
22. Ciano's diary, 6 June 1941 in Galeazzo Ciano, *Diary 1937–1943*, London, Phoenix Press, 2002.
23. Ibid.
24. DGFP/D/XII, no. 561.
25. Otto von Bismarck to Foreign Office 11 June 1941, *SCBNG*, no. 23.
26. Malcolm Muggeridge (ed.), *Ciano's Diplomatic Papers*, London, Odhams Press, 1948, pp. 446–447.
27. Ribbentrop did issue instructions soon, however, for 'contact with the frontier tribes' and the 'establishment of communications with India' to be made. See Ribbentrop to Werner Otto von Hentig, 29 June 1941, DGFP/D/XIII, no. 44.
28. Hauner, p. 361.
29. Bose to Woermann, 5 July 1941, *SCBNG*, no. 25.
30. Minutes of Bose-Woermann meeting, 17 July 1941, DGFP/D/XIII, no. 120.
31. Ibid.
32. Ibid.
33. The transfer of Indian POWs was featured predominantly in the popular German magazine *Signal* (August 1941). See also Gurbachan Singh Mangat, *Indian National Army: Role in India's Struggle for Freedom*, Ludhiana, Gagan Publishers, 1991, p. 33.
34. Hauner, pp. 312, 333. For political and intelligence activities in the area see *TUJ*, nos. 3–6.
35. Pilger to Ribbentrop, 31 July 1941, DGFP/D/XIII, no. 169. This operation was inspired by the recent success of an Italian agent in contacting the Fakir of Ipi. See Pilger to Foreign Office, 14 July 1941, DGFP/D/XIII, no. 107. See also the testimony of the wounded *Abwehr* agent upon his return to Berlin, 7 February 1942, *TUJ*, no. 61.
36. DGFP/D/XIII, no. 169.
37. *Abwehr* note, 30 August 1941, *TUJ*, no. 7.
38. Ibid., Hauner, pp. 332–333.
39. *TUJ*, no. 7.
40. Shedai to Prunas, 4 September 1941, *SCBNG*, no. 29.
41. Ibid., Shedai to Ulrich Doertenbach, 21 September 1941, *SCBNG*, no. 33.
42. 'Detailed Plan of Work', 20 May 1941, *SCBNG*, no. 17.
43. *SCBNG*, no. 29.
44. Ibid., Shedai to Doertenbach, *SCBNG*, no. 33.
45. Ibid.

46. Ibid. See also Vyas, p. 280.
47. One of the greatest myths associated with Bose in Nazi Germany was that he befriended Trott, one of the key conspirators in an attempt to assassinate Hitler in 1944. The attempt to link Trott to Bose was intended to portray the latter in an anti-Nazi light. On Trott's real sentiments for Bose see for example Bose, *The Lost Hero*, pp. 481–482, 502, 566. On Trott see Giles MacDonogh, *A Good German: Adam von Trott zu Solz*, Woodstock, Overlook Press, 1992; Christopher Sykes, *Troubled Loyalty: A Biography of Adam von Trott zu Solz*, Collins, London, 1968.
48. *SCBNG*, no. 29.
49. On Annaburg see Lothar Günther, *Von Indien nach Annaburg: Die Geschichte der Indischen Legion und des Kriegsgefangenlagers in Deutschland*, Berlin, Verlag am Park, 2003, pp. 29–51. On Indian POWs in general see G. J. Douds, 'The Men Who Never Were: Indian POWs in the Second World War', *South Asia: Journal of South Asian Studies*, 2 (2004), 183–216.
50. Compare this for example with the treatment meted out to Soviet POWs. See Michael Burleigh, *The Third Reich: A New History*, London, Macmillan, 2000, pp. 512–516; Richard Overy, *The Dictators: Hitler's Germany and Stalin's Russia*, London, Penguin, 2005, pp. 518–519.
51. *SCBNG*, nos. 29, 33.
52. Ibid., no. 29. Shedai established very cordial relations with the more nationalist inclined officers. See Mangat, *The Tiger Strikes*, pp. 51–54.
53. Ibid., no. 29.
54. 'Joint Declaration by the President and the Prime Minister' in Churchill, vol. 3, pp. 374–375. For the German reaction see Ribbentrop to Hitler, 17 August 1941, DGFP/D/XIII, no. 209 and Ribbentrop circular to German embassies, 26 August 1941, DGFP/D/XIII, no. 244.
55. On 9 September however, Churchill clarified that the Joint Declaration did not apply to India. This was to cause much disappointment and resentment in India. See Anthony Read and David Fisher, *The Proudest Day: India's Long Road to Independence*, London, Pimlico, 1998, p. 308.
56. Bose to Ribbentrop, 15 August 1941, DGFP/D/XIII, no. 213.
57. Woermann to Ribbentrop, 18 August 1941, DGFP/D/XIII, no. 213.
58. Ibid.
59. Ibid.
60. Churchill, vol. 3, p. 408.
61. Ibid., pp. 374–375.
62. Ribbentrop to German embassies, DGFP/D/XIII, no. 244.
63. Woermann minute, 6 September 1941, DGFP/D/XIII, no. 286.

64. Emil von Rintelen to Woermann, 10 September 1941, DGFP/D/XIII, no. 296.
65. Bose to Woermann, 25 September 1941, *SCBNG*, no. 34.
66. Bose to Talwar, 27 September 1941, *TUJ*, no. 16.
67. *SCBNG*, nos. 49, 50, 52.
68. Ibid.
69. Ibid., no. 49.
70. Pilger to Foreign Office, 2 October 1941, *TUJ*, no. 17.
71. Rintelen to Weizsäcker, 16 October 1941, DGFP/D/XIII, no. 404.
72. Hans Georg von Mackensen (Rome) to Foreign Office, 4 October 1941, DGFP/D/XIII, no. 379.
73. For German attempts to involve Shedai with the Indian Legion see Shedai to A. Alessandrini, 4 October 1941, *SCBNG*, no. 36.
74. See Abid Hasan, 'Netaji and the Indian Communal Question', *The Oracle*, 1 (1979), 42–46.
75. Ibid. See also Ganpuley, pp. 41–42.
76. M. J. Akbar, *Nehru: The Making of India*, London, Viking, 1988, pp. 467–468; Ganpuley, p. 37.
77. Edward S. Haynes, 'Subhas Chandra Bose and the Early Azad Hind Sangh: April–November 1941' in Verinder Grover (ed.), *Political Thinkers of Modern India*, vol. 6 (Subhash Chandra Bose), New Delhi, Deep & Deep, 1991, p. 417.
78. Bose, *A Beacon Across Asia*, p. 110.
79. On the Free India Radio see Werth, *Der Tiger Indiens*, pp. 135–137.
80. Goebbels' diary, 26 March and 6 April 1942.
81. Helmut Heiber, *Goebbels*, New York, Da Capo Press, 1972, pp. 279–280. Goebbels' control of propaganda was in many ways severely limited. See Z. A. B. Zeman, *Nazi Propaganda*, London, Oxford University Press, 1964, p. 160–161.
82. Bose, *A Beacon Across Asia*, pp. 108–111; Ganpuley, pp. 47–59.
83. Ibid., Bose, p. 108; Werth, *Der Tiger Indiens*, p. 134.
84. Gordon, p. 454. See also Hauner, p. 374.
85. HC Deb, 27 November 1941, vol. 376, pp. 879–80, London, Hansard; Nanda Mookerjee, *Subhas Chandra Bose: The British Press, Intelligence and Parliament*, Calcutta, Jayasree Prakashan, 1981, p. 134.
86. 'India's Quisling no. 1 Flees to Hitler', the *Daily Mail*, 11 November 1941.
87. One of Bose's biographers, however, alleges that Bose and Joyce played chess together but without providing evidence. See Bose, *The Lost Hero*, p. 497.
88. Ribbentrop to Hitler, 13 November 1941, DGFP/D/XIII, no. 468.
89. Ibid.

90. Minutes of Bose-Ribbentrop meeting, 29 November 1941, DGFP/D/XIII, no. 521.
91. Ibid.
92. Ibid.
93. Ibid.
94. Ibid. One source of information was Shedai who informed the German ambassador in Rome that the Counsellor of the Japanese embassy had reported that Japan's entry into the war was 'imminent'. Shedai's intention was not so much to help the Germans as it was to hasten the declaration on India. See Mackensen to Foreign Office, 1 December 1941, DGFP/D/XIII, no. 526.

3. TRIPLING THE EFFECT: BERLIN, ROME, TOKYO

1. Hauner, p. 414.
2. This resulted in agreement that the departments of the Foreign Office and the Italian Foreign Ministry specialising in India would henceforth exchange information and co-ordinate their activities. *SCBNG*, no. 43.
3. Minutes of the conference, 11 December 1941, *SCBNG*, no. 44; Hartog, p. 51
4. DGFP/D/XIII, no. 526.
5. *SCBNG*, no. 44.
6. Hartog, p. 50.
7. *SCBNG*, no. 44.
8. Ibid., Hartog, p. 51.
9. Woermann memorandum, 18 December 1941, *SCBNG*, no. 46.
10. Ibid. Bose had already been in regular contact with the Japanese embassy for several months. See the reminiscences of the assistant Japanese military attaché in Berlin, Colonel Yamamoto in T. R Sareen (ed.), *Forgotten Images: Reflections and Reminiscences of Subhas Chandra Bose*, New Delhi, S. S. Publishers, 1997, pp. 95–99. The embassy also served as a conduit between Bose and his family via the Japanese Consulate in Calcutta. See Bose, *The Great Escape*, pp. 57–58.
11. *SCBNG*, no. 46. See also *Akten zur deutschen auswärtigen Politik 1918–1945* (hereafter: ADAP) Series E (1941–1945), vol. I, Göttingen, Vandenhoeck & Ruprecht, 1969, no. 84.
12. See Oshima's reminiscences in Sareen, *Forgotten Images*, pp. 261–262.
13. Georg Thomas to Foreign Office, 18 December 1941, *TUJ*, no. 44; *SCBNG*, no. 45. This followed an already extensive report on Indian politics. See Thomas to Foreign Office, 16 December 1941, *TUJ*, no. 43.
14. Shedai to Doertenbach, 22 December 1941 quoted in Hauner, 415.

15. Ganpuley, p. 69.
16. Abid Hassan Safrani, 'A Soldier Remembers', *The Oracle*, 1 (1984), 24–65; Mangat, *The Tiger Strikes*, pp. 75–76; Hartog, pp. 53–54.
17. Ibid. See also British 'Secret Note on the HIFs (Hitler Inspired Indian Fifth Column)', 31 August 1943, *SCBNG*, no. 89; 'Indian Political Intelligence Section's Report on Indian Prisoners of War in Germany and Italy', 23 April 1943, *SCBNG*, no. 85.
18. Two of Bose's most intensely hagiographical biographers are forced to concede that the atmosphere was 'lukewarm' at best. See John Jacob and Harindra Srivastava, *Netaji Subhas: The Tallest of Titans*, New Delhi, Ess Ess Publications, 2000, p. 176.
19. Ganpuley, pp. 69–70.
20. *SCBNG*, no. 89.
21. There is little doubt that had Bose known about this he would have protested vigorously.
22. Hartog, p. 54.
23. Ganpuley, p. 76.
24. On the evolution of the Indian Legion see Günther, pp. 53–115; A. V. Raikov, 'Indian Legion in Germany' and Subhash Chandra Chatterjee, 'The Indian Legion—The First Revolutionary Army of India's Freedom' in Ratna Ghosh (ed.), *Netaji Subhas Chandra Bose and Indian Freedom Struggle*, vol. 2, New Delhi, Deep & Deep, 2006, pp. 13–36.
25. The significance of 1942 is elaborately discussed in Milan Hauner, '1942: The Decisive War Year in India's Destiny', *The Oracle*, 1 (1986), 36–44.
26. Goebbels' diary, 27 January and 12 March 1942; Willi A. Boelcke (ed.), *The Secret Conferences of Dr Goebbels: The Nazi Propaganda War 1939–43*, New York, E. P. Dutton & Co., 1970, p. 198.
27. Hitler's Table Talk, 5 January 1942, no. 94; 7 January 1942, no. 99; 12–13 January 1942, no. 105; 6 February 1942, no. 141.
28. See A. C. N. Nambiar, 'A Memorable Meeting in Paris with Netaji Subhas Chandra Bose', *The Oracle*, 1 (1982), 61–62. See also Nambiar interview in *SCBNG*, Appendix VII, pp. 434–448.
29. Bose to Nambiar, 9 January 1942, *SCBNG*, no. 53.
30. Ibid.
31. Girija K. Mookerjee, *Europe at War 1938–1946: Impressions of War, Netaji and Europe*, Meerut, Meenakshi Prakashan, 1968, p. 192.
32. Ibid., p. 194.
33. Ibid., p. 195.
34. Ibid., pp. 194–195.
35. Ibid, p. 195.
36. Ibid., p. 196.
37. Ibid.

38. Ibid., pp. 196–197.
39. Ibid.
40. Minutes of the *Abwehr* meeting, 28 January 1942, *SCBNG*, no. 57.
41. Mackensen to Foreign Office, 15 January 1942, *SCBNG*, no. 56.
42. *SCBNG*, no. 57.
43. Hauner, p. 444.
44. Minutes of the *Abwehr* meeting, 6 February 1942, *TUJ*, no. 58. See also nos. 59–60; Hauner, p. 422.
45. See Harbich, pp. 43–50.
46. Chiang Kai-shek's attempt at mediation placed the British in a very awkward political position. See Llewellyn Woodward, *British Foreign Policy in the Second World War*, London, Her Majesty's Stationary Office, 1962, pp. 421–423.
47. Maulana Abul Kalam Azad, *India Wins Freedom*, New Delhi, Orient Longman, 1997, p. 42.
48. Ibid., pp. 42–43.
49. Churchill to Linlithgow, 3 February 1942, in Nicholas Mansergh (ed.), *Constitutional Relations between Britain and India: The Transfer of Power 1942-7* (hereafter: TOP), vol. I (*The Cripps Mission January–April 1942*), London, Her Majesty's Stationary Office, 1970, no. 63. Churchill used exactly the same phrase in his memoirs. See *The Second World War*, vol. 4 (*The Hinge of Fate*), p. 179.
50. Churchill to Chiang Kai-shek, 12 February 1942, TOP/1, no. 104.
51. When Bose first met Ribbentrop he admitted that Indians sided with China in the Sino-Japanese war. See minutes of the Bose-Ribbentrop meeting, 1 May 1941, DGFP/D/XII, no. 425.
52. Bose press conference, Tokyo, 19 June 1943 in *Selected Speeches of Subhas Chandra Bose*, New Delhi, Government of India, 1992, p. 174.
53. Churchill, vol. 4, p. 80.
54. Tojo statement in the Imperial Diet quoted in Das and Subbaiah, pp. 11–12.
55. Bose to Woermann, 17 February 1942, *SCBNG*, no. 58.
56. Ibid.
57. Ribbentrop to Eugen Ott, 21 February 1942, ADAP/E/I, no. 266.
58. Ibid.
59. Hauner, p. 426.
60. German Tripartite declaration on India, 22 February 1942, *SCBNG*, no. 61. The date in *SCBNG* is incorrect.
61. Nevertheless, the Viceroy did not believe that the occupation of the Andaman islands, which shortly followed, had much impact in India. See Linlithgow to Leopold Amery (Secretary of State for India), 31 March 1942, TOP/1, no. 474.

NOTES pp. [87–95]

62. Trott memorandum, 26 February 1942, ADAP/E/I, no. 292; Hauner, pp. 431–432.
63. Bose's views appeared to be validated a few weeks later in a 'Brief Note on Subversive Activity for the Fortnight Ending April 28th, 1942' which warned of spreading 'despondency and defeatism'. See Maurice Hallet (Governor of United Provinces) to Linlithgow, 4 May 1942, TOP/2, no. 16.
64. Hauner, p. 432.
65. Karl Megerle memorandum, 26 February 1942, ADAP/E/I, no. 289; Hauner, p. 430.
66. Bose broadcast, 28 February 1942, *SCBNG*, no. 59; NCW/11 (*Azad Hind: Writings and Speeches 1941–1943*), no. 12. The date of broadcast in these sources is incorrect.
67. Ibid.
68. Bose's Free India government eventually declared war on Britain and the United States on 24 October 1943. See NCW/12 (*Chalo Delhi: Writings and Speeches 1943–1945*), no. 26.
69. *SCBNG*, no. 59; NCW/11, no. 12.
70. Goebbels' diary, 2 March 1942.
71. Azad, pp. 39–40.
72. Hitler's Table Talk, 27 March 1942, no. 175.
73. Vyas, p. 357–358.
74. Goebbels' diary, 1 March 1942.
75. Ibid., 2 March 1942.
76. Ibid., 4 March 1942.
77. Hauner, p. 436.

4. OFFENSIVE FROM BERLIN: THE CRIPPS MISSION

1. Goebbels' diary, 13 March 1942.
2. Bose broadcast, 13 March 1942, *SCBNG*, no. 63.
3. Ibid.
4. Ibid.
5. Ravindra Kumar (ed.), *The Selected Works of Subhas Chandra Bose* (hereafter: SWSCB), vol. 1, New Delhi, Atlantic, 1992, nos. 84, 85; Jacob and Srivatava, p. 167.
6. Mohandas Gandhi to Prabhabati Bose, 29 March 1942, CWMG/75, no. 538; SWSCB/1, no. 86. See also Azad, p. 40.
7. Azad to the Associated Press, 29 March 1942, SWSCB/1, no. 82.
8. Bose broadcast, 25 March 1942, *Selected Speeches of Subhas Chandra Bose*, p. 120.

9. Ibid., pp. 120–123.
10. Linlithgow to Halifax, 27 March 1942, TOP/1, no. 401.
11. See Amery to Linlithgow, 8 March 1942, TOP/1, no. 280.
12. Nehru had already been annoyed by Gandhi's condolence telegram to Bose's mother. See Bose, *The Lost Hero*, p. 536. One of Nehru's biographers, however, claims that he did write a condolence message along with Gandhi but does not provide any source. See Akbar, p. 339.
13. Azad and Gandhi to Bose, 30 March 1942, CWMG/75, no. 542; SWSCB/1, no. 83.
14. Bhim Sen Singh, *The Cripps Mission: A Handiwork of British Imperialism*, New Delhi, Usha Publications, 1979, pp. 62–64.
15. 'Note by Sir S. Cripps', 25 March 1942, TOP/1, no. 380.
16. Gandhi quoted in Read and Fisher, p. 317; D. G. Tendulkar, *Mahatma: Life of Mohandas Karamchand Gandhi*, vol. 6 (1940–1945), New Delhi, Government of India, p. 72; Louis Fischer, *The Life of Mahatma Gandhi*, New Delhi, HarperCollins, 2000, p. 448. Cripps makes no mention of this in his summary of the meeting for the Foreign Office. See 'Note by Sir S. Cripps. My Interview with Mahatma Gandhi', 27 March 1942, TOP/1, no. 397. See also Cripps' statements at a Ministry of Information press conference upon his return to London, 22 April 1942, TOP/1, no. 665.
17. Azad, p. 51.
18. R. J. Moore, *Churchill, Cripps and India 1939–45*, Oxford, Clarendon Press, 1979, p. 93.
19. Azad, p. 40.
20. Bose broadcast, 31 March 1942, Bose, NCW/11, no. 17; *Selected Speeches of Subhas Chandra Bose*, pp. 124–125.
21. Goebbels' diary, 26 March 1942.
22. Cripps to Churchill, 1 April 1942, TOP/1, no. 484.
23. Tojo statement in the Imperial Diet, quoted in Hauner, p. 438.
24. Gandhi quoted in Read and Fisher, p. 319.
25. Bose broadcast, 6 April 1942, *Selected Speeches of Subhas Chandra Bose*, pp. 127–128; NCW/11, no. 18.
26. Ibid.
27. Cripps to War Cabinet, 10 April 1942, TOP/1, no. 577; Churchill to Cripps, 10 April 1942, TOP/1, no. 582.
28. Linlithgow quoted in Patrick French, *Liberty or Death: India's Journey to Independence and Division*, New Delhi, HarperCollins, 1998, p. 142.
29. Goebbels' diary, 13 April 1942.
30. This was a view also shared by the British. Amery accused Gandhi of 'wrecking the Cripps Mission' but at the same time conceded that 'it may have been the best thing in the long run'. See Amery to Linlithgow, 9 July 1942, TOP/2, no. 241.

31. Azad, p. 40.
32. Ibid.
33. Hauner, p. 477.
34. French, p. 144.
35. It is also questionable as to what extent the cabinet itself was committed to securing a compromise. See B. R. Tomlinson, *The Indian National Congress and the Raj 1929–1942: The Penultimate Phase*, London, Macmillan Press, 1976, p. 156.
36. Amery to Linlithgow, 26 November 1941, quoted in Hauner, p. 363. This was a view echoed by Nehru who conceded that Churchill was a 'brilliant leader' but that 'his mind is the Victorian mind'. See Nehru speech in Calcutta, 22 February 1942 in J. S. Bright (ed.), *Before and After Independence: A Collection of the Most Important and Soul-Stirring Speeches delivered by Jawaharlal Nehru*, New Delhi, The Indian Printing Works, p. 217.
37. Churchill to Linlithgow, 10 March 1942, TOP/1, no. 294; Amery to Linlithgow, 10 March 1942, TOP/1, no. 304; 10 June 1942, TOP/2, no. 138. See also Auriol Weigold, *Churchill, Roosevelt and India: Propaganda during World War II*, London, Routledge, 2008, p. 42.
38. Churchill to Cripps, 11 April 1942, TOP/1, no. 597. Churchill's prognosis was premature. See War Cabinet Paper, 'India as a Factor in Anglo-American Relations. Note by the Lord Privy Seal', 27 July 1942, TOP/2, no. 339.
39. Churchill to Clement Attlee (Deputy Prime Minister), 7 January 1942, TOP/1, no. 6.
40. Churchill to Roosevelt, 13 August 1942, TOP/2, no. 532. Churchill made a similar claim on 26 August in a letter to Chiang Kai-shek. See Amery to Linlithgow, 27 August 1942, TOP/2, no. 637.
41. Nehru press conference, 12 April 1942, quoted in Gordon, pp. 477–478; B. N. Pande (ed.), *A Centenary History of the Indian National Congress 1885–1985*, New Delhi, All India Congress Committee, 1985. vol. III (1935–1947), p. 512.
42. Nehru's speech in Calcutta, 19 April 1942, Bright, p. 220.
43. See for example Nehru's speeches in Calcutta (19 April 1942) and Jhansi (29 May 1942) in Bright, pp. 222–226.
44. Henry Twynam (Governor of Central Provinces and Berar) to Linlithgow, 30 April 1942, TOP/1, no. 710; Hallett to Linlithgow, 13 April 1942, TOP/1, no. 620; 4 May 1942, TOP/2, no. 16.
45. Bose broadcast, 13 April 1942, NCW/11, no. 19.
46. Ibid.
47. Linlithgow to Amery, 9 April 1942, TOP/1, no. 559.
48. Singh, pp. 65–69.

49. Churchill to Cripps, 9 April 1942, TOP/1, no. 564.
50. Linlithgow to Amery, 27 May 1942, TOP/2, no. 91; Singh, p. 74. A few days after receiving Linlithgow's dispatch, Amery wrote to Churchill stating 'this fellow Johnson is rather too much of a good thing. Is it at all possible to prevent his return to India?' 29 May 1942, TOP/2, no. 101. Churchill responded positively asking Roosevelt's adviser Harry Hopkins to prevent the return of Johnson to India as this would interfere with British plans to assist the 'vast mass of helpless Indians from imminent invasion'. See Churchill to Hopkins, 31 May 1942, TOP/2, no. 112.
51. NCW/11, no. 19.
52. Ibid.
53. Nehru's press conference, Gauhati, 24 April 1942, quoted in Gordon, p. 477.

5. SUSTAINING THE OFFENSIVE: POLITICS, INTELLIGENCE AND PROPAGANDA

1. Ciano's diary, 14 April 1942. See also Johannes Voigt, *India in the Second World War*, New Delhi, Arnold-Heinemann, 1987, p. 132.
2. To complicate matters the draft constituted a joint declaration on India and Arabia. Hauner, p. 477.
3. Ibid., p. 478.
4. Ibid.
5. Ibid., p. 479. There was good reason for the Japanese to be annoyed. See Ciano's diary, 21 April 1942.
6. Ibid., 29 April–2 May 1942.
7. Hitler quoted in Hauner, p. 479.
8. Ibid.
9. Ibid., p. 480. See also Ciano's diary, 3 May 1942.
10. Ibid., 4 May 1942.
11. Ibid.
12. Ibid., 3 May 1942.
13. Vyas, p. 368.
14. Ciano's diary, 5 May 1942.
15. Ibid.
16. Ibid.
17. Hauner, p. 482.
18. Ibid., pp. 482–484.
19. Goebbels' diary, 11 May 1942.
20. Ibid.
21. Bose broadcast, *SCBNG*, no. 64; NCW/11, no. 20.

22. Ibid.
23. Ibid.
24. Ibid.
25. Ibid.
26. Hauner, p. 512.
27. Ibid., pp. 500–501.
28. Keppler to Kabul, 20 April 1942, *TUJ*, no. 80. See also Hauner, p. 481.
29. Indian Political Intelligence noted with barely concealed amusement that 'the world at large, perhaps more than the Nazis themselves, should be interested to know that large sums of Nazi money had been paid to further the grandiose schemes of Subhas Chandra Bose which turned out to be nothing more than paper schemes drafted by Indian communists with their tongues in their cheeks who saw an easy way to make money'. See Bose, *The Lost Hero*, p. 589.
30. Bose to Ribbentrop, 22 May 1942, *SCBNG*, no. 65; NCW/11, no. 21.
31. Hauner, pp. 483–484.
32. Ibid, p. 484.
33. Minutes of the Bose-Hitler meeting, *SCBNG*, no. 66; NCW/11, no. 22
34. Ibid.
35. Ibid.
36. Ibid.
37. For the 'Free India' reaction to the meeting see J. K Banerji, 'Subhas Chandra Bose's Meeting with the German Führer', *The Oracle*, 3 (1995), 27–29. A deliberately flawed and distorted account of the meeting, which has served as the basis for many others, is to be found in Werth, *Der Tiger Indiens*, pp. 142–143.
38. Nambiar interview in *SCBNG*, p. 446.
39. Bose memorandum, 11 June 1942, *SCBNG*, no. 67.
40. Ibid.
41. Gandhi for once was not particularly impressed now describing Bose as 'misguided'. See CWMG/76, 12 June 1942, no. 253; Linlithgow to Amery, 22 June 1942, TOP/2, no. 173.
42. Bose press conference, Berlin, 12 June 1942, *SCBNG*, no. 68.
43. Ibid.
44. Ibid.
45. For Ribbentrop's message see *SCBNG*, no. 69.
46. Bose to Bangkok delegates, 15 June 1942, NCW/11, no. 25.
47. French, p. 150.
48. Read and Fisher, p. 326.
49. The American Consul in Bombay, Howard Donavan, for one claimed in a report to the State Department in Washington on 21 May 1942, that Gandhi was worried that Bose's broadcasts would challenge his suprem-

acy in India. See M. S. Venkataramani and B. K. Shrivastava, *Quit India: The American Response to the 1942 Struggle*, New Delhi, Vikas Publishing House, 1979, pp. 152, 196.
50. Read and Fisher, p. 327.
51. See for example Hallet to Linlithgow, 10 May 1942, TOP/2, no. 43. Linlithgow himself described Gandhi's attitude as 'pro-Japanese'. See Linlithgow to Amery, 29 May 1942, TOP/2, no. 102. Linlithgow would soon describe the 'Congress way' as the 'Axis way'. See Linlithgow to Amery, 27 June 1942, TOP/2, no. 190. In a note to Churchill referring to Gandhi and the Congress leaders, Amery wrote 'we are dealing with men who are now definitely our enemies'. See Amery to Churchill, 13 July 1942, TOP/2, no. 256.
52. Churchill quoted in French, p. 166.
53. Ibid., p. 170.
54. Bose broadcast, 17 June 1942, *SCBNG*, no. 70; NCW/11, no. 26.
55. Ibid.
56. The matter was discussed during a meeting between Ribbentrop and Oshima on 24 June. See the minutes in ADAP/E/III, no. 35.
57. Hauner, p. 488–489.
58. Ibid., p. 583. For conditions in the camp see Harbich, pp. 46–49.
59. Harbich, pp. 47.
60. That is not to suggest that they were immune from the corroding effects of Nazi ideology along with other Wehrmacht troops, albeit, more visibly so on the eastern front. On this general issue affecting Wehrmacht troops see Omer Bartov, *Hitler's Army: Soldiers, Nazis and War in the Third Reich*, New York, Oxford University Press, 1992, p. 137. The full impact of serving in 'Hitler's Army' on the Indian Legionaries would become evident during the summer of 1944 in France.
61. Bose was firm about excluding religious manifestations within the Indian Legion. See Hasan, 'Netaji and the Indian Communal Question' pp. 44–45.
62. Bose to Rash Behari Bose, *SCBNG*, no. 71.
63. Ibid.
64. Ibid.
65. Bose was not alone in these efforts. See Ganpuley, pp. 83–86.
66. Mackensen to Foreign Office, 20 October 1942, quoted in Hauner, p. 582.
67. Even before Bose's arrival in Rome, the Japanese were already working to oust Shedai. See the minutes of the Ribbentrop-Oshima meeting of 24 June in ADAP/E/III, No 35.

NOTES pp. [125–130]

6. TRANSITION TO TOKYO: *I-30* TO *U-180*

1. Vyas, p. 379. See also Peter Padfield, *Himmler: Reichsführer-SS*, London, Cassell, 2001, pp. 91–92; Jan Kuhlmann, *Subhas Chandra Bose und die Indienpolitik der Achsenmächte*, Berlin, Verlag Hans Schiler, 2003, p. 46.
2. Vyas, pp. 379–380.
3. Walter Schellenberg, *Hitler's Secret Service: Memoirs of Walter Schellenberg*, New York, Pyramid Books, 1971, p. 254.
4. Vyas, pp. 380, 481, 508. Himmler's foreign intelligence service attached to the Reich Security Main Office eventually developed its own intelligence plans for India. See Reinhard R. Doerries, *Hitler's Last Chief of Foreign Intelligence: Allied Interrogations of Walter Schellenberg*, London, Frank Cass, 2003, pp. 79, 213.
5. Vyas, p. 380.
6. Peter Witte (ed.), *Der Dienstkalender Heinrich Himmlers 1941/42*, Hamburg, Christians, 1999, p. 490.
7. Boelcke, p. 263.
8. Ibid.
9. Goebbels' diary, 6, 20 April 1942.
10. Boelcke, p. 263.
11. Goebbels' Indian propaganda was increasingly unconvincing as the war went on and was not a success with the German public. This is alluded to in an extensive SS Security Service morale report to the Party Chancellery of 29 November 1943 in Jeremy Noakes (ed.), *Nazism 1919–1945*, vol. 4 *(The German Home Front in World War II)* Exeter, University of Exeter, 1998; p. 550; David Welch, *The Third Reich: Politics and Propaganda*, London, Routledge, 2002, p. 211.
12. Bose to Ribbentrop, 23 July 1942, *SCBNG*, no. 73.
13. Ibid. One week later, Ribbentrop brought up the matter with Oshima. See the minutes of their conversation in ADAP/E/III, no. 142.
14. Hauner, p. 489.
15. Ibid. See also Bose, *A Beacon Across Asia*, p. 120.
16. Hauner, p. 547. See also ADAP/E/III, no. 198.
17. Pande, p. 539.
18. Bose 'The Situation in India', *The Oracle*, 4 (1995) 42–50; NCW/11, no. 27.
19. Ibid.
20. Bose 'Free India and her Problems' in NCW/11, no. 30.
21. Ibid.
22. On Bose's preoccupation with Hindustani as a means of enforcing national unity see Suniti Kumar Chatterjea, 'Netaji, National Unity, the Language Question and the Roman Script', *The Oracle*, 1 (1979), 9–17.

23. NCW/11, no. 30.
24. Ibid.
25. Hartog, pp, 60; Hauner, p. 584–585.
26. Hauner, p. 585.
27. Gandhi quoted in Read and Fisher, p. 328.
28. Gandhi was not only speaking symbolically. Before launching the 'Quit India' campaign, he had secretly dispatched a messenger to warn Linlithgow that he would not call off his campaign unlike in the past even if violence ensued as this would be 'doing greater violence to the ideals for which he was working'. See Linlithgow to Amery, 18 July 1942, TOP/2, no. 286.
29. Gandhi was particularly annoyed over the preferential treatment meted out to him. See Joseph Boyd Irwin (Secretary to Governor of Bombay) to Sir Gilbert Laithwaite (Secretary to the Viceroy) 12 August 1942, TOP/2, no. 515.
30. Linlithgow to Amery, 15 June 1942, TOP/2, no. 148; Amery to Linlithgow, 17 June 1942, TOP/2, no. 154; Linlithgow to Amery, 19 July 1942, TOP/2, no. 288; Amery to Linlithgow, 24 July 1942, TOP/2, no. 323. The proposed deportation to Africa was, if not swiftly then vigorously, opposed by several Governors. See Sir Roger Lumley (Governor of Bombay) to Linlithgow, 28 July 1942, TOP/2, no. 343; Hallett to Linlithgow, 28 July 1942, TOP/2, no. 344; Sir Thomas Stewart (Governor of Bihar) to Linlithgow, 28 July 1942, TOP/2, no. 346. See also the earlier pre-emptive War Cabinet Paper 'Policy to be Adopted Towards Mr. Gandhi' on the need for possible 'repressive measures', 16 June 1942, TOP/2, no. 150.
31. On 'Quit India' see Francis G. Hutchins, *Spontaneous Revolution: The Quit India Movement*, Manohar Book Service, Delhi 1971; K. K. Chaudhari, *Quit India Revolution: The Ethos of its Central Direction*, Mumbai, Popular Parakashan, 1996; Y. B. Mathur, *Quit India Movement*, Delhi, Pragati Publications, 1979; A. Moin Zaidi, *The Way Out to Freedom: An Inquiry into the Quit India Movement Conducted by Participants*, New Delhi, Orientalia, 1973.
32. Linlithgow nevertheless dispatched numerous optimistic-sounding reports to London. See Linlithgow to Amery, 11 August 1942, TOP/2, no. 509; 12 August 1942, TOP/2, no. 511; 1 September 1942, TOP/2, nos. 667, 672. He described the rioters and protesters as 'hooligans'. On other occasions he could be slightly more generous describing them as 'students and riff-raff'. See Linlithgow to Amery, 14, 15 August 1942, TOP/2, nos. 544, 556.
33. For the situation in Delhi for example see British report 'Extremely Serious Situation in Delhi', 10 August 1942, in P. N. Chopra (ed.), *Quit*

India Movement: British Secret Documents, New Delhi, Interprint, 1986, no. 8.
34. Ibid., nos. 31, 49. See also Government of India (Home Department) to Amery, 5 September 1942, TOP/2, no. 698.
35. Hauner, p. 538.
36. French, p. 159; Linlithgow to Amery, 15 August 1942, TOP/2, no. 555. The potentially embarrassing issue of whipping was raised in a cabinet meeting on 12 August. See minutes in TOP/2, no. 521. The next day Amery expressed concern over the issue to Linlithgow fearing it might have an 'adverse effect in America'. See Amery to Linlithgow, 13 August 1942, TOP/2, no. 528. Lumley, the Governor of Bombay, was dismissive, however, of such concerns, describing whipping as a 'minor detail'. See Lumley to Linlithgow, 14 August 1942, TOP/2, no. 549.
37. Kennedy quoted in Lawrence James, *Raj: The Making and Unmaking of British India*, London, Abacus, 1998, pp. 564–565. Nevertheless, machine-gunning from the air was only resorted to in extremely rare and exceptional circumstances. See Government of India (Home Department) to Amery, 5 September 1942, TOP/2, no. 698.
38. Linlithgow to Churchill, 31 August 1942, TOP/2, no. 662.
39. See 'Brief Note on Subversive Activity in the United Provinces', 21 September 1942, in Chopra, no. 86. The British suspected Axis involvement in the 'Quit India' campaign but in the end discovered no conclusive evidence of any links. See 'War Cabinet Paper. India Connection of Enemy Agencies with the Recent Disturbances. Memorandum by the Secretary of State', 14 October 1942, TOP/3, no. 94.
40. Chopra, 27 September 1942, no. 106.
41. French, p. 159.
42. Linlithgow described the incident as 'shocking business'. See Linlithgow to Amery, 17 August 1942, TOP/2, no. 577.
43. Churchill quoted in French, p. 161; James, p. 567.
44. Bose had discussed the matter, however, a few days before 'Quit India' was launched. See Trott memorandum, 4 August 1942, ADAP/E/III, no. 155.
45. Hauner, p. 547.
46. For different, at times conflicting, versions of Bose's broadcasts, particularly in regard to dates, see NCW/11, nos. 28–29, 17 and 31 August 1942; *Selected Speeches of Subhas Chandra Bose*, 31 August 1942, pp. 142–148; SCBNG, no. 75, 31 August 1942; Mathur, pp. 39–40. See also Bose's broadcast of 4 September 1942 in W. J. West (ed.), *Orwell: The War Commentaries*, London, British Broadcasting Corporation, 1985, pp. 230–235.
47. Ibid.

48. Ibid.
49. Ibid.
50. For example in a radio message to Gandhi on 6 July 1944, Bose addressed him as 'Father of our Nation' while asking for his 'blessings and good wishes'. See Bose, NCW/12, no. 43. Gandhi in turn had already described Bose as a 'patriot of patriots' in an interview with the American journalist Louis Fischer. See CWMG/76, Appendix V: Interview with Louis Fischer, 6 June 1942. He even adopted the war cry, 'Jai Hind', originally used by Indian Legionaries. See CWMG/82 nos. 526, 559. On 15 February 1946, he stated: 'The hypnotism of the Indian National Army has cast its spell upon us. Netaji's name is one to conjure with. His patriotism is second to none... His bravery shines through all his actions'. See CWMG/83, no. 143.
51. For his address on that occasion see NCW/11, no. 31.
52. Bose to Schenkl, 15 September 1942, NCW/7, pp. 218–219.
53. A parallel development occurred among Indian POWs in Southeast Asia as well. See Tarak Barkawi, 'Culture and Combat in the Colonies: The Indian Army in the Second World War', *Journal of Contemporary History*, 2 (2006), 325–355.
54. Hartog, p. 63; Mangat, *The Tiger Strikes*, pp. 123–125; Ganpuley, p. 96.
55. Abid Hasan, 'With Netaji in the U-Boat: Before and After' in Madan Gopal (ed.), *Netaji Subhas Chandra Bose: The Last Phase in his Own Words*, New Delhi, Har-Anand, 1994, p. 221; Vyas, pp. 387–388.
56. Mangat, pp. 124–125.
57. Ibid., pp. 125–126.
58. Keppler to Kabul, 16 September 1942, *TUJ*, no. 98.
59. The North-West Frontier was remarkably calm as it had been for many months and would continue to be throughout the 'Quit India' campaign. See Sir George Cunningham (Governor of the North-West Frontier Province) to Linlithgow, 9 June, 8 and 25 July, 28 September 1942, TOP/2 and 3, nos. 135, 237, 326, 43. Linlithgow soon noted that Japanese intelligence infiltration from Burma was not matched by a similar German effort from Afghanistan where the Axis legations were 'concerned mainly with collection of intelligence about India and extending their influence with the tribes'. See Linlithgow to Amery, 24 October 1942, TOP/3, no. 117.
60. Minutes of the Ribbentrop-Bose meeting, 16 October 1942 in Hartog, pp. 102–106.
61. Ibid.
62. Besides police training, Bose also wanted Indians to be trained as sailors and pilots. See Toye, p. 78; Bose to Foreign Office, 8 June 1943, *SCBNG*, no. 87.

63. Ganpuley, p. 108; Hauner, p. 559; Kuhlmann, p. 262.
64. Bose to Schenkl, NCW/7, pp. 220–221.
65. Hauner, p. 585.
66. Hartog, p. 62.
67. It has been suggested that the source may have been clandestine anti-Hitler elements operating within the *Abwehr*. See Sitanshu Das, *Subhas: A Political Biography*, New Delhi, Rupa, 2001, pp. 544, 546.
68. Bose to Schenkl, 5 November 1942, NCW/7, pp. 223–224.
69. British Combined Services Division and Interrogation Centre report, 25 January 1944, *SCBNG*, no. 94.
70. Shedai to d'Ajeta, 24 October 1942, *SCBNG*, no. 77.
71. Bose to Ribbentrop, 5 December 1942, *SCBNG*, no. 78; NCW/11, no. 33.
72. See Woermann to Ribbentrop, 14 January 1943, *SCBNG*, no. 80.
73. For conflicting dates and minor discrepancies regarding this broadcast see NCW/11, no. 34, 7 December 1942; *SCBNG*, no. 79, 22 December 1942.
74. NCW/11, no. 36.
75. Bose to Bose, 8 February 1943, NCW/11, no. 39.
76. Werth, *Der Tiger Indiens*, p. 150.
77. Militärgeschichtliches Forschungsamt (ed.), *Germany and the Second World War*, vol. VII (*The Strategic Air War in Europe and the War in the West and East Asia 1943–1944/5*), Oxford, Clarendon Press, 2006, pp. 731–733.
78. Hitler quoted in Warlimont, p. 511. He was referring specifically to Indian National Army troops.
79. On this controversy which persists in India see Hugh Purcell, 'Subhas Chandra Bose: The Afterlife of India's Fascist Leader', *History Today*, 11 (2010), 45–51.

7. EPILOGUE: INDO-NAZI COLLABORATION

1. On the long and troubled relationship between Bose and Gandhi see Buddhadeva Bhattacharya, 'Gandhi and Subhas' in Muchkund Dubey (ed.), *Subhas Chandra Bose: The Man and his Vision*, New Delhi, Har-Anand, 1998, pp. 25–52.
2. Akbar, p. 368. Nehru defended troops he had once ironically described as a 'dummy force under Japanese control'. See Nehru press conference, Delhi, 12 April 1942 quoted in Gopal, *Jawaharlal Nehru*, p. 289. Even the British radical left-wing press responded with surprise to Nehru's stance. The *Tribune* for example on 8 February 1946 commented with bewilderment: 'Pandit Jawaharlal Nehru's sponsoring and participation in the defence of the

three leaders of the Indian National Army, led by Subhas Chandra Bose, has puzzled a good many of India's friends in this country'. Quoted in Gopal, *Netaji Subhas Chandra Bose* p. 241.

3. Gandhi, if he really understood the implications of Bose's actions in Southeast Asia, chose to turn them around to his convenience for on 25 July 1946 he wrote: 'today we worship Netaji Subhas Chandra Bose and his Azad Hind Fauj. We forget that Netaji himself had told his soldiers that on going to India, they must follow the way of non-violence'. See CWMG/85, no. 46. Gandhi uncritically accepted such claims by Indian National Army officers. See also CWMG/83, no. 162, 18 February 1946. Yet Gandhi also assured Louis Fischer that Bose had 'not captured the imagination of the country' and that he personally did 'not encourage the Bose legend'. See Fischer, pp. 547–548.

4. Bose has been described as Nehru's 'only potential rival for Congress leadership' in the post-war period. See Stanley Wolpert, *Nehru: A Tryst with Destiny*, New York, Oxford University Press, 1996, p. 350.

5. On the overall nature of the complex Gandhi-Bose-Nehru relationship see Reba Som, *Gandhi, Bose, Nehru and the Making of the Modern Indian Mind*, New Delhi, Viking, 2004.

6. For typical examples of glossing over Bose's involvement with Nazi Germany see Subhash Chandra Chatterjee, *Subhas Chandra Bose: Man, Mission and Means*, Calcutta, Minerva, 1989, pp. 113–116; R. C. Majumdar, *Struggle for Freedom* (ed.), Bombay, Bharatiya Vidya Bhavan, 1988, pp. 682–683; O. P. Ralhan, *Subhas Chandra Bose: His Struggle for Independence*, Delhi, Raj Publications, 1996, pp. 288–291; Jasobanta Kar, *Subhas Chandra Bose: The Man and his Mind*, Calcutta, Netaji Institute for Asian Studies, 1988.

7. See Mookerjee's chapter 'Anti-Fascist Resistance Leader' in his memoirs *Europe at War: Impressions of War, Netaji and Europe*, pp. 229–246. Also Mookerjee's 'Netaji the Great Resistance Leader', *The Oracle*, 1 (1986), 22–35. For classic examples of revisionism see Werth, *Der Tiger Indiens*, pp. 119–154; 'Planning for Revolution 1941–43' in *A Beacon Across Asia*, pp. 98–121; 'Netaji in Germany', *The Oracle*, 3 & 4 (1996), 14–42; 'An Assessment of Netaji's Policy of Co-operation with the Axis Powers during World War II' in Bose, *Netaji and India's Freedom*, pp. 249–258. See also Gautam Chattopadhyay, *Subhas Chandra Bose, the Indian Leftists and Communists*, New Delhi, People's Publishing House, 1997; N. G. Jog, *In Freedom's Quest: A Biography of Netaji Subhas Chandra Bose*, New Delhi, Orient Longmans, 1969, pp. 200–218; M. R, Vyas, 'Azad Hind Movement in Europe', *The Oracle*, 4 (1985), 15–30. Despite its title, Anirudh Gupta's

NOTES

'Netaji: A Plea for Reassessment before Rehabilitation' falls into a similar trap. See the essay in S. R. Chakravarty and Madan C. Paul (eds), *Netaji Subhas Chandra Bose: Relevance to Contemporary World*, New Delhi, Har-Anand, 2000, pp. 19–27. For an extremely flawed account of Bose's exile in Germany see S. C. Maikap, *Challenge to the Empire: A Study of Netaji*, New Delhi, Government of India, 1993, pp. 17–30.

8. For a more balanced approach see T. R. Sareen, 'Subhas Chandra Bose and Nazi Germany: An Assessment' in Chakravarty and Paul, pp. 140–172.
9. Bose speech at Tokyo University, NCW/12, no. 53; *The Oracle*, 1 (1982), pp. 3–14.
10. Author's interview with Malkiat Singh (Indian Legion), New Delhi, 12 December 1998.
11. The Legion was incorporated into the *Waffen-SS* in 1944. See Mangat, *The Tiger Strikes*, p. 199; Hartog, pp. 159–162.
12. An issue in many ways central to the intentionalism versus functionalism debate on the Third Reich. See Roderick Stackelberg, *Hitler's Germany: Origins, Interpretations, Legacies*, London, Routledge, 1999, pp. 215–217.
13. Gerhard L. Weinberg begins his one thousand page *magnum opus* on the Second World War by attacking Bose and remaining hostile throughout. See *A World at Arms: A Global History of World War II*, Cambridge, Cambridge University Press, 1994, pp. xiii, 231–232, 498, 685, 873.
14. See the Minutes of the Bose-Ribbentrop meeting, DGFP/D/XII, no. 425.
15. K. Hilderbrand, *The Third Reich*, London, Routledge, 1999, p. 55; Hauner, pp. 183–184.
16. See Woermann to Ribbentrop, 14 January 1942, SCBNG, no. 80.
17. Hitler quoted in Martin Gilbert, *Second World War*, London, Phoenix, 1995, p. 199.
18. Goebbels' diary, 3 May 1941.
19. Alan Bullock, *Hitler: A Study in Tyranny*, London, Penguin, 1990, p. 639; William, L. Shirer, *The Rise and Fall of the Third Reich: A History of Nazi Germany*, New York, Simon and Schuster, 1960, pp. 818–819.
20. DGFP/D/XII, no. 553.
21. Hitler has been described as seeing himself as a 'warlord and strategist of rare and outstanding ability'. See Werner Maser, *Hitler*, London, Futura, 1974, p. 270.
22. It was not long before Hitler began to realise the folly of invading the Soviet Union. See Magenheimer, p. 63.
23. See Guy Liddell's diary, 4 August, 4 November 1942, 19 August, 2 September, 5 October 1943, 21 June 1944 in Nigel West (ed.), *The Guy Liddell Diaries: MI5's Director of Counter-Espionage in World War II*, London, Routledge, 2005, vol. 1 (1939–1942), p. 285; vol. 2 (1942–1945), pp. 24–25, 103, 113, 122, 213.

24. Woermann did not directly refer to Bose as a leftist but he made it clear that the Forward Bloc was perceived as such. See Woermann to Ribbentrop, 12 April 1941, DGFP/D/XII, no. 323.
25. Bose was not exclusively dependent on Talwar as there were other agents working for him but their activities were equally limited when it came to subversion. See the recollections of Santimoy Ganguli *et al.*, 'Netaji's Underground in India during World War II: An Account by Participants in a Daring and Historic Undertaking', *The Oracle*, 2 (1979), 7–14; 'Netaji and B. V.', *The Oracle*, 4 (1979), 28–32.
26. Hauner, p. 511.
27. Ibid., p. 479; Minutes of the Bose-Ribbentrop meeting, *SCBNG*, no. 66.
28. Weinberg, p. 232.
29. See the comments Bose made to Nambiar after his meeting with Hitler. *SCBNG*, Appendix VII, p. 446.
30. Minutes of the Bose-Ribbentrop meeting, 29 November 1941. DGFP/D/XIII, no. 521.
31. Anthony Read, *The Devil's Disciples: The Lives and Times of Hitler's Inner Circle*, London, Jonathan Cape, 2003, p. 726; Bloch, pp. 368–369.
32. Hitler's Table Talk, 27 March 1942, no. 175.
33. See for example Fest, *The Face of the Third Reich*, p. 178.
34. Bose to Foreign Office, 18 February 1943, *SCBNG*, no. 81.
35. See Bose to Foreign Office, 8 June 1943, *SCBNG*, no. 87; Vyas, p. 379.
36. See Vyas, pp. 481–482.
37. Ganpuley, p. 108; Hauner, p. 559.
38. Govind Talwalkar, 'Among the Nazis' in B. K. and Shashi Ahluwalia (eds), *Netaji and Indian Independence*, New Delhi, Harnam Publications, 1983, p. 83; Hauner, pp. 588–589. British intelligence reports refer to the attitude and behaviour of Indian Legionaries as 'bestial' although they refrain from specifically blaming the Germans for this conduct. See *SCBNG*, nos. 97–98.
39. Minutes of the Bose-Ribbentrop meeting, 1 May 1941, DGFP/D/XII, no. 425.
40. Goebbels' diary, 20 April 1942.
41. Goebbels even sought to lessen the negative impact of Jewish persecution by playing up British rule in India. See David Irving, *Goebbels: Mastermind of the Third Reich*, London, Focal Point Publications, 1999, p. 723.
42. Most notably Werth. See Bose, *The Lost Hero*, pp. 486–487.
43. Azad, p. 40.
44. Gordon, pp. 6, 491.
45. It has been claimed that Bose 'did not view the totalitarian character and the regime's racial politics of extermination as decisive hallmarks, or he did not want to see them as such'. See Pelinka, p. 182.

46. Bose to Santosh Sen, 31 May 1937, NCW/8, p. 204.
47. Bose broadcast, 25 May 1945, *Selected Speeches of Subhas Chandra Bose*, pp. 249–250.
48. Gordon, p. 487.
49. Ibid., p. 730.
50. Bose to Nehru, 28 March 1939, NCW/9, pp. 193–216; Hauner, 'India's Independence and the Axis Powers', p. 273; Hauner, p. 67; Marshall J. Getz, *Subhas Chandra Bose: A Biography*, Jefferson, McFarland, 2002, p. 47.
51. Although Nehru claimed that 'it was not from the point of view of helping Jews' as much as getting their technical know-how. See Nehru to Bose, 3 April 1939, NCW/9, pp. 217–232.
52. On this issue see Madhusree Mukerjee, *Churchill's Secret War: The British Empire and the Ravaging of India during World War II*, Chennai, Tranquebar, 2010.

BIBLIOGRAPHICAL ESSAY

The following is only intended as a brief guide to relevant published sources on Subhas Chandra Bose, the Third Reich, Indian nationalism and, where appropriate, the Second World War. Full and additional bibliographical details are to be found in the notes.

Documents pertaining to Bose's official dealings with the German government are to be found in *Documents on German Foreign Policy 1918–1945* (London, 1949–1964). Series D (1937–1941) which covers the first part of the concerned period contains crucial notes, telegrams, conference minutes and memorandums written either by the Germans or Bose. Series E, which covers the period from 1941 onwards is available only in German under the title *Akten zur deutschen auswärtigen Politik 1918–1945* (Göttingen, 1969–1979). Even more important and useful is T. R. Sareen's *Subhas Chandra Bose and Nazi Germany* (New Delhi, 1996), which contains not only many of the documents found in the preceding volumes but others as well from Indian, Italian and British archives ranging from War Office intelligence assessments of Nazi attempts to subvert and recruit Indian POWs to Mohammed Iqbal Shedai's correspondence on Bose with Italian officials. These documents were assembled not only with the intention of encouraging further research, but as the foundation from which to develop a monograph. The remainder of German documents on the subject—albeit with an emphasis on intelligence—are to be found in Reimund Schnabel's *Tiger und Schakal: Deutsche Indienpolitik 1941–1943: Ein Dokumentarbericht* (Vienna, 1968).

On Bose himself, there is an abundance of literature, much of it of poor quality. A logical starting place is the twelve volume *Netaji Collected Works* (Calcutta, 1980–2007) edited by Sisir and Sugata Bose. An entire volume, *Azad Hind: Writings and Speeches 1941–1943* (vol. 11, Calcutta, 2002) is devoted to Bose's period in Germany although certain documents are absent. Other pertinent volumes in the collected works include *The Indian Struggle*

SUBHAS CHANDRA BOSE IN NAZI GERMANY

1920–1942 (vol. 2, Calcutta, 1981); *Letters, Articles, Speeches and Statements 1933–1937* (vol. 8, Calcutta, 1994); *Congress President: Speeches, Articles and Letters January 1938–May 1939* (vol. 9, Calcutta, 1995); *The Alternative Leadership: Speeches, Articles, Statements and Letters June 1939–January 1941* (vol. 10, Calcutta, 1998); *Letters to Emilie Schenkl 1934–1942* (vol. 7, Calcutta, 1994) and *Chalo Delhi: Writings and Speeches 1943–1945* (vol. 12, Calcutta, 2007). *Selected Speeches of Subhas Chandra Bose* published by the government of India (New Delhi, 1992; 1st edn, 1962) with an introduction by Bose's former Minister for Publicity and Propaganda, S. A. Ayer, is a useful supplement. The same is true of *The Selected Works of Subhas Chandra Bose* (New Delhi, 1992) edited by Ravindra Kumar in three volumes. Other documents can be found in Nanda Mookerjee, *Subhas Chandra Bose: The British Press, Intelligence and Parliament* (Calcutta, 1981) and O. P. Ralhan, *Subhas Chandra Bose: His Struggle for Independence* (Delhi, 1996). Asoke Nath Bose *Netaji's Letters: To his Nephew* (New Delhi, 1992) provides a valuable insight into Bose's pre-war mind while in exile. This should be supplemented by Asoke Nath Bose's *My Uncle Netaji*, (Bombay, 1989; 1st edn, 1977). Also of importance for this period is Diethelm Weidemann 'Subhas Chandra Bose's Position vis-à-vis Germany before World War II', *Asien Afrika Latinamerika*, 4 (2002), pp. 317–329.

The best biography is undoubtedly Leonard A. Gordon's *Brothers Against the Raj: A Biography of Sarat & Subhas Chandra Bose* (New Delhi, 1990). Deeply humane and compassionate in its approach, the author, however, identifies closely with his subject preventing the emergence at times of a more critical analysis. Mihir Bose's *The Lost Hero: A Biography of Subhas Bose* (Noida, 2004; 1st edn, 1982) is a lively, eminently readable and well-researched book but unfortunately suffers from a practically non-existent reference and citation system. Sitanshu Das, *Subhas: A Political Biography* (New Delhi, 2001) is also well-researched and written but with an excessively sensationalist and conspiratorial tone. *The Springing Tiger: A Study of a Revolution* (Mumbai, 2001; 1st edn, 1959) by Hugh Toye is a short, once pioneering, but now rather dated albeit still useful introduction to the subject. *A Beacon Across Asia: A Biography of Subhas Chandra Bose* (Hyderabad, 1996; 1st edn, 1973) edited by Sisir Bose, seeks to be objective but fails in portraying Bose critically. The chapter covering Bose in Germany is disappointing as are many of the writings by its author, Alexander Werth. His biography *Der Tiger Indiens: Subhas Chandra Bose* (Munich, 1971) is no exception. *Netaji and India's Freedom* (Calcutta, 1975) also edited by Sisir Bose and based on the proceedings of the 1973 international seminar on Bose held at the Netaji Research Bureau remains a valuable source of documents and papers by specialist scholars in the field ranging from Leonard A. Gordon to Joyce Lebra. This includes as well Milan Hauner's extensive 'India's Independence and the Axis Powers: Subhas Chandra Bose in

BIBLIOGRAPHICAL ESSAY

Europe during the Strategic Initiative of the Axis Powers, 1941–1942', pp. 261–304.

Sisir Bose's biography of his uncle *Netaji Subhas Chandra Bose* (New Delhi, 2005), originally published in 1986 under the title *The Flaming Sword Forever Unsheathed* is short and perhaps inevitably one-sided. More useful and important is his first hand account, *The Great Escape* (Calcutta, 1995, 1st edn, 1975). Sisir Bose played a crucial role in organising and assisting Bose's escape from India before creating the Netaji Research Bureau in Calcutta and emerging as the doyen of Boseian studies. Sayed Wiqar Ali Shah 'The Escape of Subhas Chandra Bose: Myths and Realities', *The Oracle*, 3 & 4 (1996), pp. 51–63, reveals few myths or realities besides being excessively hagiographical in its approach. N. G. Jog's *In Freedom's Quest: A Biography of Netaji Subhas Chandra Bose* (New Delhi, 1969) is elegant but propagates several existing myths surrounding Bose's presence in Nazi Germany. John Jacob and Harindra Srivastava *Netaji Subhas: The Tallest of Titans* (New Delhi, 2000) while sincere and well-meaning is in effect intense hagiography. One of the authors at least has the excuse of being a former soldier in Bose's army, not an historian. This is not the case with S. C. Maikap whose *Challenge to the Empire: A Study of Netaji* (New Delhi, 1993) is an example of Boseian studies at its worst. Marshall J. Getz's recent biography *Subhas Chandra Bose: A Biography* (Jefferson, 2002) although populist in style is a useful introduction to the subject.

Jasobanta Kar *Subhas Chandra Bose: The Man and his Mind* (Calcutta, 1900) while well meaning fails to distinguish between Boseian rhetoric and reality. Subhash Chandra Chatterjee's *Subhas Chandra Bose: Man, Mission and Means* (Calcutta, 1989) in contrast tends to succeed where Kar does not, particularly in regard to its important contribution to Bose's political and socioeconomic ideas. Govind Talwalkar briefly and very generally, if superficially, examines Bose's period in Germany in 'Among the Nazis' in *Netaji and Indian Independence* (New Delhi, 1983) edited by B. K. and Shashi Ahluwalia. Gautam Chattopadhyay, *Subhas Chandra Bose, the Indian Leftists and Communists* (New Delhi, 1997) offers a valuable, if distorted, Marxist perspective on Bose. A collection of particularly important and varied papers written mostly by Indian scholars are to be found in Muchkund Dubey's *Subhas Chandra Bose: The Man and his Vision* (New Delhi, 1998) as well as S. R. Chakravarty and Madan C. Paul's *Netaji Subhas Chandra Bose: Relevance to Contemporary World* (New Delhi, 2000). To this may be added *Netaji Subhas Chandra Bose and Indian Freedom Struggle* (New Delhi, 2006) edited by Ratna Ghosh in two volumes. T. R. Sareen's *Forgotten Images: Reflections and Reminiscences of Subhas Chandra Bose* (New Delhi, 1997) contains valuable insights from many of Bose's associates ranging from his Indian colleagues to Japanese diplomatic personnel in Berlin. Verinder Grover, *Subhash Chandra*

SUBHAS CHANDRA BOSE IN NAZI GERMANY

Bose (New Delhi, 1991), in the *Political Thinkers of Modern India* series and Anton Pelinka, *Democracy Indian Style: Subhas Chandra Bose and the Creation of India's Political Culture* (New Brunswick, 2003) offer perceptive in-depth perspectives. Jan Kuhlmann's study of Bose and the Axis powers *Subhas Chandra Bose und die Indienpolitik der Achsenmächte* (Berlin, 2003) is extremely well-researched and by far one of the best studies on Bose. Despite its promising title Hans-Bernd Zöllner's *'Der Feind meines Feindes ist mein Freund': Subhas Chandra Bose und das zeitgenössische Deutschland unter dem Nationalsozialismus 1933–1943* (Hamburg, 2000), reduces Bose's wartime activities in Germany to a few pages. More useful is T. R. Sareen's 'Subhas Chandra Bose and Nazi Germany: An Assessment' pp. 140–172, and for its revealing approach, Anirudh Gupta's 'Netaji: A Plea for Reassessment before Rehabilitation', pp. 19–27, in S. R. Chakravarty and Madan C. Paul (eds), *Netaji Subhas Chandra Bose: Relevance to Contemporary World* (New Delhi, 2000). On Bose's posthumous popularity and the controversy surrounding his disappearance at the end of the war see Hugh Purcell 'Subhas Chandra Bose: The Afterlife of India's Fascist Leader', *History Today*, 11 (2010), pp. 45–51.

Bose's wartime associates left behind their own memoirs and recollections. Bhagat Ram Talwar *The Talwars of Pathan Land and Subhas Chandra's Great Escape* (New Delhi, 1976) covers the early period. While well-written and often fascinating, this memoir needs to be read with caution as it is misleading and deceptive. After the war, Talwar for obvious reasons concealed his role as a Soviet double agent who betrayed Bose in Afghanistan. An important, rather more reliable, supplement is *When Bose was Ziauddin* (Delhi, 1946) by Uttam Chand, a nationalist who assisted both Bose and Talwar in Kabul. To this should be added Mian Akbar Shah's 'Netaji's Escape—An Untold Chapter', *The Oracle*, 1 (1984), pp. 15–23. On the attempts to set-up an underground in India and subsequent operations by Bose's followers see Santimoy Ganguli *et al.*, 'Netaji's Underground in India during World War II: An Account by Participants in a Daring and Historic Undertaking', *The Oracle*, 2 (1979), pp. 7–14, and 'Netaji and B. V'., *The Oracle*, 4 (1979), pp. 28–32.

Girija K. Mookerjee *Europe at War 1938–1946: Impressions of War, Netaji and Europe* (Meerut, 1968) is a sophisticated memoir yet in a very subtle manner extremely ideologically driven. Along with his 'Netaji the Great Resistance Leader', *The Oracle*, 1 (1986), pp. 22–35, and similar writings, it seeks to portray Bose in a rather intense anti-Nazi manner. N. G. Ganpuley *Netaji in Germany: A Little-Known Chapter* (Bombay, 1959) is more ambivalent, particularly in regard to Germany. While slow to start off and overwritten at times it remains the least self-indulgent first hand account of Bose's exile in Germany. Ganpuley's personal memoirs edited by R. R. Diwakar and S. B. Nargundkar simply titled *Ganpuley's Memoirs* (Bombay, 1983) add very little to the subject. M. R. Vyas *Passage through a Turbulent Era: Historical Reminiscences of*

BIBLIOGRAPHICAL ESSAY

the Fateful Years 1937–47 (Bombay, 1982) is a lively, at times even humorous, account with interesting anecdotes, although it does suffer from obvious excesses. His 'Azad Hind Movement in Europe', *The Oracle*, 4 (1985), pp. 15–30, is a minor contribution in contrast. Abid Hassan Safrani 'A Soldier Remembers', *The Oracle*, 1 (1984), pp. 24–65, is also a lively, witty, even entertaining account of his extensive experiences with Bose and Indian POWs in Germany. Its populist style gives it an authentic quality although it needs to be approached cautiously. His other recollections include 'With Netaji in the U-Boat: Before and After' in Madan Gopal (ed.), *Netaji Subhas Chandra Bose: The Last Phase in his Own Words* (New Delhi, 1994), pp. 218–234, as well as 'Netaji and the Indian Communal Question', *The Oracle*, 1 (1979), pp. 42–46. Unfortunately, Bose's deputy in Berlin, A. C. N. Nambiar only left behind the short and superficial 'A Memorable Meeting in Paris with Netaji Subhas Chandra Bose', *The Oracle*, 1 (1982), pp. 61–62. It is not even a particularly good account of that meeting.

On the German side, Alexander Werth's 'Netaji in Germany', *The Oracle*, 3 & 4 (1996), pp. 14–42, must be read with caution although more restrained is his 'An Assessment of Netaji's Policy of Co-operation with the Axis Powers during World War II' in *Netaji and India's Freedom* (Calcutta, 1975), pp. 249–258. Franz Josef Furtwängler, who also worked for the Special India Bureau, has left behind a sketchy recollection of Bose in *Männer die Ich Sah und Kannte* (Hamburg, 1951). A similar glimpse of Bose can be derived from Giselher Wirsing's *Indien: Asiens gefährliche Jahre* (Düsseldorf, 1968). The much eulogised Adam von Trott never left behind a memoir because he was hanged for 'treason' following his involvement in the failed attempt to assassinate Hitler in the summer of 1944. There are two excellent biographies of Trott with considerable references to Bose although in one case, very critical. See Giles MacDonogh's *A Good German: Adam von Trott zu Solz* (Woodstock, 1992) and the more severe Christopher Sykes' *Troubled Loyalty: A Biography of Adam von Trott zu Solz*, (London, 1968).

On the Nazi regime William, L. Shirer's monumental *The Rise and Fall of the Third Reich: A History of Nazi Germany* (New York, 1960), is still the best overall chronological narrative although much derided by professional historians for its insufficient analysis. Karl Dietrich Bracher, *The German Dictatorship: The Origins, Structure, and Consequences of National Socialism* (London, 1985; 1st edn, 1969), is more analytical but not as readable. More concise and to the point, yet interesting, is K. Hilderbrand, *The Third Reich* (London, 1999; 1st edn, 1979). Other, more recent, studies include Michael Burleigh *The Third Reich: A New History* (London, 2000) and Richard Overy's *The Dictators: Hitler's Germany and Stalin's Russia* (London, 2005). The former constitutes an important survey of the Third Reich while the latter is an excellent penetrative study. The four volume *Nazism 1919–1945* (Exeter,

SUBHAS CHANDRA BOSE IN NAZI GERMANY

1983–1998), edited by Jeremy Noakes is by no means restricted to the Nazi party but encompasses the state as well. It is an exhaustive source of primary materials offering many valuable insights into the regime. The published volumes of the still ongoing *Germany and the Second World War* (Oxford, 1990-) edited by the Militärgeschichtliches Forschungsamt provide an unsurpassed quasi-encyclopaedic approach to this decisive phase of the regime's history. Finally, Roderick Stackelberg's *Hitler's Germany: Origins, Interpretations, Legacies*, (London, 1999), is a useful synthesis.

On Hitler, the classic biography is Alan Bullock, *Hitler: A Study in Tyranny* (London, 1990; 1st edn, 1952), which although dated remains important. The same is true of Percy Ernst Schramm's perceptive *Hitler: The Man and the Military Leader* (London, 1971). Werner Maser *Hitler* (London, 1974), John Toland *Adolf Hitler* (Hertfordshire, 1997; 1st edn, 1976) and Joachim C. Fest *Hitler* (New York, 1974) are other major contributions. The standard work now on Hitler, however, is Ian Kershaw's *Hitler 1889–1936: Hubris* (London, 1998) and *Hitler 1936–45: Nemesis* (London, 2000).

Mein Kampf (Mumbai, 2010; 1st edn, 1925), containing Hitler's autobiographical political ramblings, while thick and plodding, is important for his perspective, however limited, on India. The several thousand pages of *Hitler: Speeches and Proclamations 1932–1945* (Wauconda, 1990) edited by Max Domarus, make in part for indispensable, if disagreeable, reading. *The Speeches of Adolf Hitler 1922–1939* (London, 1942) edited by N. Baynes are a useful supplement for the early period. Similarly, *Hitler's Table Talk 1941–1944: His Private Conversations* (London, 2000; 1st edn, 1953) edited by H. R. Trevor-Roper, offers an indispensable and fascinating insight into the workings of Hitler's mind. The same is true to a lesser extent of Otto Strasser's *Hitler and I* (London, 1940). *Inside Hitler's Headquarters 1939–45* (Novato, 1964) edited by the former staff officer Walter Warlimont, offers a close-up portrait of Hitler's operational plans and handling of the war. It should be supplemented by *Führer Conferences on Naval Affairs 1939–1945* (London, 1990). Also important is Trevor-Roper's assembled *Hitler's War Directives 1939–1945* (London, 1966). An objective in-depth analysis of Hitler's strategic calculations and plans is to be found in Heinz Magenheimer's *Hitler's War: Germany's Key Strategic Decisions 1940–1945* (London, 2002). On Hitler's specific involvement with India see Johannes H. Voigt 'Hitler und Indien', *Vierteljahrshefte für Zeitgeschichte*, 19 (1971), pp. 33–63.

On the Nazi leadership, one of the earliest studies remains as effective today as when it first came out. Joachim C. Fest's *The Face of the Third Reich: Portraits of the Nazi Leadership* (New York, 1970) is a psychologically penetrative, at times chilling, analysis of the Nazi leaders. The more conventional *The Devil's Disciples: The Lives and Times of Hitler's Inner Circle* (London, 2003) by Anthony Read is an excellent synthesis of the literature on the subject and

BIBLIOGRAPHICAL ESSAY

well worth reading. There are also important studies of specific Nazi leaders who encountered Bose. On Ribbentrop, the best biography is Michael Bloch's *Ribbentrop* (London, 2003; 1st edn, 1992) which does not seek to demolish its subject as much as try to understand it. The same is not as true of John Weitz's *Hitler's Diplomat: The Life and Times of Joachim von Ribbentrop* (New York, 1992) which is considerably more limited. Ribbentrop wrote his own, inevitably self-serving, memoirs appropriately entitled *The Ribbentrop Memoirs* (London, 1954), while awaiting execution in Nuremburg. On his relationship with the Foreign Office see Paul Seabury's 'Ribbentrop and the German Foreign Office', *Political Science Quarterly*, 4 (1951), pp. 532–555.

The standard biography on Himmler is Peter Padfield's *Himmler: Reichsführer-SS* (London, 2001; 1st edn, 1990). While extensive and well-researched it makes for distressing reading. Also important is *Der Dienstkalender Heinrich Himmlers 1941/42* (Hamburg, 1999) edited by Peter Witte. One of Himmler's senior colleagues left behind his own recollections (one rather involuntarily in the form of an interrogation) revealing among other things SS interest in Bose and India. See Walter Schellenberg *Hitler's Secret Service: Memoirs of Walter Schellenberg* (New York, 1971) and Reinhard R. Doerries *Hitler's Last Chief of Foreign Intelligence: Allied Interrogations of Walter Schellenberg* (London, 2003).

On Goebbels the classic account is Helmut Heiber *Goebbels* (New York, 1972). More recent, and lively, is David Irving's *Goebbels: Mastermind of the Third Reich* (London, 1999) but this biography needs to be read with vigilance. *The Goebbels Diaries* (London, 1948) edited by P. Lochner make for fascinating reading. *The Secret Conferences of Dr Goebbels: The Nazi Propaganda War 1939–43* (New York, 1970) edited by Willi A. Boelcke is also useful. On Nazi propaganda, the once pioneering Z. A. B. Zeman's *Nazi Propaganda* (London, 1964) remains pertinent. David Welch *The Third Reich: Politics and Propaganda* (London, 2002) is an excellent, more recent, study.

The status of Indian POWs and Legionaries requires additional research. The best account by a former officer is Rudolf Hartog's *The Sign of the Tiger: Subhas Chandra Bose and his Indian Legion in Germany 1941–45* (New Delhi, 2001). Gurbachan Singh Mangat also contributed his own important recollections in *The Tiger Strikes: An Unwritten Chapter of Netaji's Life History* (Ludhiana, 1986). He continued with *Indian National Army: Role in India's Struggle for Freedom* (Ludhiana, 1991) encompassing as well, as its title suggests, Indian troops in Southeast Asia. 'A Report on the Organisation and Training of the Free India Army in Europe 1941–42', *The Oracle*, 3 & 4, (1996), pp. 43–50, by Walter Harbich who commanded the Special India Detachment is short and formal but still important as it is the only source of information on that particular unit. Several British documents on Indian POWs and Legionaries are to be found in the already mentioned *Subhas Chan-*

SUBHAS CHANDRA BOSE IN NAZI GERMANY

dra Bose and Nazi Germany (New Delhi, 1996). Lothar Günther Von Indien nach Annaburg: Die Geschichte der Indischen Legion und des Kriegsgefangenlagers in Deutschland (Berlin, 2003) is a short but extremely valuable study. Except for length, the same is not as true of A. V. Raikov's 'Indian Legion in Germany' and Subhash Chandra Chatterjee's 'The Indian Legion—The First Revolutionary Army of India's Freedom' in Ratna Ghosh, ed., *Netaji Subhas Chandra Bose and Indian Freedom Struggle*, vol. 2, (New Delhi, 2006), pp. 13–36. On Indian POWs and troops more generally see G. J. Douds 'The Men who Never Were: Indian POWs in the Second World War', *South Asia: Journal of South Asian Studies*, 2 (2004), 183–216, and Tarak Barkawi 'Culture and Combat in the Colonies: The Indian Army in the Second World War', *Journal of Contemporary History*, 2 (2006), pp. 325–355. Omer Bartov *Hitler's Army: Soldiers, Nazis and War in the Third Reich* (New York, 1992) is a thought-provoking analysis of the German army.

An excellent overview of the Indian freedom struggle is provided by Anthony Read and David Fisher's *The Proudest Day: India's Long Road to Independence* (London, 1998). Similar but less detailed, is Patrick French's *Liberty or Death: India's Journey to Independence and Division* (New Delhi, 1998). *Raj: The Making and Unmaking of British India* (London, 1998) by Lawrence James is much less reverential. It also encompasses a much wider period. R. C. Majumdar *Struggle for Freedom* (Bombay, 1988; 1st edn, 1969) provides the standard nationalist perspective. The attempt to liberate India from outside is best covered by Peter Ward Fay's *The Forgotten Army: India's Armed Struggle for Independence 1942–1945*, (New Delhi, 1997).

On the Indian nationalist leadership, Reba Som's simple, well-written, *Gandhi, Bose, Nehru and the Making of the Modern Indian Mind* (New Delhi, 2004) is a useful introduction. On Gandhi the 100 volumes of *The Collected Works of Mahatma Gandhi* (New Delhi, 1969–1984) published by the government of India are not only indispensable but fascinating. D. G. Tendulkar's eight volume *Mahatma: Life of Mohandas Karamchand Gandhi* (New Delhi, 1960–1963) is a useful, albeit non-interpretative, chronological account. Louis Fischer *The Life of Mahatma Gandhi* (New Delhi, 2000; 1st edn, 1951) is a more intimate portrait of its subject. The interviews he carried out with Gandhi are of significant importance. The standard biography on Nehru is Sarvepalli Gopal's *Jawaharlal Nehru: A Biography* (New Delhi, 1975–1984) in three volumes. Detailed, well-written and informative it is an invaluable contribution. M. J. Akbar's *Nehru: The Making of India* (London, 1988) while elegant is much more concise and therefore limited in scope. Stanley Wolpert in *Nehru: A Tryst with Destiny* (New York, 1996) adopts a peculiar style of his own replete with ellipses and quotations but which ultimately succeeds in bringing Nehru back to life. Maulana Abul Kalam Azad, the former Congress

BIBLIOGRAPHICAL ESSAY

president, should not be forgotten. His *India Wins Freedom* (New Delhi, 1997; 1st edn, 1959) is nearly subversive in its revelations.

The Cripps Mission January–April 1942 (London, 1970) volume one of *Constitutional Relations between Britain and India: The Transfer of Power 1942–7* edited by Nicholas Mansergh provides an indispensable and exhaustive source of documents on British policy, Indian reactions and efforts to reach a compromise. Much more succinct and to the point is Bhim Sen Singh's *The Cripps Mission: A Handiwork of British Imperialism* (New Delhi, 1979) written from a nationalist perspective. *'Quit India' 30 April-21–September 1942* (London, 1971), volume two of *Constitutional Relations between Britain and India* again provides exhaustive documentation. P. N. Chopra *Quit India Movement: British Secret Documents* (New Delhi, 1986), even if poorly edited at times, contains a valuable collection of documents from an Indian nationalist perspective. Francis G. Hutchins *Spontaneous Revolution: The Quit India Movement* (Delhi, 1971) is one of the better studies. Others include K. K. Chaudhari's *Quit India Revolution: The Ethos of its Central Direction* (Mumbai, 1996); Y. B. Mathur's *Quit India Movement* (Delhi, 1979) and A. Moin Zaidi's *The Way Out to Freedom: An Inquiry into the Quit India Movement Conducted by Participants* (New Delhi, 1973). M. S. Venkataramani and B. K. Shrivastava's *Quit India: The American Response to the 1942 Struggle* (New Delhi, 1979) provides an important alternative perspective.

On the Indian National Congress, the most extensive account is the official five volume *A Centenary History of the Indian National Congress 1885–1985* (New Delhi, 1985) meticulously edited by B. N. Pande. Volume three (1935–1947) covers the relevant period. Of interest as well is B. R. Tomlinson's *The Indian National Congress and the Raj 1929–1942: The Penultimate Phase* (London, 1976).

India's role in the Second World War is the object of an excellent study by Johannes Voigt in *India in the Second World War* (New Delhi, 1987). Manzoor Ahmad *Indian Response to the Second World War* (New Delhi, 1987) is not as extensive. India and the Axis powers is dealt with by Milan Hauner in *India in Axis Strategy: Germany, Japan and Indian Nationalists in the Second World War* (Stuttgart, 1981). This monumental study is indispensable in the field of Boseian war studies and well beyond. Hauner's more focused '1942: The Decisive War Year in India's Destiny', *The Oracle*, 1, (1986), pp. 36–44 and 'One Man against the Empire: The Faqir of Ipi and the British in Central Asia on the Eve of and during the Second World War', *Journal of Contemporary History*, 1 (1981), pp. 183–212, are also important contributions. S. A. Das and K. B. Subbaiah's *Chalo Delhi!: An Historical Account of the Indian Independence Movement in East Asia* (Kuala Lumpur, 1946) covers the Japanese-controlled region before and after Bose's arrival.

SUBHAS CHANDRA BOSE IN NAZI GERMANY

For a British perspective, the already mentioned *Constitutional Relations between Britain and India: The Transfer of Power 1942–7* (London, 1970–1983) in twelve volumes is invaluable. It contains much of the correspondence between Churchill, Lord Linlithgow and the Secretary of State for India, Amery, as well as numerous other officials who helped develop British policy. American, Chinese and Indian attitudes are revealed in the process. For a more general synthesis of British policy during the war see Llewellyn Woodward's official *British Foreign Policy in the Second World War* (London, 1962).

Churchill's own grandiose, at times pompous, six volume memoirs *The Second World War* (New York, 1961–1962) provides the prime minister's perspective of the war. Admirable for its scope and depth is Martin Gilbert's practically minute by minute account *The Road to Victory 1941–1945* (Boston, 1986), volume seven in the eight volume biography *Winston S. Churchill*. Churchill's specific wartime approach to India is examined in Madhusree Mukerjee's *Churchill's Secret War: The British Empire and the Ravaging of India during World War II* (Chennai, 2010). Arthur Herman *Gandhi & Churchill: The Epic Rivalry that Destroyed an Empire and Forged our Age* (London, 2008) focuses on the feud between the two men. R. J. Moore *Churchill, Cripps and India 1939–45* (Oxford, 1979) was, and remains, a path-breaking study on overall British policy towards India during the war. Auriol Weigold *Churchill, Roosevelt and India: Propaganda during World War II* (London, 2008) focuses on the American and propaganda angles. *The Guy Liddell Diaries: MI5's Director of Counter-Espionage in World War II* (London, 2005) edited by Nigel West in two volumes provides a valuable intelligence perspective with references to Bose and Talwar.

The rather limited Italian perspective on Bose can be gleaned from Count Galeazzo Ciano's *Diary 1937–1943*, (London, 2002) and *Ciano's Diplomatic Papers* (London, 1948) edited by Malcolm Muggeridge. A few documents from the archives of the Italian Foreign Ministry are to be found in the already mentioned *Subhas Chandra Bose and Nazi Germany* (New Delhi, 1996). On the Second World War, general surveys include Martin Gilbert's *Second World War* (London, 1995) which provides an excellent day by day account. Gerhard L. Weinberg *A World at Arms: A Global History of World War II* (Cambridge, 1994) is a massive, in-depth, one volume history of the Second World War with critical references to Bose.

INDEX

Abwehr: ix, x, xiii, xiv, 40, 51, 64, 153; convenes intelligence meetings on India, ix, xi, 58, 73, 81–83, 87
Abyssinia: 18–19
Afghanistan: vii, xviii, 24, 35, 154, 157, 174–175, 180; Hitler fears British invasion of, ix, 63; and intelligence activities in, 31, 38, 40, 49–51, 58, 61, 63–64, 112, 153, 172–173
Africa: 4, 132, 141, 185
Afrika Korps: xiv, 29, 40, 46, 155
Aga Khan: 5
Algeria: 140
All India Congress Committee: xvii, 6, 17, 21, 128, 131
All India Radio: x, 67
Allies: 24, 76, 83, 90, 92, 110, 119, 123, 128–129, 131, 133, 144, 147, 160, 163–164; Bose condemns, 89, 99, 102–103, 111–112, 141
Alsace: 194
Amery, Leopold: 100, 120
Amrita Bazar Patrika: 15
Andaman Islands: 143; Japanese attack and occupy, xii, 87
Andrews, Charles F.: 78

Anglo-American Declaration: ix, 61–62, 180
Annaburg: 178, 181, 193–194; Bose visits, 76; Shedai visits, 60
Aryans: 77, 125
Atlantic Ocean: 29, 116, 127
Atlantic Wall: 144, 159
Attlee, Clement: 19
Auschwitz: 165
Austria: 18
Axis Powers: vii-viii, 24–27, 30–31, 33, 36, 41, 43–47, 53, 68, 73, 80, 84, 94, 96, 98, 101 102, 108, 110–113, 117–118, 120, 123, 127, 129–130, 133–134, 137, 140–142, 144–145, 152, 163–164, 166, 171–172, 174–175, 178, 182, 187, 197; and declaration on India, x–xiii, 49, 55–56, 59–60, 74–76, 81, 85–87, 90, 105–110, 115, 153–157, 189–191
Azad, Abul Kalam: 92, 119, 140, 160; arrested, 132; and Bose, 96–97, 123, 164; concerned with effects of Bose's broadcasts on Gandhi, 90, 100, 162; offers condolences for Bose's reported death, 94; meets Chiang Kai-

241

INDEX

shek, xi, 83; as Congress president, 83, 90, 162

Bad Gastein: visited by Bose, 18, 63, 65, 90, 92
Badenweiler: 15
Baluchistan: 113
Bangkok: 75, 84, 138; Indian nationalists convene in, 118–119
Barbarossa, Operation: xviii, 34, 37–39, 56
Bay of Bengal: xii, 87, 143
Belgium: 22
Belgrade: 35
Bengal: xii, 3, 5–6, 54, 144, 167; partition of, 1
Bengal Legislative Council: 1, 6
Bengal Provincial Congress Committee: 6
Berlin: vii-xi, xiii, xv, xvii, xix–xxi, 23–24, 26, 42–45, 50–51, 53–57, 63–65, 67, 70, 76–77, 79, 83, 86, 88, 90, 92, 96–98, 100, 105–106, 108–110, 117, 123–125, 127, 129, 131, 140–145, 151–154, 159–160, 163, 165, 172, 178, 180–181, 193, 195–196; arrival of Bose (April 1941), vii, xix, 25, 29–39, 148–149, 158, 162, 164; Bose visits (1930s), xx, 11–12, 16; Indian conference held in (December 1941), x, 73–75; arrival of Mookerjee and Nambiar, 78; visited by Shedai: ix, 58–61, 73, 177
Bevin, Ernest: 69, 185
Bismarck, Otto von: 55
Black Sea: 29
Bombay: xiv, xx, 2, 8–9, 17, 20, 131
Bonomi, Ivanoe: 7
Bose, Mihir: 27
Bose, Rash Behari: 121–122

Bose, Sarat: 23, 142
British empire: xx, 5–6, 9, 30, 32, 34, 39, 46, 48, 61, 88, 93–94, 100, 102–103, 108, 112, 148, 171, 184–185, 187, 189
Brittany: 193
Bulgaria: 59, 177
Burma: 6, 49, 75, 87, 91, 98, 113, 143–144
Byelorussians: 162

Calcutta: xii, xix, 1, 8, 11–12, 23, 81, 88, 102; All India Congress Committee meeting held in, 17; Bose appointed chief executive officer of, 6; Bose elected Mayor of, 7; Congress meeting (1928) held in, 6–7
Calcutta Corporation: 7
Cambridge: 1
Canada: 162
Cape of Good Hope: 116
Caucasus: 70, 107, 138, 155, 186–187
Cavallero, Ugo: 106
Central Legislative Assembly: x, 67
Ceylon: xii
Chemnitz: 76–77
Chiang Kai-shek: 111–112; visits India, xi, 83–84, 86
China: 19, 83, 103, 112, 143, 146
Chungking: 92
Churchill, Winston: ix, xii, xiv, 19, 37, 69, 84, 91, 93–94, 97, 99, 100–101, 103, 135, 141, 167, 184; issues Anglo-American Declaration, 61; disapproves of Chiang Kai-shek's visit to India, 84; praises Fascism, 8; critical of Gandhi, 9, 101, 119–120; fears Hitler reaching India, 46, 55; on

INDEX

invasion of Iran, 62; and 'Quit India', 132–133
Ciano, Galeazzo: xiii, 52, 106–107, 109–110, 153, 157, 181; receives Bose, viii, xiii, 54–56, 108
Concentration camps: 60, 125, 165
Congress: 5–7, 15, 17–23, 33–34, 36, 45, 52–54, 65, 68, 76, 89, 92, 94–96, 100–101, 105, 119, 122–123, 128–129, 135, 145–146, 151, 160–161; Bose as Congress president, xx, 19–21, 52, 65, 84, 146
Congress Working Committee: xvii, 15, 20–21, 128
Conservative Party: 184–185
Continental Four-Power Bloc: 148
Cripps Mission: xvii, 91, 105–106, 108–109, 119, 134, 157, 163; Bose launches propaganda campaign against, xi, 92–97; and China, 92; and Congress, 92, 96, 99–100; and Gandhi, 96–98, 100–101; Goebbels on, 92, 100; Japan responds militarily, 98; and USA, 92, 102–103
Cripps, Sir Stafford: xi, 91, 93, 95, 99, 101, 103; meets Bose, 19, 97; Bose broadcasts open letter to, xii, 97; warns Churchill of seriousness of situation in India, xii, 97–98; and Congress leaders, 92, 96, 99; critical of Gandhi in regard to Bose, 97; meets Gandhi, xii, 96–97; arrives in India, xii, 96
Croatia: 59, 143
Curzon, Lord: 1
Cuttack: 1
Czechoslovakia: 196

Daily Express: 184

Daily Mail: 12, 68–69, 184
Daily Worker: 19
Dalhousie: 17
Das, Chittaranjan: 5–7
Datta Khel: 112–113
Declaration on India: and Axis Powers, x–xiii, 49, 55–56, 59–60, 74–76, 81, 85–87, 90, 105–110, 115, 153–157, 189–191; and Bose, vii–ix, xiii, 38, 43–49, 51, 54–59, 61–63, 68–70, 74–75, 85, 90, 106, 108–109, 114, 116, 143, 148, 150–151, 153–157, 185–187; and Foreign Office, 48, 59, 88, 109–110, 150–151, 155–156, 158, and Hitler viii, xii–xiii, 47, 63, 106–107, 109, 115–116, 150–151, 153–155, 157; and Ribbentrop, ix, xii–xiii, 51, 55, 57, 61–63, 68–70, 75, 86, 106–107, 109, 114, 155–156, 185-187; and Shedai, 60–61, 76, 177
Defence of India: Act 23
Der Angriff: 166
Dresden: 193

Eden, Anthony: 19
England: 1, 3, 5, 16, 19, 31, 35, 39–40, 42, 47, 61, 63, 68, 70, 80, 95, 97, 148, 150, 155–156, 171, 175, 179, 183–187
Egypt: 46, 50, 109, 115, 195

Fakir of Ipi (Mirza Ali Khan): ix, xvii, 31, 40, 51, 58, 112, 173
Far East: 40, 46, 127, 185, 196–197
Fascism: xx, 3; and Bose, xxi, 3, 7–8, 14–15, 19, 23
Fatwah: 133
Fay, Peter Ward: 27

243

INDEX

First World War: 1, 50, 52, 122, 171, 190

Foreign Office: vii-viii, xi, xiv, xix-xx, 34, 36–38, 41–42, 44–45, 47–48, 50, 55, 57–59, 65–67, 75, 86, 100, 123, 127, 133, 137, 139, 142, 149–150, 154, 161, 178–180, 182, 194; and Bose (1930s), 11, 13, 15–17; reservations about Bose leaving Germany, 114; and declaration on India, 48, 59, 88, 109–110, 150–151, 155–156, 158; recruits Indians for the Free India Centre, 65; surprised by Tojo's statement on India, 86

Forward Bloc: xii, xvii, 24, 36, 49, 56, 102, 122, 129; founded by Bose, 21; condemns invasion of the Soviet Union, 56; as means of subversion, 31, 49, 82, 88, 113

France: x, xiii, xvii, 4, 22, 30, 32, 78, 116, 125, 144, 160, 193, 195–196; plans for Free India activities, 117

Frankenberg: x, 76, 121, 193

Free India (journal): 67, 128

Free India (movement): xiii, 65, 76–77, 88–89, 126, 131, 159–160

Free India Battalion: xvii, 123; disbanded, xiv, 139

Free India Centre: 48, 50–51, 57, 60, 63–64, 66–67, 78–79, 90, 117, 133, 136, 144, 159; inaugurated by Bose, x, 65

Free India Government: vii, xix, 29–31, 33, 36–39, 41, 44–45, 47, 50, 110, 116, 143, 146, 149–150, 154, 157–158, 164, 172, 174,

'Free India and her Problems' article: 129–130

Free India Radio: xi, 33, 38, 50, 66, 88, 95, 172

Gandhi, Indira: 146

Gandhi, Mohandas: xx, xix, 2, 7–9, 13, 17–22, 24–25, 31, 42–43, 52–53, 62, 78, 84, 89, 94, 96–98, 100–101, 105, 109, 119, 128–129, 136, 146, 149, 151–152, 154, 160–161, 164–165; admiration for Bose, 90, 100, 145, 162–163; differences with Bose, xix–xxi, 2, 5, 7, 9, 14, 20–21, 23, 34, 36, 43–45, 65, 80, 122–123, 126, 128, 149, 161; Bose praises, xiii, 9, 21, 120; opposes Bose's re-election as Congress president, 20; reserved about Bose, 17; Churchill critical of, 9, 101, 119–120; and Cripps, xii, 96–98, 100–101; Goebbels critical of, xii, 126, 161; Goering denounces, 12; Hitler on, 18, 115, 161; Mussolini praises, 9, 109; launches 'Quit India', 131–132; Shedai denounces, xi

Gandhi-Irwin Pact: 8, 18

De Gaulle, Charles: 30

al-Gaylani, Rashid Ali: 67, 69, 142, 185

Geneva: 16, 40

Georgia: 70

German High Command: vii, ix, xiv, xvii, 39–42, 44, 47, 58, 64–65, 70, 73, 83, 87–88, 127, 131, 136–137, 140, 142, 194, 197

Germany: viii-x, xx–xxi, 3–5, 10–11, 13, 15–20, 22–27, 29–38, 45–48, 51, 55–57, 59–62, 67–70, 74, 76, 78, 80, 82–83, 85, 87, 94, 107–108, 110, 114–115, 120, 122, 127, 131, 141–143, 146–148, 153–167, 171, 177–187, 189–191, 193

Gestapo: 138, 159

INDEX

Ghadar: 52
Ghulam Siddiq Khan: 67
Goebbels, Joseph: vii, xiii, 38, 66, 77, 90, 92, 100, 126–127, 150, 166; praises Bose, xi, 89–90, 97, 126, 158; critical of Gandhi, xii, 126, 161; opposes Indian government-in-exile, 110
Goering, Hermann: Bose rebuts remarks on Gandhi, 13, 20; denounces Gandhi, 12
Gordon, Leonard A.: 27
Great Britain: xx, 4, 10, 30–32, 37–39, 43, 46, 50–51, 59, 67–68, 87, 89, 92–93, 98, 101–103, 111, 122, 141, 144, 159, 171–172, 190–191; Free India government declares war on, 143; possible peace settlement with Germany, 30, 37, 43, 148; reasserts control in the Middle East, 55; Ribbentrop's dislike of, 42
Greece: 29, 54; High Command plans to deploy Indian Legion in, xiv, 131
Greenwood, Arthur: 19

Haguenau: 194
Halder, Franz: vii, 40
Halifax, Lord: 18–19, 96
Hamburg: xiv, 136
Harbich, Walter: 41, 83
Hardinge, Lord: 122
Haripura: 20
Hauner, Milan: 27
Haushofer, Karl: 13
Hawaii: 73
Hess, Rudolf: 13
Himmler, Heinrich: 158–159; arranges Gestapo training for Indians, 138; receives Bose, xiii, 125–126

Hindenburg, Paul von: 126
Hinduism: 125
Hindustani: 30, 65, 130, 181
Hirohito, Emperor: 164
Hitler, Adolf: ix–x, xii-xiii, 3–4, 6, 10–14, 16, 22, 24, 34, 40, 42, 46–48, 52, 55, 62, 68–70, 73, 87–88, 90, 101, 108–109, 112, 117, 120, 127–128, 138, 148–149, 164–165, 185–188; fears British invasion of Afghanistan, ix, 63; receives the Aga Khan, 5; approves Bose's transfer to Asia, xii, 106, 116; impressed with Bose, xii, 90, 116, 158; receives Bose, 5, 114–116, 164; admires British empire, xx, 5; fascinated with British India, xx, 4; advises British to shoot Gandhi, 18–19; sceptical of Gandhi's tactics, 115, 161; approves German declaration on India, viii, 47, 150; postpones German declaration on India, 63, 150–151; orders invasion of India, vii, 39, 152; considers recognizing Indian government-in-exile, vii, 38–39, 44, 149–150; Indian Legionaries swear oath to, 136; ridicules Indian National Army, 144; critical of Indian nationalists, 3–5, 10; irritated with Japanese over Tripartite declaration on India, 106; preoccupied with Japanese advance towards India, 77; orders German penetration of the Middle East viii, 47; critical of Nehru, 115, 117, 161; Nehru critical of, xii, 104; argues with Ribbentrop, 156; receives A. L. Sinha, 16, opposes Tripartite declaration xii-xiii, 106–107, 109,

245

INDEX

115–116, 153–155, 157; *Mein Kampf*: 3, 5, 11, 20, 70, 116
Holland: 22, 30, 194–195, 197
Hungary: 59, 177
al-Husayni, Mohammad Amin, (Grand Mufti of Jerusalem): 67, 69, 142, 185

Independence Day: xi, xv, 8, 79, 141–142
India: vii–xiv, xix–xx, 1–5, 9–18, 20–26, 29–46, 49–54, 56–57, 61, 63–70, 73–80, 82–85, 88–104, 109, 111–113, 115–120, 122–123, 125–147, 150–155, 159–164, 166, 171–175, 178–183, 185–187, 190–191, 195; Abwehr convenes intelligence meetings on, ix, xi, 58, 73, 81–83, 87; Chiang Kai-shek visits, xi, 83–84, 86; Churchill fears Hitler might reach, 46, 55; Cripps warns London seriousness of situation in, xii, 97–98; and declaration on, vii–xiii, 38, 43–49, 51, 54–63, 68–70, 74–76, 81, 85–88, 90, 105–110, 114–116, 143, 148, 150–158, 189–191
Indian Army: xvii, 31–32, 40, 43, 81–82, 88, 98, 113, 121, 137, 139, 151, 174–175,
Indian Civil Service: 1–2
Indian Legion: x, xiv, xviii, 41, 50, 74–75, 78, 113, 121–122, 131, 136–137, 139–140, 144, 159–160, 162, 177–178, 180–181, 193–194, 196–197
Indian National Army: xvii, 36, 82, 84, 88, 143–144, 145, 149
Indian National Congress: xiv, 6–8, 10, 18–23, 31, 36, 52, 54, 65, 74, 78–79, 83–84, 100–101, 119, 128, 132–133, 154; and All India Congress Committee, xvii, 6, 17, 21, 128, 131; Azad president of, 83, 90, 162; and Bose, 5–7, 15, 17–23, 33–34, 36, 45, 52–54, 65, 68, 76, 89, 92, 94–96, 100–101, 105, 119, 122–123, 128–129, 135, 145–146, 151, 160–161; Bose president of, xix–xx, 19–21, 52, 65, 84, 146; and Congress Working Committee, xvii, 15, 20–21, 128; and Cripps Mission, 92, 96, 99–100; Nehru president of, 17
Indian Ocean: xv, xviii, 116, 137, 140, 143, 158
Indian POWs: viii–ix, xiv, 40–44, 53, 57, 60, 64–66, 70, 74–76, 78, 82, 121, 123, 138–139, 178–181, 193–197
Indian Princely States: xviii, 95, 130
Iran: ix, 51, 61–63, 113, 157, 184
Iraq: vii, 46–47, 49, 51, 55, 63, 67, 69, 142, 150, 155, 184–185
Ireland: 48, 93, 130, 138
Irwin, Lord: 8, 18
Italy: xx, 3, 7, 9, 12, 15, 18, 52, 54, 59, 61, 74, 87, 108, 110, 120, 140, 143, 155, 177–179, 180, 189–191, 193, 196

Japan: x–xii, 46, 61, 71, 73, 76, 91, 101, 104, 106–107, 122, 148–149, 151, 153, 189–191; and Bose, x, xx, 33, 40, 46, 59, 74–75, 77, 81–88, 90, 93, 98–99, 105, 108–110, 112–116, 119–120, 123–124, 127–128, 137, 139–140, 143, 157–158, 162–164, 177, 185; attacks India, xii, 87, 98–99, 144, 146, 164
Jana Gana Mana: 65, 79
Jews: 159, 165–167

INDEX

Jinnah, Mohammed Ali: 74, 96
Jodl, Alfred: 107
Jog, N. G.: 27
Johnson, Louis: 102–103
Joyce, William (Lord Haw Haw): 68

Kabul: viii, xiv, xix–xxi, 24, 26, 40, 49, 50–51, 58, 63–64, 153, 172
Kaiserhof Hotel (Berlin): xi, xv, 79, 141
Karachi: 8–9
Keitel, Wilhelm: 88, 107
Kennedy, John: 132
Keppler, Wilhelm: 59, 178
Kernesky, Alexander: 185
Khan, Mohammed Jamil, 181
Kiel: 143
Kirti Kisan: xviii, 53–54
Königsbrück: 136, 138, 193–194, 197
Kuhlmann, Jan: 27

Labour Party: 184
Lansbury, George: 19
Laski, Harold: 19
Lawrence of Arabia: 153
League Against Imperialism: 10
League of Oppressed Nations: 10
Libya: 29, 40, 54, 140, 178–179, 195
Linlithgow, Lord: xii, xiv, 22, 96, 99, 100, 111, 119, 132
London: xii, 2, 5, 8–9, 18–19, 29–30, 79, 83–85, 90, 97, 99, 103, 119, 153, 180
Lorient: xiv, 127
Luftwaffe: 35, 127, 159, 197

Madras: 6
Malaya: xvii, 82
Marathas: 126,
March on Rome: 14
Marxist: 26, 67, 159

Mazzotta, Orlando: xix, 178–180, 182
Mein Kampf: 3, 5, 11, 20, 70, 116, 186–187
Meseritz: 83
Middle East: viii, 32, 46–47, 55, 62, 150, 155, 162
Molotov, Vyacheslav: 37
Mookerjee, Girija K.: 27, 78–81, 117
Moscow: vii, xix–xx, 3, 24, 26, 37, 64, 73, 153, 196
Muhlberg: 194
Munich: 11, 13, 15, 18
Muslim League: xviii, 74, 96, 123, 135, 138
Mussolini, Benito: xiii, 3, 22, 41, 52, 106–107, 153, 157, 185; and Bose, xiii, xx, 8, 12, 14–15, 18–20, 54, 59, 108–110, 114, 117, 120, 164–165; and Gandhi, 9, 109

Nagpur: 133
Nambiar, A. C. N.: x, 77–79, 116–117, 196
Naples: 18
National Congress Radio: 133
Nazi party: xx, 4, 10–12, 14–15, 20, 142
Nehru, Jawaharlal: xi, 8, 25–26, 74, 83–84, 96, 100–102, 105, 119, 128, 132, 140, 146, 149, 152, 154; and Bose, xix, xx–xxi, 3, 5–7, 15, 17, 36, 52, 65, 68, 88, 92, 96, 101, 105, 115, 117–118, 145–146, 149, 160, 164, 166; critical of Bose, xii, 21, 101–104; Bose critical of, 14, 85, 89, 101, 103, 123, 128–129; as Congress president, 17; critical of Hitler, xii, 104; Hitler critical of, xii, 90, 115, 158, 161

INDEX

Nepal: 49
Neubruck: 194
New Delhi: 96, 146
'Night of the Long Knives': 14
Nitti, Francesco: 7
Normandy: 144
North Africa: viii, xiv, 29, 43, 46, 57, 74, 113, 121, 123, 133, 139, 140, 184, 195, 197
North-West Frontier: x, xiv, xviii, 24, 31, 35, 40, 58, 74, 83, 113, 138, 151–153, 173
Norway: 30, 180

Orissa: 1
Oshima, Hiroshi: x, 75

Palestine: 50, 130, 177–178
Paris: 77–79, 117, 196; Bose visits, 63
Pearl Harbour: x, 73
Pelinka, Anton: 27
Poland: xx
Presidency College: 1
Punjab: 181

Quadruple Alliance: 148
Quisling: x, 24, 68–69, 119, 147, 154, 163, 166, 184
'Quit India': xiv, 131–137, 153

Radio Himalaya: xi, xviii, 52, 63, 66, 140
Raeder, Erich: 40
Rajputs: 126
Rangoon: 87, 91–92
Regenwurm: 83, 121
Rennes: 193
Ribbentrop, Joachim von: viii–x, xiii–xiv, 30, 35, 47, 51–52, 55, 57, 64, 68, 83, 86, 88, 100, 113, 118, 121–122, 127, 131, 133, 137–138, 140, 148, 151, 156, 158, 161; receives Bose, vii, 42–46, 69–71, 114, 137–138, 183–188; and declaration on India, ix, xii–xiii, 51, 55, 57, 61–63, 68–70, 75, 86, 106–107, 109, 114, 155–156, 185–187
Röhm, Ernst: 13–14
Romania: 59, 177
Rome: ix, 14, 58, 60, 64, 73, 86–88, 92, 105, 121, 137, 139, 151, 164, 180–181, 195–196; Bose visits viii, xiii–xiv, xx, 12, 14–15, 35, 51–57, 107–109, 123–124, 139–140
Rommel, Erwin: 29, 40
Roosevelt, Franklin D.: ix, 101, 103, 119, 132; and Bose, xii, 61, 102, 141
Rosenberg, Alfred: 11
Round Table Conference: 8–9
Roy, Manabendra Nath: 21
Royal Air Force: 35, 133
Russia: ix, xx, 3–5, 34, 37, 46, 57, 61, 68–69, 80, 82, 103, 115, 148–149, 152, 156, 162, 184–185, 196

Sturmabteilung: 14
Salt March: 7, 14
Salzburg: xiii, 106, 109
Sareen, T. R.: 27
Saxony: 197
Schenkl, Emilie: 54; and Bose, viii, 15, 52, 67, 139, 142, 144, 159
Schmitt, Kurt: 13
Shedai, Mohammed Iqbal: ix–xi, 76, 177–182; and Bose viii, x, xiv, 52–54, 58–60, 64, 73–75, 117, 123–124, 139–140, 160, 179–180, 182
Shillong: 6
Sikhs: 121, 126, 183
Singapore: xi, 33, 40, 84–86, 88, 94, 98, 143

INDEX

Singh, Ajit: viii, 52
Singh, Bhagat: 8
Singh, Gurbachan: 181
Singh, Labh: viii, 52
Singh, Sant: 181
Sinha, A. L.: 16
Slovakia: 59, 177
South Africa: 48, 187
Southeast Asia: xii-xiii, 25–26, 33, 36, 73, 82, 105, 116, 138, 143, 146, 149, 157–158, 163–164
Soviet Union: viii-ix, xviii, 39, 62, 128, 143, 148–149, 152, 154, 157, 160; and Bose, viii, xx–xxi, 3, 7, 24, 26, 30, 32, 34–37, 45–46, 51, 56–57, 64, 80, 89, 113, 115, 148, 153, 156, 159
Special India Bureau: ix–xi, xiii, xviii, 57–60, 65, 73, 86, 105, 108
Special India Detachment: xviii, 83, 121, 123
SS: 67, 125–126, 146
Stalin, Joseph: 180
Strasser, Otto: 4
Suez Canal: 22, 46, 70, 155, 187
Sykes, Christopher: 26
Syria: viii, 55, 63, 155, 185

Talwar, Bhagat Ram: 51; and Bose, viii-ix, xiv, 49, 63–64, 113, 137, 153
Thailand: 87, 143
'The Situation in India' article: 128–129
Thierfelder, Franz: 15–17
Tiflis: 70, 186
Tiger, Operation: ix, 40, 51, 58, 64, 87
Tilak, Bal Gangadhar: 6
Time: 20
The Times: 184
Togo, Shigenori: 106

Tojo, Hideki: xi-xii, 84–86, 98–99, 105, 108, 143, 164–165
Tokyo: x, xii, xx, 74–77, 81–82, 85–88, 90, 92, 94–95, 99, 105–107, 113–114, 116, 118, 120, 122–124, 127–128, 138–139, 143, 146, 151, 157–158, 163–164, 180
Tokyo University: 146
Tribal Territory: viii-ix, 31, 38, 50–51, 58, 64, 137, 152, 173
Trott, Adam von: 59–60, 63, 177–178
Turkey: 45

U-180: xv, xviii, 143
Ukrainians: 162
United States: x, 34, 61, 68, 71, 73, 87, 89, 96, 101–103, 111–112, 141, 143, 148, 162, 183, 185

Venice: 10, 55–56
Vichy: 55, 94, 140
Vienna: vii, 10–12, 14, 184
Völkischer Beobachter: xviii, 10, 12, 15

Wardha: 97
Washington: 92, 96
Waziristan Radio: xviii, 133
Weimar Republic: 126
Weinberg, Gerhard L.: 26, 154
Werth, Alexander: 27
Westminster: 94
White House: 103
Wilhelmstrasse: xix
Woermann, Ernst: viii, x–xi, 32, 35–37, 51–52, 55–56, 59, 63, 74, 85–86, 153, 178; receives Bose, viii-x, xix, 29–30, 34–35, 51, 57, 62, 75, 114, 131, 156

Yamamoto, Bin: xi, 81–82, 136, 143

Zandvoort: 194–195, 197

249